THE GRACED HORIZON

Nature and Grace
in
Modern Catholic Thought

Stephen J. Duffy

A Michael Glazier Book
THE LITURGICAL PRESS
Collegeville, Minnesota

THEOLOGY AND LIFE SERIES

Volume 37

A Michael Glazier Book published by The Liturgical Press

Cover design by David Manahan, O.S.B.

Cover photo by S. Annette Brophy, O.S.B.

Copyright © 1992 by The Order of St. Benedict, Inc., Collegeville, Minnesota. All rights reserved. No part of this book may be reproduced in any form or by any means, electronic or mechanical, including photocopying, recording, taping, or any retrieval system, without the written permission of The Liturgical Press, Collegeville, Minnesota 56321. Printed in the United States of America.

1	2	3	4	5	6	7	8	9

Library of Congress Cataloging-in-Publication Data

Duffy, Stephen.
    The graced horizon : nature and grace in modern Catholic Thought / Stephen J. Duffy.
        p.   cm. — (Theology and life series)
    "A Michael Glazier book."
    ISBN 0-8146-5705-2
    1. Grace (Theology)—History of doctrines—20th century.
    2. Nature—Religious aspects—Christianity—History of doctrines—20th century. I. Title. II. Series.
    BT761.2.D84   1992
    234—dc20   92-474
                                                                  CIP

For
Steve & Ann

Contents

Prologue

Even though the theology of nature and grace is out of fashion in a day when dogmatics is out of favor, concern about the nature/grace relationship remains a theological perennial. No dimension of Christian life or thought can be addressed without recourse, at least implicitly, to a theology of nature and grace. The nature/grace dialectic can never be purely academic, a relic of the past. At stake is the ontology of the human person in relationship to the free, always surprising gift of God's presence and power to the world of creatures. Grace qualifies all divine/human relationships in such a way that they are freely initiated by God and in no way dependent upon the creature. Both God's creative activity and God's saving activity are graces. The former grounds the participation of everything in being; the latter brings to fulfillment the beings that are, for a variety of reasons, alienated from, even resistant to, the ground that alone is their fulfillment. In every case, grace is always a strangeness, a gift, a surprise.

In the present century, a renaissance in Roman Catholic theology sparked renewed interest in the theology of nature and grace. Critical historical studies and the philosophical breakthroughs of Maurice Blondel (1861–1949) and Joseph Maréchal (1878–1944) opened doors too long closed and by mid-century, from the early 1940s through the 1960s, a heated debate raged over the theology of nature and grace. Vatican Council II is not intelligible without an understanding of this controversy. With this dispute, Catholicism turned a corner. The often bitter conflict served to overcome both the juridical, naturalistic poison of Jansenism, which was so damaging to Catholic life, and the rationalistic poison concocted by unreconstructed "Thomists" as an antidote to safeguard the gratuity of grace. The inner logic of this "Thomism" had reified nature and made of it a closed system for which the "supernatural" could only be the invasion of a foreign body from without and, therefore, able to be dispensed with. Exiled from everything human, the "supernatural," these paleo-Thomists thought, becomes all the more divine and gratuitous. This extrinsicist view failed to see God as the author of both nature and grace and of nature in view of grace. It also failed to see that it had rendered the "supernatural" a superficial appendage to the natural, which it left essentially untouched, the two related only by an external divine decree.

More important yet, since theory always mediates praxis, the extrinsicist theology could not be without practical consequence. The sad irony is that it led to an unconscious collusion between the exponents of secularism and the theologians who, driven to ensure the gratuity of grace, relegated it to a realm far beyond nature's borders. Such a dualism, wrongheadedly thinking it had checked its enemy, naturalism, had in fact surrendered the field to it in protecting the transcendence of grace by its banishment.

In the 1940s, with the gradual ascendence of "la nouvelle théologie," as its opponents labeled it, there was a reversion to a more Platonic anthropology, via a *ressourcement*, a retrieval of Thomas and early Christian thought. This christened Platonist anthropology read the divine signature inscribed in human being and experienced as a lack, a desire, an erotic drive, a restlessness buried in the depths of all consciousness. Undergirding all experience is an original experience which binds the hunger for God with the wellsprings of all human cognition, affectivity, and action. Again, theory mediates praxis.

This anthropology led to a revivified theology of nature and grace, one that would only emerge stronger from the fires of debate, then to provide the needed theoretical justification of Catholicism's emergence from its ghetto at mid-century and of its new openness to the world and to religion's "cultured despisers." For a century and a half, from Lamennais to the Modernists, challenges to the Church's withdrawal from and negativity toward the modern world had been defeated. But now the revitalization of theology and the swift currents of modernity could no longer be resisted. The post-Tridentine dualisms that had turned Catholicism against the world and sundered the religions and the secular could now be exorcised. The pre-Vatican II Church as sub-culture began to collapse. The quotidian and the religions were now seen to reside not in separate zones, but to suffuse each other. A renewed theology transformed the plain truth of the humdrum into poetry, and poetry into revelation. Borne, too, on the swelling tide of this renewed theology of nature and grace would be the new liberation theologies of the century's last decades.

In many ways the present work is a period piece, for it is content, as an historical and interpretative work, to chronicle the nature/grace debate of the mid-twentieth century, which was a rehearsal for the drama of Vatican II. For the most part, the focus is narrowed to the literature of those years. The opening chapter maps out the basic issues, their historical development in post-Tridentine scholasticism, and a typology of approaches. Thereafter, chapters are devoted to the two major players, Henri de Lubac (1896–1919) and Karl Rahner (1904–1984), and to other representative voices: Hans Urs von Balthasar, Juan Alfaro, Edward Schillebeeckx, and Eulalio Baltazar.

The central question addressed by these thinkers, the relationship between nature and the utterly gratuitous destination of human persons to union with God, has been nudged into oblivion since mid-century. However, the question has not, and never will be, definitively resolved. It is misguided to think it is no longer an axial question. The "nouvelle théologie" controversy was not merely an esoteric, intramural squabble. Quite the opposite. No tempest in a teapot, the controversy concerned a challenge to the narrow, cabalist theology of the court theologians who prevailed in Roman circles up to the eve of Vatican II and who were still active in the halls and on the floor of the council. Ironically, in light of the *ressourcement*, theirs was the "new theology," fostering as it did an exiled Church, a sclerotic *Schultheologie*, and worst of all, a dualism that rendered grace alien, scarce, and ultimately, superfluous. What the challengers espoused was an inclusive, world-affirming theology that sought the integration of nature and grace.

The happy outcome of this controversy was the negation of the idea that religion exists for the inner consolation of the privileged, pious few. Reappropriating buried treasure in its own tradition, Catholicism came to see again that the power of Christianity could not be imprisoned in the private sphere or pushed into the margins of life. Unfortunately, a loss of nerve and a virulent restorationism have, in the last two decades of this century, marked something of a return to the old dualisms that interiorize and privatize religion, thus again willy-nilly conceding "the world" to secularism, as the school theology had done, and making the supernatural a peripheral adornment to life, which is primarily natural and secular. Secularism and dualistic theologies again become unwitting bedfellows.

Finally, if anything is obvious, it is how far we are from having reached a definitive resolution to the endlessly complex problem of nature and grace. Truth to tell, it is not a problem at all, but a mystery. We are never home and dry. Our study of the mid-century problematic and its distillates merely suggests possibilities for reflection that might lead to a more integral perspective, which is, of course a necessity, since one's theology of nature and grace plays upon all the registers of life and thought. While the old dualism will no longer do, it is less than clear what alternative theological options will emerge.

Certainly, what emerged from the mid-century debate is not wholly adequate. For one thing, its anthropocentrism continues theology's long-standing bifurcation of historical and natural reality. Future theologies of nature and grace will have to take account of God's presence and power in the whole expanse of creation, from the vastness of galaxies yet unknown to the elusiveness of infinitesimal particles of matter. The gracing of human history is but a brief epoch in the immensity of the universe. The term "nature" in the nature/grace dyad urgently needs expansion. Were it not for the physical world and its processes human history would amount to nothing. The human community and its eschatology are but a small part of the larger community that is the organism of the universe. The reality of grace and the broad theatre of its engagement has yet to be articulated with scope appropriate to the magnitude of its energy or to the changes that mark the modern (and post-modern) person's self-understanding vis-à-vis nature. The reality of grace is intelligibly proposed only if the grammar and rhetoric of the proposal are commensurate with the actuality of human being in its assessment of how it feels, works, and thinks in its universe, orbiting amid the stars and probing the genetic code. Humans are who they are not merely in virtue of some structure of their being or in virtue of their relationship to God; they are who and what they are because of where they are as well. There is a need, then, for the theology of nature and grace to be so explicated within self- and world-understanding as to transcend its inherited anthropocentric grammar and rhetoric. The presence, power, and hope of grace will then be located within humanity's life in the world-as-creation as well as within humanity's hearing and receiving God's Self-communicating and

forgiving word. And so there is much unfinished business remaining.

Meanwhile, theology must always go backwards even while it
attempts to reinterpret nature and grace forward into contemporary experience. I have attempted to render intelligible a debate where in our own time the tradition changed course or,
perhaps some would say, returned to a course that it had, with
devastating consequences, strayed from. The opacity and intricacy
of the issues involved are not of my invention. The debate and
the long history that is prologue to it bear their own complexity
and illegibility; our study simply mirrors as much. Moreover, one
duty of students of history and theology is to resist the tidal pull
of the pious imagination to oversimplification.

1

The Problem of Nature and Grace: The Issues and Terms of the Debate

Many debates which mark the history of theology are ultimately debates about nature and grace. The problem of nature and grace is the problem of finding a bridge across the abyss separating God and humanity, of locating the image of God in the human person, and of discovering how the human person makes its way back to God. While discussions of the relationship between nature and grace have been most abstruse, they are, nonetheless, discussions freighted with practical ramifications. From the sixteenth to the twentieth century the problem of nature and grace was technically resolved in such a way as to generate a variety of dualisms that were to bedevil Christian life, the dualisms of the sacred and the profane, the religious and the secular, the Church and the world, faith and reason. Only recently have new viewpoints on nature and grace begun to exorcise these old dualisms. It is these new viewpoints that concern us in this work. But to better comprehend more recent theologies of nature and grace one must know something of the history of the problem and of the issues and terms of this complex debate.

I. *Nature and Grace in Historical and Ecumenical Perspective*

The problem of nature and grace is perhaps the only problem on which Roman Catholics and Protestants have gone their separate ways with little sense of sharing a common problem or criteria of judgment. Tradition, scriptures, Christology, the papacy, the sacraments have all been objects of ecumenical dialogue, but not the nature/grace relationship. For Roman Catholics the technical problem came to the fore only in the post-Reformation era. The impetus was provided by discussion of Cardinal Cajetan's commentary on the *Summa Theologica* written in the first decade of the sixteenth century.[1] The relationship between nature and grace became the topic of a heated intramural controversy in post-Tridentine Catholicism. Only Roman Catholics fully stated the problem and explained the options in depth. While the positions of earlier thinkers were difficult to assess, the problem was newly formulated. From the time of Michael du Bay, or Baius (whose teaching was condemned in 1567) to the time of Cornelius Jansen and Pasquier Quesnel (whose teaching was condemned in 1653 and 1713, respectively) the debate grew more intense.[2]

The distinction between nature and grace is rooted in the conviction that what we become in our relationship with God cannot derive solely from our own capabilities for self-growth. Hence human nature must somehow be supplemented by grace, the free Self-communication of God. The life offered by grace is said to be "supernatural" in three senses: a) God's being is ontologically superior to all created being; b) a direct and perduring relationship with God surpasses human cognitive and affective capacities; and c) life with God under grace is freely given and beyond all claims or requirements that flow from human nature itself. In a word, the life of grace transcends the being, powers, and exigencies of the human person. All agreed on the first ground for the supernatural character of grace. Precisely the preeminence of divine being made it the only completely satisfying telos for human life, which, though finite, knows the difference between anxious, threatened, finite being and infinitely perfect being. All further agreed on the third reason for the supernatural character of grace. Grace is of necessity a love freely given; it is unowed to nature and unnecessary for its functioning. God in grace comes to be newly known, not as Creator only but as covenant partner.[3]

However, a difference of opinion arose over the second ground due to varying conceptions of humanity's natural powers and the

[1]On the history of this problem, cf. H. de Lubac, *Augustinianism and Modern Theology* (London: Geoffrey Chapman, 1969) and *The Mystery of the Supernatural* (New York: Herder & Herder, 1967). I am indebted to the insights of E. Te Selle, "Nature and Grace in the Forum of Ecumenical Studies," *Journal of Ecumenical Studies* 8 (1971) 539-559.

[2]DS 1901-1980; 2001-2007; 2400-2502.

[3]Thomas Aquinas, *ST*, I-II, 109, 3, ad 1; I, 60, 5, ad 4; I-II, 62, 1, ad 3.

way they are complemented by grace. The theology that came to possess the field in the Roman Catholic view of human nature and its powers was based on the Aristotelean theory of knowledge and especially on its contention that all intuitive knowledge entails a certain identity of the knower and the known (the after-image in the mind following sensation, the abstraction into which it is converted by understanding, and at the apex of the process, the self-transparency of interior acts with the mind becoming present to itself). Knowledge, no doubt, exceeds intuition. Knowledge involves varieties of knowing. If we start with intuition, we go well beyond it to form propositions in which we distance ourselves from the known reality. Sense impressions lead to judgments through which we project our attention toward the object which initiated our sense impressions. But the focus here is intuitive knowledge. According to Aquinas, the highest intuition the finite mind can achieve is immediate awareness of itself. God can be apprehended only mediately, indirectly, inferentially as ground of being.[4] On this basis it is not difficult to see why grace offers nature a means to transcend its limits. On this basis no finite mind can attain of itself immediate, direct knowledge of God. Thus grace supplements nature by providing a power to achieve a cognitive and affective level of activity transcending the natural. Grace renders nature capable for the first time of a direct relationship with God *in via* and of an immediate relationship *in patria*. Given this understanding of human nature, the introduction of extrinsic, "superadded" powers (*habitus* was the Aristotelean category invoked) becomes not fantasy but necessity. The elevation of natural powers is a must if one is to be capable of a range of activities otherwise impossible. Grace, Roman Catholic thinkers came to maintain, is gratuitous not merely because of our sin, but primarily because of the poverty of our being. This assumption for the most part went unquestioned down to the present, though its articulation varied.[5] Recent Catholic theology has, as we shall see, struggled to extricate itself from extrinsicism by stressing the immanence of God, yet all the while holding to the three grounds for the supernatural alluded to above. The transcendence of life with God, it is thought, must include a transcendence of one's natural powers.

[4]Thomas Aquinas, *Contra Gentiles*, III, c. 45–48; *ST* I, 12.

[5]This assumption, so fundamental in the Catholic theology of grace since the medieval period, is not found in Augustine. Cf. E. Te Selle, "Nature and Grace in Augustine's Exposition of Gen 1:1-5," *Recherches Augustiniennes* 5 (1968) 95–137.

Most post-Tridentine Catholic theological schemes made their own this assumption, perhaps the most crucial one concerning the transcendence of the supernatural.

By the seventeenth century the common or "standard" view had come to rest in the *duplex ordo* theory of Cardinal Cajetan (1469-1534) and Domingo Bañez (1528-1604) largely through the Spanish commentators on Aquinas. In this line of thought the life offered by grace so transcends nature's powers that it has never entered the human mind or heart, so that the sole end humanity can seek is one commensurate with its powers. When grace appears, it offers not just new powers, but a new telos for human life. A second view, in rivalry with the standard view but edged into the shadows until its revival in the twentieth century by Maurice Blondel, Joseph Maréchal, and Henri de Lubac, held that the human person has a positive, unconditioned desire for the mode of existence offered by grace but the desire remains inefficacious because human nature, while *capax Dei*, cannot bring the desire to fruition. What grace furnishes is not a new end, but new active powers for attaining the very end desired by nature. A modification of this second view suggested that grace complements human capacities. Humanity not only has a positive desire for God as sole, ultimate end but also possesses, at least in principle, the powers to attain God. Humanity falls short neither with regard to the end nor with regard to the means. What grace does is to arouse and sustain the activity that one is capable of by nature, but which, in the absence of grace, would be called into question or blunted by a sinful world since human beings are defectible.[6]

One reason this problematic may seem foreign to some students is that theology today does not find talk about beatific vision easy. Yet contemporary theology does invoke themes bearing affinity to it. Notions like "the Absolute," "the Ultimate," which furnish a critique of all attempts to locate a focus of loyalty, a ground of satisfaction anywhere short of God, or notions like "the Kingdom," "the Eschaton," or "the God of the absolute future" correspond to beatific vision. The pertinence of these older discussions of nature and grace may come to life if they are translated into the existential or political language of contemporary theology. It matters very much whether God and the Kingdom

---

[6]Te Selle alleges that this was the view of Augustine and, before him, of Athanasius. Origen, Clement of Alexandria, Irenaeus, and Justin held a similar view. Cf. Note 1.

are directly relevant to human life or, as the *duplex ordo* or "two floors" tradition suggested, enter in some alien fashion through revelation and grace; it matters whether humanity is intrinsically able, in principle, to live with a view to God and the Kingdom, or, as the theory of inefficacious desire holds, must without grace be content with a provisional commitment. We are never finished with the problem of nature and grace and there is much to learn from the controversies over it. What is at stake ultimately is the crucial matter of theological anthropology.

Protestant theology, unlike Catholic theology, presents no clearly identifiable technical viewpoint on nature and grace. The reformers were wary of futile speculation on matters such as the beatific vision. They also approached nature much more existentially than did Roman Catholic thinkers with their substantialist philosophy. Finally, Protestant thinkers, while generally shying away from philosophical thought, were impressed by the reticence of the scriptures on this issue.

Is there any point of contact? How are we to conceive human life before God? The "standard" Catholic view certainly had its own conception. It understood nature by contrasting it with grace. Nature is what remains when grace is bracketed. Often the primordial human situation was referred to as a state of integrity (*natura integra*). The standard view also assumed that graced nature is a nature enriched, improved, elevated by powers (*virtutes*) superadded to it and enabling a level of life surpassing its intrinsic abilities. The condition of postlapsarian humanity is seen as wounded and corrupted (*natura vitiata*). But mark well that the "standard view" saw this as a deprivation of the superadded gifts (*spoliatio in gratuitis*) and, secondarily, as effecting a malfunctioning of human nature's natural capacities (*vulneratio in naturalibus*). The extrinsicism is glaring. For it is implied that the life of grace is not lived from the inner center of one's being and that its presence or absence do not really affect the human person centrally. Modern Catholic thinkers have, as we shall see, tried to avoid this extrinsicism whereby grace is an ornament added or subtracted without inner effect on humanity.

Protestant theologians, on the other hand, in opposition to substantialist Scholastic thinking, usually insisted that nature is to be identified with the primordial or ideal state of humanity and that nature itself has been corrupted by sin. Thus the function of grace is primarily redemptive or medicinal, restoring humanity to its nature and destiny (*natura reparata*), not elevating and adding new powers, but liberating humanity's own powers so that they will be oriented to the God of whom they are capable and for whom they were meant. Human love for God is the perfection of nature itself, which must, however, be sustained by grace. The chief reason for grace is not the sublimity of the end sought but the feebleness of the will seeking it.[7] The powers of human nature cannot be lost; they are the very substance of human life. They may, however, be modified by the varying situations in which a human person is found and by the fundamental orientation a person takes (*natura integra, natura vitiata, natura reparata*). The function of grace is to direct these intrinsic powers to God in all situations and to support them, lest in their mutability they defect from their true end, God.

There are examples of this type of thinking in Melancthon's *Apology for the Augsburg Confession* (1530–1531) and in the *Institutes* of Calvin (1539).[8] Luther objected to Scholastic talk of superadded gifts. For him both original righteousness and the corruption of sin are "of man's essence." Neither is adventitious; both characterize the total being, down to its depths.[9] The *imago Dei*, as the perfect operation of the human mind in the primordial state, belongs to human nature, even though it is a special divine work.[10] Obviously, the Augustinian understanding of nature employed by Protestant thinkers is more fluid than the substantialist understanding found in Catholic thought and it reflects an awareness that human nature not only adapts to changing circumstances but is interiorly modified by them, whether they be states of grace, sin, or redemption. In general, Roman Catholic thinkers, more preoccupied with refurbishing Scholasticism than with a humanistic study of the Fathers, were perplexed by the Protestants' stance and understood them to hold that faith and love are native to every person and arise from nature with inevitability as the person de-

[7] J. Healey, *Jansenius' Critique of Pure Nature* (Rome: Universitas Gregoriana, 1964), 71–77.

[8] *Apologia Confessionis Augustanae* art. 2, secs. 9, 12, 17, 23; *Institutes* II, ii, secs. 4, 12, 16. The reformers' notion of nature is more existential than substantialist, hence nature is understood more in terms of the human relationship to God than in terms of alterations of structures of a prior and continuously existing identity or essence. The true self is excentrically rather than "inwardly" located. Cf. W. Joest, *Ontologie der Person bei Luther* (Göttingen: Vanderhoeck & Ruprecht, 1967), 233–274.

[9] *In Genesim* 3.7.

[10] Ibid., 1.26. See A. Hasler, *Luther in der katolischen Dogmatik: Darstellung seiner Rechtfertigungslehre in dem Katholischen Domatikbuchern* (München: Huber, 1968), 116–128.

velops.[11] This appeared to jeopardize the gratuity of grace. It is to this question that we now turn. In mapping out in greater detail the two major positions concerning gratuity within Catholicism we hope to provide a grasp of the issues and the terms that must be understood if we are to comprehend twentieth century Catholic attempts to recast the technical doctrine of nature and grace. It was that recasting that provided post-Vatican II Catholicism with a theoretical justification for its new, more open stance vis-à-vis modernity.

II. *The Interiority and Gratuity of the Christian Vocation*

Christian hope hangs upon Jesus Christ, the resurrection and the life. It looks to a life that will be an immediate, personal communion with God, "face to face" (1 Cor 13:12). The pledge of this future was placed on Christian tongues by Jesus: "Pray then like this: Our Father who art in heaven" (Matt 6:9). Christians feel called to a new intimacy with God. The Father of Jesus is the Father of every Christian (John 20:17). Christians are and will be the children of God. This is a destiny which is not imposed, but comes as a vocation (Heb 9:15). In the scriptures the call is often addressed to those who have heard the verbal message of the apostles. But Christianity also maintains that God wants all to be saved. All are called to share in the divine life. The call is universal and must somehow be known by all. Is the call, therefore, interior, and is it already a grace? These two questions concerning the interiority and gratuity of the call to grace we must now address. Their import is not one of idle theological speculation. On the responses given to these questions will depend the attitudes one takes to the dualisms of the religious and the secular, the ecclesial and the mundane. The broadly outlined responses in what follows will prepare us for the more detailed discussions of individual theologians.

A. *The Interiority of the Christian Vocation*

Does the call remain exterior to us or is it interior, assuming the form of an aspiration, a profound attraction? Certainly Au-

---

[11]Cf., e.g., C. Jansenius, *Augustinus*, in "De Statu Purae Naturae," Bk. I, c.15, col. 747.

gustine thought the call was interior. "You have made us for your-self, O Lord, and our hearts are restless until they rest in you."[12] An opening has been hollowed out in us by the creating God and God alone can fill it. One might object that here Augustine makes reference to the rest that comes with any possession of God, even one that is inferior to immediate union, e.g., the repose that comes from the joyful contemplation of God as reflected in creatures. But in the same work, Augustine mentions the vision of his mother, Monica, at Ostia.[13] This vision did not achieve the full-ness of the beatific vision. Yet it is of the same order, an antici-pation, a prelude. It is clear to Augustine that there is as yet no full repose for his mother or himself in this state of anticipation. Ostia is a beginning, a preparation; it is only in the heavenly ex-perience that Monica will still her restlessness. The restlessness and the desire for God implied in all this appears to be absolute. It is not "conditioned." Our desire is absolutely oriented to God, at least on God's part, if God has posited all the conditions of proximate possibility for the desire's fulfillment. There is noth-ing in the Augustinian texts to suggest that Augustine, explicitly or implicitly, had any reservations. His sense is this: "In creating us, You have made us for Yourself, You have effectively destined us to union with You and You have freely offered the means, hence our desire to possess You is unconditioned." For clarity's sake it will be advantageous to study more closely the terminology involved here since it is employed in the modern approaches we are to examine later.

The term "conditioned desire" recurs frequently in debates con-cerning nature and grace. It refers to the natural tendency of human intelligence, pursuant upon the realization of the condi-tions for a remote possibility of union with or a vision of God. What are these conditions? Simply the existence of created spirit, for human intelligence, essentially having unlimited being for its formal object, is by that very fact open to the free communica-tion of infinite Being, and even desirous of that communication. The conditions of a remote possibility of union may in fact be realized, but the proximate condition, viz., God's will to Self-communication, might remain in suspense. There would then be in the subject an initial orientation, a tendency toward union as a radical possibility but not yet proximately possible: a conditioned

---

[12]*Confessions* I, 1; XIII, 8; *The City of God* XI, 13.

[13]*Confessions* IX, 10.

desire. An absolute desire, on the other hand, is a tendency pursuant upon the realization of the proximate conditions by God. It is a living tendency, unelicited, and independent of the subject's knowledge (had only by revelation) of the realization of the condition. However, since the fulfillment of the absolute desire hangs on the free response of the subject, it remains, in this sense, conditioned by human freedom.

What can Scripture tell us about the interior dimension of this desired union? Scripture does seem to remark directly on the interiority of the union. "We [Jesus and the Father] will come to him and make our home with him" (John 14:23). But is the call to union itself already interior? The restlessness that Augustine speaks of appears to be a constitutive determination of concrete human being, an *existential*, and not merely a free and contingently elicited act, an *existentiell*.[14] Existentials, the constitutive dimensions of human being, are anterior to all free, personal decisions and so deeply rooted that one cannot opt to acquire or destroy them according to one's liking. Thus the Augustinian inquietude for God precedes all deliberate will acts and survives any free rejection of God. Does Scripture speak of this radical, interior inquietude? Does it interiorize the divine call to this extent?

Scripture knows well the *search* for God.[15] But if one closely examines the texts which can be adduced, nothing warrants finding in them the assertion of an existential inquietude. There is reason to think, too, that the question itself is anachronistic.[16] Paul's allusion to seeking God in Acts 17:27 is fairly typical. It has the ring of a Hellenistic intellectual searching. There is hope of a manifestation of God through creatures. On the other hand, the context is thoroughly biblical and this gives to the "seeking" a strong Israelitic tonality. The reference is not only, nor even

---

[14]Much more will be said about the notion of an *existential* in chapter 4. A distinction has usually been made between abstract nature, or humanity as such, and concrete nature, or historical humanity. Abstract human nature is humanity with all its essential components, lacking which it would lose all possibility of being. Concrete human nature is humanity with all its components, including those which are necessary (or essential) and those which are contingent and due to historical circumstances over which the subject has little or no control, e.g., the proclivity to evil effected by history and culture or by original sin as it was traditionally understood.

[15]Cf. L. Malevez, "Interiorité et gratuité de la vocation chrétienne," *Ephemerides Theologicae Lovaniensis* 48 (1972) 54–55.

[16]I enter this caveat because the problems and questions of later theologies do not always fall within the horizon of the biblical text or of its authors. Most often post-Tridentine Catholic theology did not heed or was not aware of this caveat.

primarily, to a Greek way of knowing God in intellectual contemplation, and the seeking in question is not Augustinian restlessness, nor is its finality the immediate vision of God. To seek
God is for Paul to seek a practical knowledge of the sovereign
rights of the one true God, a knowledge from which will flow
adoration, obedience, and love. What is central is not an existential attraction, but conscious (existentiell) steps toward a knowledge of divine dispensation.

Are the scriptures more helpful concerning *desire* for God? Israel appears moved by a profound desire for God. There is the
desire to acquire wisdom (Prov 5:19); the nostalgia for Jerusalem (Ps 137:5); the desire to go up to the holy city or to the Temple
(Ps 128:5; 122:1); the desire to know the Word of God (Ps 119:20,
131); the desire which polarizes all energies and unmasks all illu-
sions and deceits (Amos 5:18; Isa 58:2). But here again we are
dealing with exclusively personal desire, the desire of one who
has freely formed it in one's own heart. We are not given to understand that the evil doer would remain, even in the depths of evil,
under the sway of an attraction to or nostalgia for the Absolute.
And when Paul, e.g., speaks of his "desire to depart and be with
Christ" (Phil 1:23), the desire is not the desire of concrete humanity as such, but of a person reborn in the Spirit. One might
want to appeal to 1 Cor 15:49: "Just as we have borne the image
of the man of dust, we shall also bear the image of the man of
heaven." One might add that between these two images, united
in one divine plan (Rom 8:29; Eph 1:3-4), there exists a hidden
link. Though severed by sin, the two remain dynamically bound
together. The earthly Adam, our concrete human nature, tends
to union with the heavenly Adam. This dynamism exists in every
human, in every natural image of God. We have here a tenuous
indication, perhaps, of the Augustinian existential desire.

Perhaps Romans 8:19-23 presents the clearest witness to an aspiration or desire for God that is rooted in the existential depths
of human being rather than arising at the level of conscious reflection and choice. The text is concerned with the aspiration of rational creatures, even if the accent is on the "groaning" of
material creation. Only in incarnated rational beings capable of
becoming the children of God does "groaning in travail" become
a free aspiration. Union with God is the telos of this aspiration
since the text designates those aspiring as children of God and
members of the family of God. No doubt the aspiration is clearer
in those believers who are already in Christ, who "have the first

fruits of the Spirit.'' But the aspiration is not their privilege alone. The "whole creation has been groaning." We seem, too, to be dealing with an interior reality that goes with the condition of creatureliness. Perhaps, however, it is not absolutely essential; perhaps it is a supernatural, gratuitous endowment. These are questions later thinkers will raise, as we shall see in detail. Nonetheless the aspiration or desire appears here as a circumstance of our historical nature, as a constitutive of our concrete being, all the more so as the scriptures affirm the creation of all things, humanity included, in Christ. It is true that the text speaks of creatures "subjected to futility." But should we conclude from this that the "groaning" is explained only by the wound of sin? Certainly sin makes the union for which humanity groans a freedom from bondage. It imprints a character on the aspiration, but it does not give to it its being. It seems due to God alone who has created humanity for Godself. Perhaps, then, there is in every person, according to Pauline thought, a restlessness for God that goes before every deliberate search and is its source and can be considered an existential determination of concrete humanity. Augustine's "You have made us for Yourself" can, perhaps, find a scriptural prelude.

It would, however, be rash to rest one's case on this or that text of Scripture. As noted above, it is anachronistic to address the questions of much later theological debates to these texts. Any certitude one may claim for the interiority of the call to union derives less from scriptural warrants than from theological reflection. The argument runs as follows. We learn from revelation that God wants the salvation of all. We learn by rational reflection on the divine simplicity that the decrees of God relative to created beings are not really distinct in themselves but only in their terms, or effects. If the divine decree of creation destines all for the Kingdom, this destination, to be distinguished from others, had to translate, it seems, into a certain effect in the depths of human being. To the immanent divine decree there corresponds in us a disposition, an ordination to the goods promised. This ordination can be conceived of as a desire, for the Kingdom is not immediately conferred in all its plenitude. It is offered as an end, as the last end. The inner disposition which renders it connatural to us takes the form of a tendency, an attraction. And it is necessarily absolute. It is not conditioned except in the hypothesis that the destination is not yet effective on God's side or that God is limited to creating first a pure nature ordered to a wholly natural end, and only later calling it to a superior end. But Christians believe the call is effective and is not put off by the foreknowledge of sin. It is the human foreseen as sinner that God calls to possession of the divine Self. In the concrete nature of fallen humanity there is an interior, absolute desire of the Kingdom that correlates with the universal salvific divine will. This determination is an *existential*. It is prior to all personal options and persists through all possible acceptances or rejections of one's end. Whatever one does, one remains interiorly ordered to absolute communion with God. Not that one is in a "state of grace," to use the traditional language. But one is always in a graced order and under the influence of the offer of grace. To some degree this existential determination seeps into consciousness. It is an attraction and all attractions are necessarily consciously experienced in some measure. In this case it is perhaps confusedly experienced as an appreciation of the goods of the Kingdom. More often this attraction will be lived rather than reflected upon. But it can rise to the level of reflection and clear articulation, as in the case of Augustine's "You have made us for Yourself, O Lord, and our hearts are restless. . . ." We shall see later how theologians have fleshed out this argument.

B. *The Gratuity of the Christian Vocation*

This brings us to a second question: is this interior call the gratuitous gift of grace? The question is complex and can surface in more than one form. That God effectively communicates God's own life to humans is an event of grace and wholly gratuitous. The divine summons to this communion, it has been argued, arouses in the human being a desire. Are the call and the desire an expression of grace distinct from the gift of creation? An absolute desire demands satisfaction. It is a prayer that is lived before being reflected on. Would the existence of created spirit be inconceivable without this unconditioned openness to the divine in itself? Certainly human desire or attraction cannot constrain God by demanding the gift of union, thus removing from the divine Self-communication its character as a free gift of grace. But is that precisely the danger to be feared, the threat to divine freedom, if the desire is an essential element of the human spirit? This is not immediately obvious. Even though essential and constitutive, could not the absolute attraction remain a humble demand, a prayer?

Another way to frame this question is to ask: is the interior attraction natural or supernatural? Karl Rahner, as we shall see, refers to it as a *supernatural existential.* The notion of an existential has been briefly adverted to already. But what does "supernatural" mean?[17] Many begin with the term "natural." Customarily it is referred to any of the necessary components of human nature, e.g., the power to form concepts after beginning with sense data, or the ability to choose freely. Suppress these functions and you are no longer in the presence of incarnated spirit. Similarly, according to some, the Augustinian attraction to the possession of God is a natural constitutive of the human condition. Deprived of it, our nature would find itself in a state of contradiction. Consequently it conditions the possibility of human nature and its call to existence. God cannot create humans without destining them to union with Godself. Creation is gratuitous. So too is the destination to union. But the latter has no other gratuity than that of creation itself.

Is "naturalness" so understood to be disavowed from the outset? To get a better grip on this question we need first to clarify the gratuity of the communion to which humanity is called. The debates have generally distinguished two things: destination to union and its actual conferral. All are called to and destined for union but not all enter the joy of union. All, it has until recently generally been asserted, are not infallibly saved. What has Catholic theology thought of the actual enjoyment of union with God? It has generally declared it to possess a gratuity distinct from the gratuity of creation. God's coming to dwell in us (John 14:23) is a pure grace to which we can lay no claim. And the gratuity is not simply by reason of our sinful condition which has forfeited any title to union. The gratuity in question has deeper roots. It

---

[17]Some today consider the term no longer useful. It suggests the very debatable idea of a two story existence, one imposed upon the other, as though the divine generosity is exercised by successive additions. If it is true that the divine design does not involve two successive moments in God, nor two gifts in its term (Christian existence), gifts which would be closed and complete in themselves (nature and grace), still the real distinction between nature and grace as two incomplete principles (potency and act) of one, undivided Christian existence remains for many a valid medieval development. If so, the distinction must be expressed. But in what terms? Some propose that "theological," "eschatological," "Christique," or "Christian" be substituted for "supernatural," and that "supernatural order" be replaced by "Christian mystery." But do any of these substitutes express as well the gratuity of grace? And will it suffice simply to append "gratuitous" or "gracious" in view of the fact that most consider creation as already gratuitous? What needs articulation is precisely the gratuity proper to grace. Cf. L. Malevez, "Interiorité et gratuité," 59.

derives primarily from our condition as creatures. Nothing in created being as such grounds a right to the Kingdom. Catholic thinkers did not pretend to find all this clearly in the scriptures, but they thought they found there at least an orientation in this direction. There is, e.g., the theme of adoptive filiation (Rom 8:15; Gal 4:7; Eph 1:14, 18 etc.). It is thought to be a gift over and above being created. It is not given with creation and there is no right to or exigency for it (Eph 2:8). Thus adoption as children of God moves us to conceive of a deeper gratuity. Of itself it does not signify the restoration of lost goods to an unworthy child, but the dispensing of a heritage to those, who even though innocent, have no right to it. There is also the theme of the divine invisibility. "No one has ever seen God; the only Son, who is in the bosom of the Father, he has made him known" (John 1:18; Matt 11:27). "Not that anyone has seen the Father except him who is from God; he has seen the Father" (John 6:46). These passages, it is argued, announce more than the simple fact that no one knows the Father. They also declare an incapacity and the absence of any right to see the Father. If anyone does come to know God (in the strong biblical sense of "commune with"), it will be by the free gift of the Son. This freedom of God's Self-revelation is affirmed, it seems, without regard to humanity's status as sinful. We can, further, place all this in a much larger context. God "dwells in unapproachable light" (1 Tim 6:16). One might see in this the liberty of God vis-à-vis created being as such, prescinding from any fall. The created being is powerless to lift itself to the divine level and unjustified in making the demand of any gift.

Such are the scriptural intimations.[18] One must again enter the caveat concerning the anachronism that may be involved in such a reading. Nonetheless, Catholic theologians considered the scriptures as warranting an affirmation of the singular gratuity of the gift of union with God. It does not respond to any exigency in the human being, neither as sinner nor even as purely human. It is sheer grace, healing to be sure, but primarily elevating, since it introduces humanity to a level of being that it cannot pretend to if left to itself. Such was the order of grace as most Catholic theologians conceived it.

[18]Ibid., 60-61.

III. *Divergent Theories: A Typology*

We have seen the general thesis that the actual conferral of union with God is marked by a gratuity distinct from the gratuity of creation. And we have taken note of the distinction between the conferral of union and destination to union. Are we to affirm a singular gratuity for the destination to union as well as for the union itself? All are called to the Kingdom and this call engenders in all a corresponding attraction that is necessarily absolute. Is this circumstance essential, natural to and identical with the created spirit? Or is it an "event" distinct from creation and therefore supernatural? This is an open question and we are free to come down on either side of the question of the possibility of created spirits who are not destined to union with God. One needs to hold, however, to the gratuity of the actual gift of union itself. When God communicates Godself, the gift is gratuitous and not purely a response to any exigency found in us. This implies that not even an absolute attraction in us can be counted as a demand for union. At least it is not immediately obvious that a natural absolute attraction necessarily creates an exigency.

Traditional Christian thought concerning the gratuity of salvation can be stated thus: those who are saved are saved by the grace of God. But the formula conceals an ambiguity. The offer of salvation is one thing, its effective accomplishment another. Is it only the latter that is gratuitous? Catholic disputes over nature and grace have presented two major and radically divergent viewpoints. A close examination of these two positions will further acquaint us with the issues and terms of the nature/grace debate. One position affirms that the divine Self-gift, perfected in the future life, but already initiated in the present order, is absolutely gratuitous, but there is in every individual an absolute desire for the divine Self-communication which is necessarily integral to the structure of the human spirit and which enjoys no other gratuity than that of creation. Let us call this position X. The other and more standard viewpoint, which we will refer to as Z, maintains that the destination to union is itself gratuitous with a second gratuity over and above that of creation. The absolute desire cannot be counted among the constitutive conditions of the human spirit, which could meaningfully exist without it. X denies a unique gratuity to the destination to union; Z affirms it.

Do we find X held, perhaps, by some members of the Augustinian school in the eighteenth and nineteenth centuries? Two varia-

tions appeared in the Augustinian camp.[19] Whether the destination
to divine union is essential, natural, and indistinguishable in its
gratuity from the gratuity of creation is perhaps a question that
some Augustinians neither asked nor resolved as such. Some did
claim that the human being cannot have any other last end but
the possession of God.[20] But what do they mean by "cannot
have"? Simply this: *de facto* the rational creature is destined for
the possession of God and once this destination is conferred, how
possibly conceive of any other finality? The Augustinians, then,
did not maintain a metaphysical impossibility. They were not saying it is impossible for God to create humanity without destining
it to divine union because such destination is a constitutive of
human nature. Starting from this premise, they assert that since
humanity is ordered to the vision of God, the means required for
that end must be given, among them the graces that theology calls
supernatural.[21] In more negative terms, since humanity is ordered
to the vision of God, it cannot be found in a state of pure nature,
which for the Augustinians means not a condition of non-
ordination to vision, but a state destitute of the means of grace
necessary to the pursuit of its end.[22] It must be noted that in their
eyes this requirement of grace does not find its source in us but
in God. Otherwise, how would grace remain grace? God owes
it to Godself, to the divine ordinary power, i.e., to the divine
power joined with wisdom and goodness (*ex decentia divinae bon-
titatis*) to provide humanity with the wherewithal to attain its end.
The Augustinians never rooted the claim to grace in humanity.
One can understand why their position has never been the object
of magisterial censure.[23] If they affirm the necessity of the means,
they do not clearly affirm the metaphysical necessity of destination to the end. They seem generally to bracket the question of
the unique gratuity of this destination. As a result this Augustinian line does not exactly coincide with X, which rejects this
gratuity.

Here and there some Augustinians did envisage the question
of metaphysical necessity, the question whether humanity must

[19]H. de Lubac, *Augustinianism and Modern Theology*, 273 ff.

[20]Ibid., 274–275.

[21]Ibid., 275–276.

[22]Ibid., 277.

[23]Ibid., 297 ff.

be destined to a supernatural finality.[24] If they did respond affirmatively, they embraced X, which rejects the special gratuity of the destination while claiming nonetheless to safeguard the gratuity of the gift of union. These Augustinians would hold to the thesis that the order of grace stands compatible with the necessity of destination.

A. *Arguments against the Gratuity of the Call*

The scriptures are silent on the contingency or necessity of human destination to divine union. One can hold one view or the other as long as one holds that in fact the love of God has called all equally to the Kingdom. The question of gratuity is, according to X, properly framed only if we ask: how is salvation gratuitous for concrete, historical humanity already called to union with God? If one claims the destination is a grace for a nature that could exist without it and without absolute desire, nothing much is achieved. For one has not yet come to the real problem, the problem of gratuity relative to concrete humanity already called.[25] X, unlike Z, never envisages a purely possible human existent; it knows only historical humanity. One might object against X that to hold that an absolute attraction to divine union is a necessary dimension of created spirit is to compromise the gratuity of the union. If the human being necessarily aspires to God, God, it seems, is bound to communicate Godself. X finds in this objection a misunderstanding of the phenomenology of love. And therein is found the first argument for X's thesis. In human relationships a love inscribed necessarily in the heart of the subject loving (e.g., the love of a mother for her child) does not jeopardize the liberty of the being that is loved. If love is true, it does not demand a return of love. It seeks a response that is its own master. This same pattern marks divine-human relationships, even more so. The person desiring God is not confronted by a liberty univocal to its own created liberty but by the incomparable liberty of a transcendent being, a liberty that is absolutely sovereign. In the desire for divine intimacy the Christian cannot but sustain the complete gratuity of the divine gift. There is desire without any exigency, for any demand would destroy the entire relationship.

---

[24]Ibid., 276, n. 49.

[25]This element in X's argument is borrowed from de Lubac. As we shall say in chapter 3, there is reason to think that de Lubac is a proponent of X. Malevez exonerates him. See L. Malevez, "Interiorité et gratuité," 64–65, fn. 18.

29

Thus a necessary tendency to the Kingdom in historical nature does not imperil the order of free grace. Paradoxically, the inverse is the case; the more the aspiration is deepened and identified with nature's will, the more it respects the freedom of the divine gift.

This brings us to X's second argument, or better, counterargument. Z does not necessarily hold that historical humanity has ever lived in a state of pure nature. Indeed, most who defend Z adamantly deny it. They claim that humans have never existed otherwise than in an order of grace, destined to the vision of God. But for the proponents of Z this is a simple fact, not a necessity. The notion of pure nature does not designate any existent. It is in their eyes purely a limit concept, one useful for understanding and articulating the gratuity of our factual destiny. This is all well and good, say the proponents of X, but the embarrassing insufficiency of Z is not thereby eliminated.

This alleged possible nature cannot be conceived without attributing to the human spirit as such a natural finality, inferior to the supernatural finality of concrete humanity which has effectively been called by God to share the divine life. But who does not see that in making the transition, even if only mentally, from the sole existent finality to an abstract, possible finality one changes substantially the subjects in question? A finality is essential, intrinsic. Change it and you are no longer in the presence of the same I, nor even of the same nature. Between the human being that I actually am and the human I might be who is not destined for union with God there is no real identity. The difference between the one and the other, moreover, cannot affect only the individual I; it cannot fail to affect human nature itself.[26] Is there not a contradiction lodged in the heart of Z? Z wants the nature not destined for God to be substantially identical with the nature that is. This is impossible. Thus X argues the invalidity of Z on the ground that the latter's efforts to articulate the gratuity of grace are centered on a hypothetical being that is other than the concrete humanity that has been summoned. It has not clarified gratuity in reference to historical humanity.

Finally, X may argue that in placing destination to participation in the divine life among the necessary structures of the created spirit, it guarantees to that spirit its unity. If the absolute

---

[26] Again, we have an argument borrowed from de Lubac that can be used in support of X, which shows again the ambiguity of his position.

attraction is, as Z would have it, only a contingent, superadded modality, the human spirit will follow two aspirations, each one independent of the other. Substantially it will tend to a natural finality inferior to divine union. Accidentally it will be the possession of God that it pursues. The juxtaposition of the two finalities is incomprehensible and effects a wrenching inner division in the human spirit between restlessness for God on one side and on the other side, a disinterest in God, a restlessness to possess the world connatural to it. But can the spirit be so divided in its being? No doubt, some Christian philosophers have held that the natural spiritual life of the human is controlled by a conditioned desire to see God and they add that revelation has already apprised us that the conditions have been fulfilled. God has freely chosen to unite us with Godself. Hence our conditioned desire is transformed into an absolute desire and the unity of the human spirit is assured in grace. But proponents of X see this as a futile solution. For those who would follow these philosophers must recognize that in the logic of their view, the absolute desire for God is verified only on a supernatural level which is, as it were, an accidental and supernumerary structure. In the depths of nature nothing is changed. Such an approach cannot meet the demand for unity in the inner life of the human being. By the superadded attraction it will tend toward God; by its own natural finality it will gravitate toward the world. Such a schizophrenic condition is intolerable.

We have briefly considered three arguments for X, a conceivable position, yet adopted by very few Catholic theologians in the past. This is remarkable if one considers the considerable weight of the above arguments and the fact that the scriptures do not clearly reject it. But by a kind of instinct Catholic theologians have generally opted for Z. This option may find a fragile grounding in Scripture. Its primary justification resides in discursive theological reflection.

B. *Arguments for the Gratuity of the Call*

What all Catholic theologians have asserted above all is the gratuity of the effective elevation of historical humans who have already been destined to divine union. But what of the gratuity of the destination itself? One might appeal to the scriptural theme of free divine election. Sometimes the election appears to be an absolute election. ". . . For the sake of the elect, whom he chose, he shortened the days. . . . False Christs and false prophets will arise . . . to lead astray if possible the elect" (Mark 13:20, 22). Later the theologies based on this text would understand by the "elect" those for whom glorification is already assured and effective. If this is the case, the theme of absolute election does not enlighten us. Even if this text and others like it proclaim the gratuity of election, it would equivalently be an affirmation of the gratuity of effective glorification. It does not tell us anything about the destination to election and glorification. Moreover, God wills to save all. Does this will or intention entail, according to the Scriptures, its own gratuity distinct from that of the will to create? On this question the theme of absolute election leaves us unenlightened. Here and there in Scripture we seem to find in the divine election a conditioned will. Some (Christians) appear absolutely chosen for justification, but not necessarily for glory. Glorification is somehow tied to their fidelity. In this case we seem to see a divine love which, while not absolutely saving, is distinguished (at least for those chosen) from simple divine creative love. Nevertheless our question remains. Nothing is affirmed about the destination of all humans (even of those not chosen for glory, if indeed there are such). Of this destination we still do not know whether it also enjoys a unique gratuity of its own.

Lacking anything explicit and clear, however, the proponents of Z might claim some faint indications of the gratuity of the destination to the order of grace. Take, for example, John 3:16: "God so loved the world that he gave his only Son." The world is permeated by God's creative love. But it becomes the object of a new love when the Father sends his Son. Here is an outburst of love incomparable to the creative love. Here is a love in which God offers all the possibility of salvation in Christ. It is an offer of love, a destination distinct from the creative love. Not that these two loves are temporally separated, as though the second could only follow the first chronologically. But even if they coincide in time, they are not identical. The love that creates us, argue the defenders of Z, does not necessarily carry in it the love that offers intimate divine Self-communication. The summons to union, to adoption by God is an undreamt of occurrence that the simple call to existence does not carry with it. Z also invokes the texts already cited on the invisibility of God, especially Matthew 11:27: ". . . no one knows the Father except the Son and anyone to whom the Son chooses to reveal him." This text was appealed to above to buttress the gratuity of union with God. God has freely given Godself; this Self-donation responds to no human exigency and is gratuitous not only because humanity is sinful, but also and primarily because humanity is created and God is transcendent. But do these texts go further still? Do they indicate not only the absence of any exigency in the creature but also of any obligation on God's part to make a Self-revelation merely in virtue of creation? God is, according to Z, free to remain hidden and silent. Certainly, asserts Z, humanity has been, in fact, created only with a view to the divine Self-revelation and covenant. This destination gives rise in the human being to a correlative desire and attraction that is absolute. This commits God, and it is a novel commitment, one not necessarily implied in creation. The absolute attraction is not, therefore, one of the necessary structures of the created spirit. In a word, Matthew 11:27 and texts like it suggest to the defenders of Z the gratuity of union and of the very destination to union as well.

Do these few and questionable indications of Scripture directly assert the gratuity of the destination to union? It is doubtful. Perhaps one could say at very most that the assertion is indirect. The scriptures do sufficiently and clearly ground the gratuity of actual union with God, according to Z. Z strongly insists on grounds of Scripture and theological reflection that the gift of grace enjoys a gratuity distinct from the gift of creation. But Z wants further to maintain that the two gratuities of union and destination to union are linked in interdependence. If an absolute destination to union appears among the necessary structures of created spirit, it is due to the gratuity of effective union. Attack the gratuity of one and you attack the gratuity of the other. God is obliged to Godself in the absolute offer of participation in the divine life. God promises Godself to humans on the condition of their acceptance in faith. If the offer is accepted, God owes it to Godself to share the divine life. To ask whether God, having so committed Godself, could now make the conferral of union yet another gratuity is to pose a question that lacks sense. On God's part salvation is already assured in the act of destination, which only the bad faith of humans can check. On condition of human acceptance God owes it to Godself to will effective union; more precisely, God has already willed it. In light of this, Z attempts to lay bare the weakness of X.

Z does not contest the phenomenology of love invoked by X. It is true that one destined to divine union and absolutely aspiring thereto asks of God God's free Self-communication. However, in so doing, one does not solicit a gratuity distinct from that already in the call and destination, for such cannot exist. By the very fact that God is already committed, the actual Self-gift cannot be the object of a new divine gratuity. The prayer implied in the absolute desire is saying: "Deign to give Yourself in virtue of the absolute love You already committed Yourself to when You called me." So X's phenomenology of love is valid. Love does seek a freely given love in return. Yet in the case of the God who has called, the freedom and gratuity of divine union cannot be other than that of the call and destination itself. Here we come to the heart of the matter. According to X, the destination has no other gratuity than that of creation. God cannot call spirit-beings to existence without calling them to union with the divine. But Z counters that since the freedom of the actual conferral of union cannot be distinguished from the divine freedom in destining humans to union, the gratuity of the divine Self-communication itself would not be distinguished from that of creation. If God necessarily calls to union the created spirits that are freely created, God already confers it upon them, or at least he cannot not absolutely promise it, if they do not reject it. If historical humanity is, solely by reason of creation, necessarily ordered to union, then union is no longer the object of free grace. Grace is no more; there is only the freedom of the divine creative act.

Defenders of Z find in this their most telling point against X. To avoid compromising the grace of elevation to union with God one must consider the destination to grace as already a unique gift distinct from the creative divine love. Correlatively, the absolute attraction stimulated by the destination is not a necessary structure of any created being. It is a supernatural attraction, a supernatural existential.[27] The gift of union comes from God not simply as creator, but as savior. Only the one drawn by the Father comes to Christ (John 6:44). The attraction that draws one to Christ comes from God, who in arousing it does something other than creating or calling into being. God's attraction draws us into

---

[27]The real distinction between the order of grace and the order of creation is not a distinction between two divine gifts which are wholly independent. Creation is oriented to gracing, for humanity is called to existence only in view of its call to union with God. The divine plan is a unified whole, though it has been customary to place a real distinction between its diverse moments. Thus a double gratuity has been seen in the call to being and the call to union, the latter not following necessarily from the former. Terminology and syntax sometimes mislead and a separation, even a reification, of the two divine gifts results.

the inner divine life of the Trinity. If this is so, if the attraction in us is already a work of grace, the movement it begets in us is not due to any moral activism, for nature cannot merit a pure gratuity. Rather than activism, it is abandonment and acceptance that are pivotal. Proponents of Z contend, therefore, that more is at stake here than winning points in an arcane theological debate. The position one takes on the interiority and gratuity of the call to union carries serious practical import. Z finds the viewpoint of X tinged with semi-Pelagianism. To hold that the interior attraction is not uniquely gratuitous is to undermine the importance of Christian abandonment to and receptivity before God. No longer attributing directly to God the élan that draws one to union the one relies on oneself and considers oneself the principle of salvation if the natural desire of salvation is already the seed of salvation.

C. *The Question of a Double Finality*

Some proponents of Z have distinguished in the concrete dynamism of existence two finalities. The first is that of the absolute, supernatural attraction to God; the second, that of nature in its orientation to its proportionate end. On what does Z base this distinction? On the supernatural character of the absolute attraction to God. This attraction modifies nature profoundly, but it remains a supernatural determination, distinct from nature as its substratum. It is nature that now aspires to union with God; it is nature which is supernaturally finalized. But nature, according to Z, is distinct from the absolute attraction, which does not define it. Nature still retains the finality which defines it. This last assertion needs elucidation, for it is not without its own difficulties.

Although for Z the absolute attraction is not essential, it is absolute and it may appear to remove any possible natural finality for the spirit. Is there, according to Z, something essential in the spirit relative to union with and vision of God? Z would respond affirmatively by asserting the existence in the human being of an obediential potency (sometimes considered a positive opening) or, as others would have it, a conditioned, natural desire for God. The latter came increasingly to be affirmed. The conditioned desire is viewed as the natural tendency of the human mind pursuant upon the realization of the conditions necessary for the remote possibility of vision and antecedent to the condition of its proximate possibility. The condition of this proximate possibility is the free divine decision to call humanity to union, the gracious willing of the salvation of all. The Christian believes in faith that this condition has been posited. God has called all and this call and destination coincides temporally with the act of creation. Though humanity could exist without being called it has never in fact so existed. As a consequence, Z contends, the call is not inscribed in us as an unconditioned aspiration. The call itself gives rise to the absolute, interior attraction. Here precisely is where difficulty crops up. Are we to say that in historical humanity, summoned to share the divine life, there coexist two desires for union with God, the conditioned desire of nature as such and the absolute desire of nature as supernaturally elevated? This would be absurd. What one must say is that the conditional tendency that might have been is by reason of the divine summons an absolute desire for vision. There is no question of a union which is only radically possible. Consequently, there is no purely conditioned desire. Union has become a proximate possibility and there is only the absolute desire for it. This, of course, brings Z to another difficulty. Does the suppression of the conditioned desire by the absolute attraction not amount to the suppression of any natural finality for the sake of the sole, supernatural finality? Can the human spirit be drawn by two diverse finalities?

The conditioned desire, however, is a tendency of nature towards an end, God in God's own self, that it can only receive and never attain. It is the side of the human spirit that is receptive, infinitely open to a reality that it cannot possess except as gift. It is this passive dimension of our natural finality, argues Z, that is suppressed by reason of the gift of absolute desire. Not that the absolute attraction relates us to God as other than the term of a pure Self-donation. God remains grace vis-à-vis the absolute desire. But whereas the conditioned, natural desire would set humanity in a position of radical and remote receptivity with regard to a God who has not committed Godself to it, the unconditioned desire sets humanity in a posture of proximate receptivity to a God who is knocking at the door. It is this passage (logical, not chronological) from radically possible and distant to proximately possible and near that Z expresses in terms of suppression.

But Z might further claim that the natural finality is not exhausted in conditioned desire for God. The very functions of mind and heart which, with regard to God, cannot but be receptive are at the same time powers for relating to their own proper mundane objects and for transforming them.[28] The exercise of these powers follows a natural, interior finality. They pursue an end and effectively achieve it. Not God in Godself, but the world, which is to be possessed in all the modalities of human knowledge and enjoyment. (If God is offered here as an end, it is indirectly and mediately, in and through the world as reflecting the divine.) If absolute desire eliminates in the natural finality the element of conditioned desire, it does not affect the human faculties in their tendencies outward to the proper objects of their knowledge, control, and creativity. Some might want to add that the absolute desire does not arise in the human spirit without bringing with it its own proper demand of sovereignty. God cannot become the goal of human aspiration without the sublation and subordination of all other human aspirations, real or possible. These sublated aspirations may pursue their proper goods but these multiple pursuits must submit to being placed in service of the absolute desire for the "one thing necessary." In this subordination and coordination these so-called "natural goods" tend to lose their character as ends and become pure means.[29] Intramundane activity ceases to obey a natural finality; intramundane ends are sublated by the supernatural end. Only such integration can protect the human spirit from threatening divisions and progressively unify it.

But there are some who think that by so ordering themselves the intramundane ends do not cease to be what they are; they are not reduced to the level of simple means. The world, even in a graced order, still possesses in itself the two conditions of a true end. First, the world could have been offered to humanity as its proper good in a purely natural order. Objectively, it is, therefore, a good, an end in which humans realize and fulfill themselves. No doubt, once introduced into a supernatural order, it acquires by virtue of its relation to the supernatural end an enhanced value. Nonetheless, its essential goodness remains independently of this elevation and lives on in the heart of the divine union. *Gratia supponit et perficit naturam.* Secondly, the human

---

[28] In what follows it is evident that Z and X do not adequately work out the relation and integration of the finalities. For a fuller integration cf. C. Davis, *God's Grace in History* (New York: Sheed & Ward, 1966). The failure at proper integration had not a little to do with the triumphalism that has often marked the history of Catholicism.

[29] One should feel some malaise over the term "natural." How to determine what is "natural"? This is difficult philosophically and culturally, and made no easier by the presence of grace, as we shall see.

subject, though living in a graced order, retains its eager enthusiasm for the world. Certainly the absolute desire of the heart inspires love for the incomparable Good. But this desire, which is not essential, is really distinct, asserts Z, from its substratum, the subject which it determines. The attraction does not suppress nature. And nature, the profundity of the absolute desire notwithstanding, retains its openness to its connatural good, interaction with the world. What more could be required for the world to retain its character as a true end? Objectively and subjectively it meets the requisite conditions.

According to some proponents of Z, then, there is a double aim in the created spirit. In X the spirit can have but one finality: the possession of God in Godself and of the world in and through God, not the possession of the world in itself as a good in which the subject realizes itself. Since the absolute desire for God is by no means a superadded reality for X, it does not allow for a subject that might aspire to another and proportioned end, for the absolute desire constitutes the total aspiration of the subject. It is not inconceivable that X might assign a positive role to our relationship to the world. In a universe of corporeal spirits it could well be, X might contend, that the corporeal spirit cannot make its way to God except through a certain mastery of the world. But for X this would only be a point in passage, a mere means, but never an end. It would not correspond to any hunger or desire in the subject. Thus X and Z differ in their conception of ends. This difference leads to another. For they also differ in their estimation of human activity in the world.

IV. *The Christian and the World*

We have already observed that the absolute attraction to some extent emerges in consciousness. This attraction, more often lived and pre-thematic, is clarified at the level of reflexive consciousness, as in the case of Augustine. But the attraction lies deeper than we can ever probe. We feel an obscure certainty that we can never blot out the attraction. We experience ourselves as called to surrender and acceptance, to the commitment of ourselves to a powerful benevolence. But mingled with this call one hears another. We are lured and tempted by activism. Humanity is drawn to know and master the world by means of science, technology, culture, and the building of the earthly city. Various fields of activity come before humanity, each with its own principles, methods, and autonomy, and they solicit our respect. In this situation, what are we to make of the theological positions of X and Z? Z admits that the supreme end of humanity is union with God as a pure gift of grace. Z is in no way disconcerted by a call to surrender. From the start such abandonment has a place in Z's system. Receptivity is the movement of the human being in response to the exclusively divine origin of union. Z is also in a position to give to the call to action a positive, favorable sense. On one hand, for Z, the supernatural finality coexists with humanity's intramundane orientation. The two are distinct and the former qualifies the latter. But humanity, says Z, ought not, in the name of its elevation to grace, renounce its relationship to the world. The world remains its counterpole and its necessary good. On the other hand, Z sees in this relationship to the world, the end suited and accessible to our natural powers of action. This finality offers and promises itself not to a posture of abandonment or surrender, but to our action in the world. Hence for Z the call to interaction with the world is something good, and by action alone can one achieve the good promised by relationship to the world.

X for its part maintains there is no end other than the possession of God in Godself and the world cannot be sought except in God.[30] On this score, X gives pride of place to abandonment, because for X, as for Z, the supernatural end, the divine in itself, is a gift of pure grace which lies open only to our capacity for acceptance.[31] Abandonment, moreover, is not pure passivity; it is the fullness of commitment. Though it is not activity in the world—the mastery and transformation of our environment—it is nonetheless the sovereign expression of our freedom. However, if X honors abandonment and the pure action of spirit, it has an

---

[30]"In God" has here an ontological sense. Of itself it can signify possession of the world in a way conformable to the will of God. This would give it a moral sense, which could be accepted by Z as well as by X. But here X primarily means by "in God" a possession of the world in and through God as an ontological milieu in which the created spirit knows all creatures.

[31]X might be reproached for betraying the need for abandonment, since, for X, attraction to the divine is essential and natural. This appears to leave little room for abandonment. In a semi-Pelagian mode, one depends on oneself for one's religious élan. Yet X does maintain that union with God is supernatural and comes only as a grace. Thus abandonment reappears. For X union with God is in one sense natural and in another sense supernatural: natural in that it corresponds to a human attraction that is essential, supernatural in that it is a pure gift of grace, the naturalness of the attraction notwithstanding.

altogether different reaction to our so-called "worldly" activity.
X appears to devalue it. On the one hand, humanity has but one
end: God in Godself and the world in God. On the other hand,
intramundane action (science, technology, building the city) is
given, by its very nature, to the possession of the world in itself
and not in God. Thus worldly activity does not, of itself, bring
us to participate in the sole true good that alone can sate us.
Should, X, therefore, call us to renounce worldly action? In the
context of our present condition X must admit that through this-
worldly activity humans, without well knowing how, wend their
way to their unique end, and that in some obscure way such activity can contribute to the coming of the Kingdom. Its necessity
is its justification. Such a justification, however, hardly aggran-
dizes it. It remains true that life and action in the world will never
attain the goodness that can make of it an end. At most it will
have the very relative goodness that makes it a simple means. The
world and its beings will never be worthy of being loved in themselves. One gives oneself to the world only to the extent that it
is impossible to escape from it. For X, it seems, worldly engagement can at best be tolerated in a kind of resignation to human
weakness and limitation (and, perhaps, fault) and to our exile
while we await redemption and release.

Given these corollaries of the two typological Catholic positions on nature and grace, one might turn to the thought of Vatican II for guidance on the place and import of activity in the
world. In these conciliar texts perhaps the position of Z appears
to have the upperhand. Chapter III of Part I of the *Pastoral Constitution on the Church in the Modern World* addresses the question of human activity in the universe (nn. 33–39). It is directly
concerned with action in the world, not with religious sentiment,
i.e., the abandonment and receptivity whereby one opens oneself to the immediate possession of God. It is concerned with the
action by which humanity "subjects to itself the earth and all that
it contains, with the action, individual and collective, and altogether monumental, whereby humans through the course of centuries have labored to better the circumstances of their lives" (n.
34, par. 1). Taking possession of the world is, it seems, immediate and direct, not just "in God." It is declared good, simply so,
and in agreement with the mission confided by God to humanity;
good not expressly by reason of its relation to the possession of
God (certainly this relationship qualifies its goodness, but here
it is neither envisaged nor mentioned), but good because it per-

fects humanity. "When one acts, one's work transforms not only things and society; one develops oneself as well. One learns much, cultivates one's resources and goes outside and beyond oneself" (n. 35, par. 1).[32] If it is true that of itself intramundane activity offers a certain good or perfection (i.e., prescinding from its reference to life in God), then there is no ground for devaluing it. Without a doubt it is not completely autonomous. "Hence the norm of human activity is this: that in accord with the divine plan and will, it should harmonize with the authentic good of the human race. . . ." (n. 35, par. 2). It is also the case that often enough disorderly human passions menace this required authenticity (n. 37). But such disorder is not inscribed in action by necessity and so the intrinsic goodness of participation in building a world stands.

The conciliar documents seem to side more with Z than with X on this matter. For X, the immediate possession of the world, although not evil, does not offer any good that might draw us. At most we might resign ourselves to being in the world as a transitional testing ground and an enigmatic necessity for the arrival of the Kingdom. The world has only a kind of borrowed goodness. And even that is often admitted with great reserve. All this squares poorly with a mode of thought that exalts human activity and encourages participation in it. "Far from thinking that works produced by humanity's own talent and energy are in opposition to God's power, and that the rational creature exists as a kind of rival to the Creator, Christians are convinced that the triumphs of the human race are a sign of God's greatness and the flowering of God's own mysterious design" (n. 34, par. 3). Z, it seems, does fuller justice to such a view.

Here Z might appeal to a confirmation from experience. That interaction with the world remains a proper and proportional end, that it is good in itself, that the need to engage talents is not merely to be tolerated but appeals to our deepest desires, all this is borne out in the joy that flows from our interaction with the world of things, and, above all, persons. In acting on the world to transform and better it, one tastes the pleasure of life, certainly mixed with a sense of precariousness—the world and interaction with it is not the absolute—and yet all together permeated by an experience of fulfillment and accomplishment. The joy experienced

---

[32]Here there is need to guard against a certain anthropocentric or even egoistic instrumentalism whereby other created beings, things and persons alike, are approached as mere means to the prospering of oneself or one's group.

in work and interaction indicates that one is harmonized with one's own being, that one is as one ought to be. Certainly hearing and responding to the call to action is not without its danger. Ordered by a supernatural attraction to union with God, it is to this call that one must attend above all. An inner space must be given over to the transcendent. In a nature scarred by the wounds of sin there has to be the fear that the intramundane will all too readily absorb all of one's energies. But foreseeable deviations do not cancel out the certitude of the principle at stake: of itself and in itself engagement in worldly activity is good and the sense of joyful fulfillment it arouses is a sign of its goodness.

At this point we can summarize the thrust of the discussion. The temptation to prefer X to Z is strong. Why keep safeguarding this supernatural dome that crowns the edifice of the Christian life? It seems of little use to claim, as Z does, that it corresponds to an expectation of nature. The very language used, and the reality itself, do not cease to suggest the very dangerous idea of a detachable element coming from the outside to crown the life of the spirit. On the other hand, Z attaches a great deal of importance to showing that the gratuity of the call and the destination condition the gratuity of the union itself. Z argues that the supernaturality of the attraction is required for the protection of the order of grace. Further, some proponents of Z, the much more common view, have, more recently, called attention to the threat that X is to the order of nature. In so doing they touch a sensitive nerve for the modern person who is so concerned with terrestrial values and the crucial significance of humanization of interaction with the world of nature and people. The question addressed to every modern is whether he or she wants to be, to use Teilhard's words, a "child of the earth." These proponents of Z conclude that if one agrees with X that the desire for God in Godself is essential to the created spirit, and that consequently union with God in Godself is humanity's natural end, then primacy must be given to the value of abandonment to God and other-worldly detachment from the world of exile in which one is delayed.

V. *The Possibility of a Graceless World*

Finally, we must attend to a question that runs through all the debates concerning nature and grace. Do the gratuity and supernaturality of the human destination and attraction entail as a corollary the possibility of a pure nature? To respond, a distinction was usually drawn. The destination to union is a grace and the attraction is supernatural. Neither of them conditions the possibility of the created spirit according to traditional Catholic positions on nature and grace. Created spirit does not necessarily entail them as it does intelligence and freedom. Human nature would be meaningful independently of an absolute attraction. Nonetheless, it is generally held that historical humanity has never existed without the absolute attraction. Hence we can form the concept of a nature not called, not elevated to the order of grace and we can do so in the very act of forming the idea of the gratuity of the call. This we call the concept of pure nature. In this first sense, the term designates precisely human nature envisaged as independent of the attraction that historically qualifies it supernaturally. It is a heuristic concept enlisted to protect the gratuity of grace. No actual instance of pure nature is known to us. There exists only concrete nature under the actual determination of the call and attraction to grace.

One might, however, understand the concept of pure nature in another way. One might assimilate human nature in all its dimensions to natures, animate or unanimate, that are inferior to it. Each nature is a species. *Pure* human nature will then refer to humanity insofar as it fully manifests all the characteristics of the natural beings. Is such a way of understanding human nature necessary to explain the gratuity of human destination to divine union? In the philosophy of some Scholastic theologians "nature" designated, in a hierarchy of beings, a particular degree of being, and each nature ranked in this scale has tendencies strictly commensurate with its capacities for action. Natures aspire only to that which they are capable of achieving. The end that each nature pursues must be proportioned to its operative faculties and its appetites and desires are not geared to goods it could only receive but never attain of itself. There can be in the realm of nature no inefficacious desires. In a word, natures are closed systems, turned back upon themselves, each locked in its own species.

But can humanity be thus assimilated to the other "natural" beings?[33] One cannot deny that by reason of its corporeal dimen-

[33]Some Scholastics thought it could. Cajetan is the initiator or at least the leading proponent of the concept of human nature as completely closed and self-sufficient. After him came Suarez, John of St. Thomas, and others. Cf. H. de Lubac, *The Mystery of the Supernatural*, 187 ff.

sion humanity does largely share the condition of the other natures. Yet by reason of its spirit, humanity transcends the others. To show this, one might appeal to the human acts of intellection and choice and the formal limitlessness they manifest. Cognition presupposes as its principle a spiritual power that is open, by desire, to the infinite fullness of being, a fullness that the created spirit is incapable of giving itself. This dynamic movement towards the plenitude leads humanity to transcend itself. There is perhaps an even simpler indication of all this, a kind of argument from absurdity. Suppose human nature is closed in on itself, much the same as all other natures. Should we say that it is simply and absolutely thrown back on itself, that it cannot be elevated to the grace of divine vision? This perhaps is unwarranted. According to the Scholastics, although natures are closed systems, they are nonetheless able to submit to a certain extraordinary divine action in virtue of a passive capacity which renders them docile and obedient in the face of this divine action. This passive or obediential potency (*potentia obedientialis*), when it is exercised, permits something miraculous to appear. Having naturalized the human spirit, having viewed it as a closed nature, these Scholastics go on to claim that humanity possesses an obediential potency relative to God's elevating action and therefore remains open to grace.

Does this way of explaining the divine/human relationship do justice to the characteristics of this union as they are put forth in the tradition? It seems to misconstrue them in two ways. First, God wants all to be saved. Destination to union is universal. Even if the union is supernatural, it is difficult to think of it as miraculous, for it is difficult to think of the world of created spirits as elevated to its heights by reason of an ongoing, universal miracle. Secondly, union with the divine penetrates the heart of human being. "We will make our home in him" (John 14:23). The union is profoundly interior. One seems to eliminate this interiority if one makes elevation to grace simply a detachable superstructure superimposed on a nature that is closed in on itself and self-sufficient. One also eliminates by the same token any reasonable expectation of an obligatory acceptance of the proffered grace, which can only appear alien to a closed, self-sufficient nature.

What follows from all this? First, some will argue that the divine/human rapport ought not be worked out in terms of an obediential potency, a conceptual construct entailing the notion of a closed nature rendered docile to miraculous divine action. If one insists on this construct, it should be understood, in the case of humanity, as a positive openness, a tendency and aspiration to union. But this especially seems to follow. The notion of pure nature as closed is not necessarily linked to the gratuity of the call to grace. Indeed, not only is it not required, it is to be avoided. If we naturalize humanity without reservation, if we assimilate it to the closed systems of the so-called natural beings, we remove the interiority and universality of the union. Pure nature in the sense of a closed nature seems, then, impossible at worst and heuristically useless at best.

That human nature is not closed means that it is open to a good that it can only receive, i.e., the absolute Good as its supernatural end. Human nature not only has an openness to the supernatural, but, according to some theologians, a tendency, an aspiration to it. Can this openness and tendency be identified with the absolute attraction or desire? As we have seen, it has generally been maintained that this attraction is gratuitous and supernatural, as is the call which gives rise to it. Otherwise, the gratuity of the union itself is compromised and the whole order of grace collapses. If this is so, the opening of nature as such to the supernatural is, strictly speaking, only a disposition for the absolute attraction. What nature is immediately open to is not so much actual union with God but supernatural aspiration to union. Nature as open can be the subject of absolute desire for God. Some theologians, however, are not content, as we said, to speak merely of an openness. They discern, by means of a transcendental analysis, as we shall see, a natural aspiration in the spirit to divine union, a natural desire for the vision of God. But they enter an important qualification. This is not the absolute Augustinian desire. It is a conditioned desire, a seminal orientation whose full development depends on a factor over which the desire itself has no control and which it cannot set in motion, viz., the free condescension of absolute being to communicate itself.

The idea of a conditioned desire is not without its problems. It may be superior to the idea of a simple opening. The latter escapes less well the unacceptable idea of a closed human nature whose desire is measured by the end it can effectively procure. But does not the idea of a conditioned desire imply a nature which could go on always unfulfilled, never attaining its end? It would be given to asymptotic progression with no possibility of passing its limit. This is unacceptable to those for whom becoming without end is repugnant.[34] Perhaps the proponents of a conditioned desire have never adequately weighed this difficulty. It must be dealt with if one wants to hold at the same time both the unique gratuity of an absolute destination to union and the impossibility of a closed human nature. Because human nature cannot be closed, there has to be in it aspiration and desire. On the other hand, because this natural desire cannot be an absolute attraction, lest, being natural, it bring tumbling down the entire edifice of grace, it must be conditioned. The absolute attraction is, as we shall see, a supernatural existential according to Rahnerians. It is, however, not inconceivable from another angle to see in this a "natural" desire. Some Scholastic thinkers did view material natures as closed. But human nature is essentially open to the totality of being. Consequently, the absolute attraction, gratuitous as it is in relation to human nature and its limitless openness, corresponds nonetheless to that which is specific and proper to nature and in this sense it could, without detriment to its gratuity, be called "natural." This usage has not been accepted. The absolute attraction is gratuitous for a nature, it is contended, that is intelligible and possible without it. A word is needed to articulate this. And the word "supernatural" presents itself. The absolute attraction is supernatural; the conditioned attraction is natural.

In conjunction with the notion of pure nature, we must return again to the position of X. We saw how one of its arguments, the one based on the phenomenology of love, is met. Now we have to assess the other two. First, X reproaches Z for sundering the unity of the human being's inner life. Z seems to assign two ends to the human spirit, each one apparently independent of the other. There is the natural end, knowledge and mastery of and interrelationship with the world and there is the supernatural situation, the summons and destination of humanity to intimate union with God. Is the reproach against Z warranted?

It is true that Z sometimes does distinguish a double finality and even fails to interrelate them adequately. By its essential constitution, nature aspires effectively only to possession of the world. That is nature's proportionate end and supernatural elevation does not suppress it, but by reason of the supernatural attraction nature aspires to immediate possession of God. This double finality marks a double movement in the life of the spirit: one which con-

[34]Ibid., ch. 10.

duces to action in the world and a spirit of conquest, the other to a posture of acceptance and surrender. But, argues Z, nothing warrants translating this distinction in terms of a divided self. For the supernatural end does not manifest itself to the spirit through a conscious attraction without making its superiority to the natural end known. Not only is it superior, it is controlling. The Kingdom subordinates nature to itself and places it in its own service. The supernatural end exercises a priority that establishes a hierarchy of finalities and introduces into the life of the spirit a principle of unity. The word "principle" should be underlined. The unified self is not a ready-made endowment that one passively receives. It is a rule, a challenge that demands recognition and acceptance. It is a task. We have to actively submit nature to the supernatural attraction and actively place the natural spirit of conquest at the service of surrender and of the Christian life. If we do so, our lives become progressively integrated under the supremacy of the Kingdom as ultimate end. One can speak of a distinction of ends, but the ends are ordered. There need be no division or tearing of the inner self.

Z tacitly presupposes in its response that the ends of nature are objectively such that it is possible for the human person to actively, subjectively place them in service of the supernatural end. Is this assumption grounded? Can human interaction with the world cooperatively contribute in any way to the Kingdom? Here Z is in need of views only recently opened to us by a renewed theology of terrestrial realities. The union of humanity with God calls for a progressive transformation of the worldly milieu to which it is tied. Humanity ought to seriously commit itself to an increasing humanization of its world. Otherwise grace, which is always incarnate, is stunted and fails to achieve its full development. Certainly, human culture and the secular city are not the Kingdom. Nor can city-building of itself bring in the Kingdom, which remains pure grace and is open directly only to our spirit of acceptance and surrender. Yet all authentic human effort disposes us for the Kingdom. All victories over the opaqueness and gravity of nature prepare for the fullness of union with nature's God. It is a preparation that the grace of God works in and through us. These assertions have validity on the personal level but on the social level as well. Bergson is relevant at this point. ". . . that true, active mysticism aspires to radiate, by virtue of the charity that is its essence, is certain. How could it spread, even enfeebled and diluted as it must necessarily be, in a humanity obsessed by fear of not eating its full? Man will rise above the earth only if a powerful instrument provides him with the requisite fulcrum. He must be serious about matter if he hopes to detach himself from it. In other words, the mystical summons up the mechanical."[35] Building the Kingdom requires of humanity a certain mastery of the world. One must be a child of the earth to become a child of heaven. World and Kingdom are not two isolated realities that divide the self.

There is one final argument of X that Z must face. We have seen that in Z's view the gratuity of salvation cannot be conceived of apart from the special gratuity of the destination to grace, a gratuity distinct from the gratuity of creation. In turn the gratuity of the destination begets the hypothesis of pure nature. The destination is gratuitous for the being that we are; it cannot be counted among the necessary structures of human being. Humanity is meaningful and possible without it. The objection of X to this line of thought is that recourse to the hypothesis of pure nature doesn't really further the cause of Z. The finality of pure nature is different from the finality of concrete, historical nature. And finality is something essential. Change it and you change the being itself. Pure nature is an altogether different being from the historical being destined for union with God. What light, then, can this hypothesis provide? The analysis of pure nature, if it is even possible, concerns a possible entity substantially unlike historical humanity. And it is concerning this concrete existent that the question of gratuity must be resolved.

The objection seems valid, Z replies, if it is levied against pure nature in the second sense, i.e., human nature assimilated to non-spiritual natures, to a closed system locked in on itself, where tendencies are measured by capabilities for action and achievement. Such a human nature would desire only that which it can achieve on its own; it would entail an absolute ontological indifference to divine union, which is beyond its grasp. It would differ substantially from the elevated humanity that is in love with the absolute.[36] Does the objection of X hold also for pure nature which is open, the only nature that Z admits? As a "pure" nature it

[35]H. Bergson, *The Two Sources of Morality and Religion* (Garden City: Doubleday, 1935), 309.

[36]One might appeal to the hypothesis of the obediential potency (in the strict sense), with its docility and its compliance with the miraculous transforming action of God (praeter ordinem naturae). But this miracle does not confer the dual character of interiority and universality that marks the elevation of concrete, historical human nature. The two are different beings. There is closed nature, superficially elevated and extrinsically refinalized and there is historical nature, which in the depth of its being is a living desire for God.

would tend neither absolutely nor efficaciously to divine union. Being open, however, it would enjoy a real capacity for supernatural destination, a capacity, which, far from being a simple obediential potency (a non-repugnance), is already a positive orientation, an authentic though conditioned aspiration for God. An absolute destination does not substantially alter such a nature; rather, it completes it. A new finality supervenes, but it presupposes and perfects the possible natural thrust of human being. It brings human being into an order that is immeasurably superior, but it is still the same human being that it advances. In all this, however, there is need to avoid certain traps which the imagination can set for us. Talk about a gratuitous destination and a supernatural attraction as a gift to nature evokes the idea of an aim superimposed from without and filling up a void. This could leave Z open to an objection. Even if the position of Z is that the new finality simply actuates a positive capacity, it is still the case that, coming from without, it works some violence on the being that it determines. But Z insists that the new finality is not imposed from without. It is the call of God (or, more exactly, the objective correlative of this call). God is always already present in the depths of the being called. The destination arises from within. The finality which draws us activates, in its term, an inherent capacity of the subject and, in its source, derives from God who is immanent, *interior intimo meo*. It is from within the subject itself, in its intrinsic creaturely dependence, that the destination to union with God arises. There is a difference, a change from what might have been. But the principle which effects the change comes from within the being itself which is changed. Violence is not done to human nature; its identity is respected.

Z recognizes that the subject thus elevated, while remaining identical with itself and its nature, is profoundly transformed. Employing Scholastic language, it understands the new form that is the absolute attraction as an accidental modification of the human substance. The term "accidental" ought not mislead us. For Scholastic philosophy considered the faculties of will and intellect as accidents of the human essence. Did that mean they were considered to be merely superficial determinations? Evidently not. The term "accident" does not necessarily indicate a purely surface reality. For neo-Scholastic theologians the same is true when attraction to the vision of God is said to be accidental. The person who knows this attraction retains human identity. But the accidental determination is ontologically rooted, anterior to all

activity of the subject. In its profundity it is radically and intimately transformative as it draws us to an end incommensurable
with any proportioned natural end, the possession of God's own
Self. The attraction draws us to search for that which we already
desire. "You would not be searching for me if. . . ." There is
a double experience engendered by the attraction: the experience
of the long-already-thereness of its term in our spirit and the experience of the ecstasy and surprise of discovery that never ceases.

Having briefly noted the history of the nature/grace debate and
having exposed at length the issues and terms of the debate and
the lines drawn by the two major positions, we are now in a position to examine in detail the resurgence of the discussion among
Roman Catholic theologians in the decades following World War
II. These were heady and exciting years for a newly awakened
Catholicism as it attempted to adapt itself to modernity. The new,
more positive openness that has marked post-conciliar Catholicism is due in no small measure to the theology of nature and
grace that began to develop in the pre-conciliar period. This "new
theology" (nouvelle théologie) marked the end of the static theology of nature and grace that had been in vogue since the era
of the counter-Reformation.[37] Without this development Vatican
II's *Dogmatic Constitution on the Church,* its *Pastoral Constitution on the Church in the Modern World*, and its *Declaration
on the Relationship of the Church to non-Christian Religions*
would have been without theological underpinning, or even,
perhaps, inconceivable. It is this theological infrastructure that
we want to lay bare. As with most infrastructures, it is assumed
to be there but seldom examined. Our study offers an exposition
and critique of the approaches taken by representative major
players in the nature/grace discussions of mid-twentieth century
Roman Catholicism, Henri de Lubac, Karl Rahner, Hans Urs von
Balthasar, Juan Alfaro, Max Seckler, Edward Schillebeeckx, and
Eulalio Baltazar. The listing is not exhaustive, only representative. Least of all is there any indication that the discussion is
closed. The relationship of nature and grace is a perennial among
theological problems. Because it is, it will always be a growth in
which are found old things and new.

---

[37] On the renaissance in Catholic theology inaugurated by the "nouvelle théologie,"
cf. T. Schoof, *A Survey of Catholic Theology, 1800–1970* (Paramus: Paulist, 1970),
175–228; R. Aubert, *The Church in a Secularized World* (New York: Paulist, 1978),
535–623; J. Connolly, *The Voices of France* (New York: Macmillan, 1961).

2

The Reemergence of the
Problem of Nature and Grace
in the Twentieth Century

More than four decades have elapsed since the publication of
Henri de Lubac's mind-changing book, *Surnaturel.*[1] In the two
decades following its publication, Catholic theologians were prolific on the subject of nature and grace.[2] What occurred following de Lubac's work was a complete break with the counter-
Reformation theology of nature and grace.

[1]H. de Lubac, *Surnaturel: Études Historiques* (Paris: Aubier, 1946). This work was
a shot heard throughout the Catholic theological community.

[2]Cf., e.g., J. Alfaro, *Lo Natural y lo Sobrenatural* (Madrid: Consejo Sup. de In-
vestigaciones Cient., 1952); "Persona y Gracia," *Gregorianum* 41(1960) 5–29; "Transcendencia e Immanencia de lo Sobrenatural," *Gregorianum* 38(1957) 5–50; E. Baltazar,
Teilhard and the Supernatural (Baltimore: Helicon, 1966); H. Urs von Balthasar, "Der
Begriff der Natur in der Theologie," *Zeitschrift für Katholische Theologie* 75(1953)
452–464; H. Bouillard, "L'Idée de Surnaturel et le Mystère Chrétien," in *L' Homme
devant Dieu: Mélanges offerts au Pere H. de Lubac* (Paris: Aubier, 1964), 153–166;
G. De Broglie, "De Gratuitate Ordinis Supernaturalis," *Gregorianum* 29(1948) 435–463;
P. Donnelly, "On the Development of Dogma and the Supernatural," *Theological
Studies* 8(1947) 471–491; "Discussion on the Supernatural Order," *Theological Studies*
9(1948) 213–249; "The Surnaturel of H. de Lubac," *Theological Studies* 9(1948) 554–560;
"The Gratuity of the Beatific Vision and the Possibility of a Natural Destiny," *Theo-
logical Studies* 11(1950) 374–404; E. Gutwenger, "Natur und Übernatur," *Zeitschrift
für Katholische Theologie* 75(1953) 82–97; B. Lonergan, "The Natural Desire to See
God," *Proc. of Jesuit Philosophical Association*, (1949) 31–43; L. Malevez, "La Gratuité
du Surnaturel," *Nouvelle Revue Théologique* 75(1953) 561–586, 673–689; J. Maréchal,
"De Naturali Perfectae Beatitudinis Desiderio," in *Mélanges Maréchal*, I (Paris: Desclée
de Brouwer, 1950), 323–337; K. Rahner, "Concerning the Relationship between Nature and Grace," *Theological Investigations*, I (Baltimore: Helicon, 1961) 297–317;
E. Schillebeeckx, "Het niet-begrippelijke moment in de geloofsdad volgens Thomas
van Aquino," *Tijdschrift voor Theologie* 3(1963) 167–195; W. Shepherd, *Man's Condition: God and the World Process* (New York: Herder & Herder, 1969).

I. *Historical Antecedents*

Karl Rahner pointed to three historical factors that fostered a renewed study of the nature-grace dialectic.[3] There was first the philosophical work of Joseph Maréchal and those who bore the stamp of his influence.[4] Maréchal made an original study of Thomistic epistemology, relating it to the work of Kant. Maréchal's study was rooted in his understanding of intellectual dynamism, i.e., a tension in thought toward reality by reason of its teleological drive, independently of conceptual structure. One might summarize Maréchal's relevance to the nature-grace problematic in three affirmations: (1) the concept is of itself static and receives its full meaning only when immersed in the vital tendency of the intellect to know all truth; judgment reflects the total dynamic movement of nature, not merely to this particular object, but to the antecedent finality of the rational potency itself; (2) the conceptual, experiential image points to a transcendent noumenal reality which is subsisting truth; (3) subsistent truth is identified with God. For Maréchal repose in a particular affirmation is known not to be total insofar as it does not exhaust the intellect's drive. The possession of a particular truth is merely a subordinate end, a moment in the pursuit of a more comprehensive end. At the heart of all intellectual striving is an insatiable and obscure desire for total being, total truth.

According to Maréchal, then, what makes humans to be what they are and experience themselves to be is a radical orientation to God. The climax of the cognitive dynamism is the equation of the possession of total truth with the beatific vision. Spirit is thus seen to be a real, even if conditioned, desire for the vision of God. The human person is a longing for absolute being. Not that God is desired as an object not yet achieved, but rather as fulfillment of an existence in which there is already a preliminary experience of God's presence. The force of this thrust is implicitly felt and pre-conceptually affirmed in each human act. For Maréchal this *a priori* condition is the key to understanding spiritual being. The desire for God is, in his view, a transcendental condition for all cognition and volition. In other words, every affirmation or acceptance of finite being derives from the *a priori*

---

[3]K. Rahner, *Nature and Grace: Dilemmas in the Modern Church* (New York: Sheed & Ward, 1964), 119–123.

[4]J. Maréchal, *Le Point de départ de la métaphysique*, Vol. V: *Le Thomisme devant la philosophie critique*, 2 ed. (Paris: Desclée de Brouwer, 1949).

condition making possible that affirmation; and it is this *a priori* that remains the possibility for affirming and accepting a consequent orientation toward God as implicit in the human spirit. It is not difficult to see why Maréchal's position spawned a debate concerning its compatibility with the Church's teaching on the supernaturality and gratuity of the direct vision of God. Nonetheless, a twofold benefit accrued from Maréchal's work: the orientation to God began to be once again understood not as an "extra," but as a central principle in the human make-up, and study was stimulated as to how grace affects persons already so disposed to God in their very nature and being.

Secondly, one must factor into the renewed nature-grace study the wealth of historical investigation of how the natural-supernatural distinction became an accepted theorem in Catholic theology in the post-Tridentine period. Only gradually was the distinction developed. Obviously this is no criterion of its legitimacy. Even more gradual was its application to and implication in numerous individual theological problems. Nevertheless, the adoption of this distinction, however justified and necessary, was far from being a model of theological development pure and simple. Historical study has led us to ask whether in charting the movement of this development we do not find lost in its wake much that was of value in previous theological understanding, as well as a sharp shift in emphasis relative to other facets of human divinization by grace.

Summarily, the nature-grace distinction was often inflated to total dichotomy. So radical was the discontinuity between the two that human nature stood over against grace, a new quasi-nature, thus endowing humans with the internal incoherence of a dual finality. Paradoxically, the very conceptualization that was meant to safeguard the uniqueness and transcendence of grace tended to destroy those qualities.[5] Nature and supernature were juxtaposed, two species of one genus. Grace, the supernature, merely reproduces to a superior degree all the features which characterize nature itself, for if the state of pure nature is merely a transposition of the existential order, conversely, the supernatural order may easily become the transposition of a purely natural order. Further, created grace became the focal point in the heat of a polemic that blinded theologians to the paramount consideration that should have been paid to uncreated grace and its relation to

[5]Cf. H. de Lubac, *The Mystery of the Supernatural*, ch. 3.

created grace. And insufficient attention was given the large and intricate question of the nexus between the incarnation and human gracing due to a preoccupation with the effort to accent the gratuity of grace by setting actually graced humanity in stark contrast to a possibly ungraced humanity.

In the third place, Rahner notes that the renewed dialogue between Catholic and Protestant theologians did much to impel a reapproach to the question of the relationship between nature and grace. The issue had driven a wedge between the two camps since the sixteenth century. Protestant studies fostered investigation of the nature-grace problematic indirectly through their reconsideration of the theology of the Fall and of the process of justification. Protestant theologians asked themselves what else is a human person apart from being a sinner? To what extent does a person remain a sinner once justified? To what extent was the image of God in humans destroyed by the Fall and restored by Christ? What does today's person have in common with the Adam of Genesis 2 and 3? On the other side, Catholic theologians, insufficient in number, however, engaged in a reevaluation of Protestant postures, both old and new.

These then are the historical factors that loomed large in reawakening interest in the relationship between God's grace and human being. However, it ought to be noted that all three factors are themselves permeated by and function within the context of a certain contemporary spirit which itself was a stimulus in this direction. The desire today is for a synthetic understanding of humanity, a holistic picture that integrates the many aspects of human being made known to us by "regional" fields of study. Further, perhaps due to a more existential and/or empirical approach to life, people today want to experience grace in experiencing themselves and their communities, ecclesial and non-ecclesial. Such a mentality obviously influenced theologians. Hence the effort of some theologians to show that in concrete existence and experience grace cannot be neatly sealed off from the so-called "natural" levels in a person, but that it must penetrate all activities, both conscious and unconscious.

Finally, an observation at once diagnostic and prognostic. The theology of nature and grace was influenced in no small way by the Church's effort to formulate a positive theology of the world which would respect the autonomous existence of the secular. The constitution on *The Church and the Modern World* of Vatican II is a prime example and the culmination of much previous effort. Aware of past futility, not to mention outright error in swimming against the tide of social change, or in retreating from an encroaching world of science, politics, and autonomous human development, the Church was searching for a way to baptize the inevitable march of history and to integrate social evolution into the evolution of the Kingdom. All of this gave rise to the knotted problem of the relation of the Church to the world, the sacred to the profane, the eternal to the temporal, the Christian to the human, the sacred to the secular. It would seem that the age-old problem of these dualities is in function of the more remote theoretical problem of nature and grace. Only to the extent this latter problem is satisfactorily thematized can safe guidelines be drawn for a sound practical approach to the former. Certainly, practical attempts will be made to achieve a proper sacral-secular relationship on the level of living long before the theologizing is at an end. Certainly too, through the dialectic of life and theology the resulting experience will offer no little light to theologians.[6]

Moreover, it would seem that theologians, if they are to refine the secularization theology born in the 1960's, today and in the years ahead will have as one of their principal concerns a reconceptualization of the nature-grace problematic. Numerous Christians experience a schizophrenic tension, torn as they are between the poorly harmonized mundane and religious aspects of their existence, trying to hold on to both ends of the chain, confident the two are somehow joined in the hiddenness of God. The secularist, on the other hand, cannot accept a supernatural "beyond." It must somehow be seen as situated at the core of personal life if it is to have any possibility of achieving meaning. All this implies that the immanence of grace must be more forcefully accented, yet without detriment to its transcendence.

The temptation is always strong to collapse the distinction between the natural and the supernatural. More precisely, the temptation is to engage in a process of reductionism by opting to collapse the sacred for a glad affirmation of the secular. But while the terms may be changed to something with a more contemporary ring, and the understanding of them changed so that reductionists become more patient of the distinction, the reality of the "theorem of the supernatural"[7] seems to some implied in Scripture

---

[6]Cf. H. de Lubac, "Nature and Grace," in T. Burke, ed. *The Word in History* (New York: Sheed & Ward, 1966), 22–40.

[7]B. Lonergan, "St. Thomas' Thought on Gratia Operans," *Theological Studies* 2(1941) 301.

and a valid, permanent acquisition of the medieval era of theology. Hence there will be need to avoid the tendency to monistic reductionism, so often the risk run by the anthropological and existential orientations which have been so fruitful in modern theology. Theology must speak of God as well as humans, of the theological as well as of the psychological, of grace as well as nature.

II. *The Critique of the Post-Tridentine Theology of Nature and Grace*

One of the predominant concerns of the Catholic theology of grace in the post-Reformation era was to combat the view wrongly ascribed to the Reformers that grace made no intrinsic difference in humans. For the Catholic theologian grace was a permanent spiritual entity intrinsic to the justified. The model traditionally employed to explicate grace was human nature. In the human person there is a multiplicity of individual actions, but there was thought to be an abiding substratum, a human nature that is the principle of these actions. In analogous fashion for the supernatural order, it was thought, one must posit as underpinning the multiple transitory actions and the intermediary powers eliciting and elevating them in a way comparable to nature's faculties, a perduring entity or "nature," better known as sanctifying grace. The end result of this conceptualization was a certain extrinsicism, a kind of "superstructure" understanding of grace.[8] Grace is seen as grafted on to nature; it is a new "nature" or "essence" superadded to human nature. The structure of the new nature, grace, is patterned after that of human nature, upon which it is superimposed. Both are tripartite, with their underlying essence, powers or faculties, and the actions issuing therefrom.

Now, however, one describes grace and explicates its relation to nature, it must always be understood as the totally free gift of God, a gift that is most meaningful for humanity. Immediately the mind has set for itself a twofold task and the performance of one may very easily cause serious difficulties for the other. In other words, the mind faces the perplexing problem of balancing in unresolved tension the terms of an irresolvable antinomy. The

---

[8]The extrinsicist approach could be found in almost any manual of theology in use at the time and even among the better monographs. See, e.g., C. Journet, *The Meaning of Grace* (New York: P.J. Kenedy, 1960) and M. Scheeben, *The Mysteries of Christianity* (St. Louis: B. Herder, 1946).

first task is to show that grace, the divine life communicated to human persons, is distinct from and transcendent to nature. Otherwise the gratuity of grace is jeopardized. It must be shown that grace is not a human accomplishment nor merely the outgrowth of human nature. But one must also see to it that grace is not simply an extrinsic addition to human nature, a kind of optional additive. Otherwise, the real immanence of grace is sacrificed. If one does not forge an intimate bond between nature and grace, it becomes difficult to see the meaningfulness of grace and to maintain that human persons have but one finality. If grace is purely an additive to nature, already complete in itself and verifiable in any possible order, if humanity is meaningful apart from Christ and his grace, then one is free to accept or spurn the offer of grace.[9] If nothing in concrete humanity inevitably orientates it toward the deification that grace promises and initiates, then one suffers no substantial loss in declining the offer of a graced destiny. Persons are at liberty to develop those structures that *are* their nature, to opt for a purely "natural" destiny, to ignore the invitation tendered by a voluntaristic God as a disturbing intrusion forced upon their already intelligible situation, and all this with no intrinsic havoc worked upon themselves. For when a natural order is simply juxtaposed alongside the supernatural order, and the former is presented as absolutely autonomous and self-sufficient, the latter must by necessity be thought of as extrinsic, accidental, foreign, and an unintelligible superadded element for which the human person is not made.[10]

In the past, theologians who explained the nature-grace relationship in terms of the construct known as "pure nature," or in terms of rational nature as a closed whole whose active capacities, tendencies, and finalities are in strict correlation, have, especially since the Baian controversy, almost exclusively delimited

---

[9]A definitive natural beatitude was of no concern to medieval theology because it was considered non-existent and because efforts to conceptualize it were forced, it was thought, to borrow from the true finality. The possibility of a pure nature having as its end an abstract knowledge of God was first championed by Cajetan and fed into the mainstream of Catholic theology through its use in polemics against Baius and Jansen. Cf. R. Bruch, "Das Verhältnis von Natur und Gnade nach der Auffassang der neueren Theologie," *Theologie und Glaube* 46(1956) 81–102; H. de Lubac, *The Mystery of the Supernatural*, pp. 181–216. The work of J. Alfaro (cf. note 2) showed definitively Cajetan's deviation from his predecessors.

[10]"On this view man is only made and destined for it *after* he has received grace, and then only in a way entirely abstracted from experience." K. Rahner, "Concerning the Relationship between Nature and Grace," 300.

their focus to the transcendence of grace, its utter discontinuity with nature. Certainly the end to which humans are destined, the vision of the Godhead, is not unqualifiedly natural, for it transcends the range of created intelligence. Otherwise it would not be a participation in what is proper to the divine Persons. Yet the price dearly paid in protecting the transcendence of grace was the immanence of grace. Impaled on a dilemma, post-Reformation theologians opted for what they considered the more important polarity, the safer extreme, but for all that an extreme. Once grace becomes so completely extraneous in an effort to highlight its transcendence Christian proclamation is evacuated of all urgency, for it can no longer be heard as heralding a perfection that answers to anything intrinsic to humanity. Yet the supernatural order does exist precisely to effect an absolute fulfillment for humans. It ought to involve the immanent perfection of one's highest powers. If one is not to reduce humanity to a mere locus of extrinsic divine operation, the inner, tripersonal life of God must be immanently perfective of personal inner being, not a totally alien additive to a being already integral in itself.

Obviously, too, any extrinsicist approach could hardly be consonant with the new era in theology, anthropological as it is in its orientations. Any proffered destiny must be presented as fulfilling, as meaningful, and of value for humans.[11] The superhuman goal that Christianity sets before people becomes wholly unacceptable if it is seen as anti-human, or at best superfluous. It was precisely the failure and the poverty of the Catholic theology of grace that in this respect provided a thinker of Paul Tillich's stature with ground to accuse Catholic theologians of what he terms supernaturalism.[12] This unfortunate and unnecessary dualism spawned numerous sad consequences in various areas of Christian life.[13]

In the same line of argument, the extrinsicist approach, in its efforts to construct a protective rampart around the gratuity of grace, resorted to invoking the dictum: God does not create a na-

---

[11]It was M. Blondel's conviction that the Christian apologetic should keep this point uppermost. *Letter on Apologetics and History of Dogma* (New York: Holt, Rinehart, Winston, 1964). On Blondel relative to the problem of nature and grace, cf. W. Shepherd, *Man's Condition*, 58-70.

[12]P. Tillich, *Systematic Theology*, 3 vols. (Chicago: University of Chicago, 1951-1963), I, 64-65; II, 5-10; III, 113-115, etc.

[13]Cf. H. de Lubac, *The Mystery of the Supernatural*, 233-234; L. Malevez, "L'Esprit et le désir de voir Dieu," *Nouvelle Revue Théologique* 69(1947) 3-31.

ture in vain. *Deus non creavit frustra; natura non potest esse inane.* In other words, those things necessary for the creature's perfection are owed to it; the creature is simply unintelligible without them. Once the argument is so marshalled, it follows that the supernatural cannot be necessary to humans and at the same time preserve its gratuity. For what is necessary is demanded. But the supernatural cannot be demanded. Therefore it is not necessary, but wholly gratuitous if bestowed. Furthermore, since the Creator creates no nature in vain, human beings could live and find meaning apart from filiation in relation to God.

The difficulty encountered in this approach has already been implied in our observations above. How, once the argumentation is accepted, can the supernatural be valued as a person's highest perfection and yet be unnecessary? One does not elucidate the mystery of grace by eliminating one of the unmanageable polarities found within it. If being God's adopted child is one's most perfect fulfillment, it would seem it should also be one's deepest need, as Scripture, according to some, indicates, especially since it seems to proclaim the priority of the incarnation and being "in Christ" over creation in the divine intention. The order of grace is not a divine afterthought; nor does it involve God in second-guessing Godself after human alienation through sin. If grace is not one's deepest need, the perfection without which one is most incomplete, then how can God's gratuitous Self-communication be truly significant? How can the inviting word evoke a grateful response in the hearer? Conversely, if the gift of grace cannot be isolated from human completeness, then how is humanity intelligible without it?

The ramifications of the old extrinsicist view on the nature-grace relationship for other areas of theology were fairly evident. In this context, e.g., how can original sin, as traditionally understood, be a serious wound, intrinsic to human nature? For how could loss of the supernatural through violation of a purely juridical divine decree be of any consequence to a nature for which it is superfluous in the first place? Is *homo peccator* different from *homo in statu purae naturae* merely as *spoliatus a nudo*? Is what *homo peccator* experiences of himself here and now exactly what one would have experienced in an order of pure nature?

In conclusion, we have briefly delineated the crucial difficulty with the presentation of the nature-grace relationship which, until this century, had gone without serious challenge. The historical factors mentioned in the previous section, the radical inadequacy of the theory as described here, linked to the ambiguity of historical progress, which seems to point up humanity's incapacity to achieve true progress in culture and civilization when left to itself, all this led Catholic theologians to reconsider this classical problem. The question now is not so much whether one has an exigency for grace; nor whether there is a natural appetite to see God. Rather, the modern problematic assumed a new form. It is this: even prior to receiving from without the first salutary grace, are human beings already internally affected by grace in the interior of their being? More concretely one might ask: is it possible that the radical similarities found by anthropologists and students of comparative religion to exist between non-Christians and Christians are explainable in terms of some element or elements that are more than merely "natural"? It is within this framework that the gratuity of grace came to be discussed, and in a way that saved the transcendence of grace, while placing new stress upon its immanence.

III. *The Intervention of the Magisterium:* Humani Generis

The theological problematic being what it was, it was only to be expected that theologians and philosophers, in readdressing themselves to the matter would give anew emphasis to the immanence of grace. As in all else, there is an ebb and flow in theological development. The Christian vision is so rich that the historical moment and its needs can usually bring into focus only certain given aspects of a mystery, while, without negating them, more or less relegating their dialectical counterparts to a less conspicuous position.

So strongly rooted was the post-Tridentine presentation of the gratuity of grace in the formal hypothesis of pure nature that once contemporary theology commenced to elaborate the graced human condition without appeal to this relatively recent hypothesis, the impression was easily given that gratuity was being denied. To remind all that the gratuitous quality of grace must be preserved Pope Pius XII in his encyclical *Humani Generis*, issued on 12 August 1950, reiterated the truth that God can never be under any obligation to Self-communication to intelligent beings. Pius warned against those who "undermine the true gratuity of the supernatural order when they claim that God could not create intellectual beings without ordering and calling them to the beatific vision.''[14]

To capture the spirit of the time in which *Humani Generis*, a twentieth century syllabus, was issued one must take cognizance of the theological renaissance of that period, generally known as the "new theology" ("la nouvelle théologie").[15] Like all historical trends the "new theology" was the gradual realization of a vision, an intuition never grasped totally or clearly by any one theologian, a constellation of disparate elements. No one thinker associated with the "nouvelle theologie" ever formulated the components of the constellation. Probably no two would have committed themselves to it had it been formulated. De Lubac's controversial *Surnaturel* was a concrete symbol of this theological ferment in France, where its exponents could number such outstanding names Henri Bouillard, Jean Daniélou, Yves Congar, M.D. Chenu, Yves Montecheuil, A.-M. Dubarle, Teilhard de Chardin, all of whom would eventually play large roles in influencing the thought of the Second Vatican Council.

The *Humani Generis* mentioned no names, condemned no individual, nor any particular book.[16] Nevertheless, some saw the papal admonition as directed primarily at Henri de Lubac, whose *Surnaturel* was the culmination of a number of studies that were to open wide new vistas to the theological community in the years ahead. Noting the condemnation and recalling previous

[14]D.S. 3891. "Alii veram gratuitatem ordinis supernaturalis corrumpunt, cum autument Deum entia intellectu praedita condere non posse, quin eadem ad beatificam visionem ordinet et vocet." Paragraphs 25–28 of the encyclical form a syllabus of errors. H. Rahner remarked concerning these errors: "Frankly, I do not know in which school that is still Catholic such errors are tolerated." "Hemmschuh des Fortschritts? Zur Enzyklika *Humani Generis*," *Stimmen der Zeit* 117 (1950–1951) 165.

[15]One can capture the mood of the time in the reactions to *Humani Generis*. See, e.g., R. Aubert, "L'encyclique *Humani Generis*," *Revue Nouvelle* 12 (1950) 302–309; C. Boyer, "Les leçons de l'encyclique *Humani Generis*," *Gregorianum* 31(1950) 526–539; A. Dondeyne, "Les problèmes philosophiques souleves dans l'encyclique *Humani Generis*," *Revue Philosophique de Louvain* 49(1951) 5–56; P. Donnelly, "The Encyclical *Humani Generis*: Its Import for Seminary Professors," *Bulletin of National Catholic Educational Association* 48(1951) 82–95; M. Flick, "L'enciclica *Humani Generis* e falso progresso del pensiero Cattolico," *Civiltá Cattolica* 101(1950) 577–590; M. Labourdette, "Les enseignements de l'encyclique *Humani Generis*," *Revue Thomiste* 58 (1950) 32–55; C. Vollert, "Humani Generis and the Limits of Theology," *Theological Studies* 12(1951) 3–29; G. Weigel, "The Historical Background of the Encyclical *Humani Generis*," *Theological Studies* 12(1951) 218–230.

[16]H. Rahner commented that "It would be wholly against the mind of the encyclical itself to use it as a quiver supplying arrows for anyone feeling eager to shoot." He admitted, however, that the encyclical looked first to France, yet gave general norms for all. "Hemmschuh des Fortschritts?", 169.

Roman strictures such as Pius V's condemnation of Baius and Pius X's *Pascendi*, commentators, on this point concerning the gratuity of grace more than on the many other concerns of the encyclical, thought of France, and "with politeness and courtesy they nodded, some shyly and some not so shyly, in the direction of de Lubac."[17] De Lubac himself detested the epithet "new theology." He insisted he and his colleagues were not rejecting an "old theology" in order to substitute a wholly new and different one for it. And de Lubac claimed that his work, far from denying the gratuity of grace, had served not only to preserve, but to foster it, even more so than the accepted extrinsicist view that bears the brunt of his attack.[18]

Pius XII did not question the fact that the present creation is a supernatural order, and that in this order of sin and redemption historical humanity has, and always had, a supernatural destiny. Since, however, the fear haunting many at the time was that a doctrine of immanence was being given a disproportionate emphasis, it might be well to recall briefly the distinction between the *doctrine* of immanence and the *method* of immanence.[19] The *method* of immanence is based upon the principle enunciated by Aquinas: "Nihil potest ordinari in aliquem finem, nisi praeexistat in ipso quaedam proportio ad finem."[20] This method attempts to show that humans, in the present order, have need of the supernatural, to which they are already in the depth of their being secretly ordered by God, since they have been actually called, gratuitously, to share the divine life. Such an avenue of approach is traditional. St. Augustine summed it up well with his "Fecisti nos ad Te et irrequietum est cor nostrum donec requiescat in Te." The method of immanence is, in a word, founded upon the realization that whatever penetrates a person's inner life and informs all operations as an entitative factor (grace) must correspond to an orientation prior (at least logically) to the operation of that factor. The doctrine of immanence, on the other hand, is some-

[17]G. Weigel, "Gleanings from the Commentaries on *Humani Generis*," *Theological Studies* 12(1951) 540. Cf. L. Renwart, "La 'nature pure' a la lumière de l'encyclique *Humani Generis*," *Nouvelle Revue Théologique* 74(1952) 337-354. Renwart saw the encyclical as a continuation of the teaching of Pius V, Pius VI, and Pius X.

[18]H. de Lubac, *The Mystery of the Supernatural,* 63-67.

[19]Cf. A. Valensin, "Immanence" in A. d'Ales, ed., *Dictionnaire Apologétique de la Foi Catholique,* 4 ed., (Paris: Beauchesne, 1925-1928), II, cols. 569-593 for a discussion of the problem in the historical background.

[20]*De Veritate* q. 14, a.2.

thing else altogether. Far from admitting the supernatural is a wholly gratuitous divine response to a tendency in the human heart which God has freely finalized in a sharing of the divine life, it maintains that the supernatural is simply the outgrowth and prolongation of nature and "qu'il suffira de juxtaposer à une analyse approfondie des necessités de la vie sensible, intellectuelle, morale et sociale, l'exposé parallèle du dogme catholique, pour avoir une demonstration chrétienne."[21] The doctrine of immanence very definitely seemed to militate against the authentic transcendence of grace.

The distinction here briefly reviewed should be kept in mind when the position of any given theologian is measured against the *Humani Generis*. Standing now at a distance from the *Humani Generis*, it is only fair to say that de Lubac and his followers saw themselves as employing only the method of immanence, never the doctrine. Disciples of lesser insight and endowed with a certain imprudence in speech and writing may at times have betrayed the soundness of the master's teaching.[22]

Granted, the legitimacy of the method of immanence, the problem that theologians have been grappling with since the time of *Humani Generis* is this: is it still possible to conceive of grace as unexacted if the theologian presupposes an unconditional reference to grace, and if grace is so constitutive of historical humanity's makeup that it is unthinkable without it? Certainly de Lubac, and those who were in basic agreement with him, had no intention of jettisoning the gratuity of grace. But the question remains whether the theorem of an unconditioned orientation to grace in nature is consistent with the gratuity as postulated by the *Humani Generis*.

Our proposal is to examine the treatment of the nature-grace relationship as developed in several twentieth century Catholic theologians. While it is useful and even necessary for an adequate picture to take the measure of the historical precedents of the development, an historical investigation of the classical theologians and the fresh contributions of earlier twentieth century thinkers

---

[21]A. Valensin, "Immanence," col. 578.

[22]Perhaps this is the case with the anonymous "D" whose "Ein Weg zur Bestimmung des Verhältnisses von Natur und Gnade," *Orientierung* 14(1950) 138-141 was taken to task by Rahner. De Lubac felt that Rahner mistakenly thought "D" was de Lubac. See *The Mystery of the Supernatural*, p. 139, note 36. U. Kuhn, *Natur und Gnade: Untersuchungen zur deutschen Katolischen Theologie der Gegenwart* (Berlin: Lutherisches Verlaghaus, 1961), 116, identified "D" as Pierre Delaye.

such as Gratry, Bergson, Blondel, Rousselot, Maréchal, and de Broglie is not undertaken here because it would render our task too unwieldy and because such an investigation has already been undertaken by others.[23] We shall see that among the authors who form the field of our study every effort was made to avoid the post-Tridentine extrinsicism deriving from an essentialistic, static outlook which tended to view grace as a reality merely superimposed upon nature, or as an additive wholly discontinuous with nature, which is disposed for grace only to the extent that no repugnance to the superadded perfection is verifiable in it. In such a perspective the bond between nature and grace had at best only the intensity of freedom from contradiction, a non-repugnance. Yet the Magisterium, through the *Humani Generis*, warned that extrinsicism is not to be overcome by sacrificing the divine primacy and initiative in the elevation of human persons to union with the Trinity. Any theological hypothesis attempting to better explicate the bond between nature and grace so that the graced person is better seen as achieving the harmonious integration of its human being must be careful to retain the gratuity of grace.

More specifically, then, it is not our purpose to deal with the whole complex of questions surrounding the relationship between nature and grace. The task we have set for ourselves is more modest, viz., to determine how theologians in the period following the *Humani Generis* understood the gratuity of grace. The working hypothesis underlying our study is that although theologians agreed on the gratuity of the divine Self-gift, and although various ones safeguard it in their own way, nevertheless, the approach to gratuity changed and the counter-Reformation theology of gratuity was radically challenged. This change stems from the fact that the starting point and focus is historical human nature existing in this concrete economy and the effects of grace upon it, rather than upon any formalized, abstract conceptual construct known as "pure nature." There has been a shift from the

[23]To the work of Alfaro cited in note 2 we can add the following sampling. P. Bastable, *Desire for God* (Dublin: Burns, Oates, Washbourne, 1947); J. Buckley, *Man's Last End* (St. Louis: B. Herder, 1949); A. Dondeyne, *Contemporary European Thought and Christian Faith* (Pittsburgh: Duquesne University, 1958); H. Rondet, *The Grace of Christ* (New York: Newman, 1967); W. O'Connor, *The Eternal Quest: The Teaching of St. Thomas Aquinas on the Natural Desire for God* (New York: Longmans, Green, 1947); V. Doucet, "De naturali seu innato supernaturalis beatitudinis desiderio iuxta theologos a saeculo XIIIo usque ad XXum," *Antonianum* 4(1929) 167-208; J. O'Mahony, *Desire for God in the Philosophy of St. Thomas Aquinas* (Cork: University Press, 1929).

metaphysical to the historical. What is operative here is the methodological principle that the theologian must take the data of revelation and formulate hypotheses on the basis of what actually is, rather than in the basis of what could have been. Flight from the real does not illumine the revealed darkness.

We hope, then, to verify our hypothesis by exposing and reflecting upon the alternative solutions of a sample of Catholic theologians who addressed the problem in the crucial two decades following de Lubac's *Surnaturel*. Our choice of theologians for study is based upon their generally representative value and upon the fact they made the most significant contributions toward a deepened understanding of this complex problem. These were, therefore, the criteria for choosing to study the work of Henri de Lubac, Karl Rahner, Hans Urs Von Balthasar, Juan Alfaro, Edward Schillebeeckx, and Eulalio Baltazar. It was de Lubac's work that brought the issue to a head, and it is Rahner's work that has probably been most significant insofar as he forged new conceptual tools for dealing with the problem. Most Catholic theology today reflects the thinking of these theologians, and especially of Rahner, in one way or another. Von Balthasar, for example, offers a nuanced agreement with the Rahnerian theory, while Schillebeeckx voices a common objection against it. Eulalio Baltazar is of interest, finally, because his is a bold new approach that attempts to break loose from a no longer viable Scholastic framework that he sees ensnaring all other approaches.

Whatever differences may exist among these theologians it is clear that all adhere to the distinction between nature and grace. Further, none of them views nature, the condition of God's Self-donation, as abstract pure nature, or as a reality totally intelligible in itself and experienced by us separately. Rather, concrete nature is seen to be what God posits as possible partner, but in such a way that in relation to it, the gift of God's own Self remains as it must be, free and gratuitous. There has occurred, therefore, a change in perspective relative to the whole problematic. Grace is viewed as primary rather than secondary in the divine intention. Humanity exists because grace contingently is, not vice versa. Gratuity is related to human nature here and now; not to some possible world of pure nature. In fact, the counter-Reformation theory of "natura pura" is relegated by these theologians to a wholly secondary and marginal position. In a word, the whole treatment of the problem is more existential and less formalistic and conceptualistic. Humanity and its historical situation are front and center rather than some abstract notion of a nature that occupies the never-never land of what-might-have-been. Let us proceed to examine the theologians who in varying degrees exemplify this shift in emphasis. Having done that we shall be in a better position to formulate the change in gratuity maintained in our working hypothesis and adumbrated here.

3

Grace as the Heart's Desire:
Henri de Lubac's *Surnaturel*

Henri de Lubac did more than any twentieth century Catholic theologian to bring about a reexamination of the problem of nature and grace.[1] De Lubac's *Surnaturel* did not suddenly appear on the scene. It had been aborning for some time. During the 1920's and 1930's the relationship between the natural and the supernatural orders was a burning question. Several times in the 1930's and early 1940's de Lubac had addressed himself to the issue and to its impact on the construction of a Christian humanism.[2]

The end product of these investigations was *Surnaturel* in 1946, an historical study of the concept of the supernatural and those doctrines and theological concepts intimately bound up with its development. The work was not meant to be definitive; it was put together, as he himself tells us, in haste, and as a mere sketch.[3] *Surnaturel* is divided into four sections. The first presents a com-

---

[1]Reference to de Lubac's principal works on this topic has already been made in Chapters 1 and 2. See also D. Burke, *The Prophetic Mission of Henri de Lubac: A Study of his Theological Anthropology and its Function in the Renewal of Theology,* unpublished doctoral dissertation (Washington: Catholic University, 1967). To contextualize de Lubac's work politically, see J. Komonchak, "Theology and Culture at Mid-Century: The Example of Henri de Lubac," *Theological Studies* 51(1990) 579–602.

[2]"Apologétique et Théologie," *Nouvelle Revue Théologique* 57(1930) 361–378; "Deux Augustiniens fourvoyés: Baius et Jansenius," *Recherches des Science Religieuse* 21(1931) 422–433, 513–540; "Remarques sur l'histoire du mot 'surnaturel,' " *Nouvelle Revue Théologique* 61(1934) 350–370; "La recontre de 'superadditum' et de 'supernaturale' dans la théologie médiévale," *Revue de Moyen Age Latin* 1(1945) 27–34. De Lubac returned to the problem in a more recent work of haute vulgarisation. See *A Brief Catechesis on Nature and Grace* (San Francisco: Ignatius Press, 1984).

[3]*The Mystery of the Supernatural,* 65–68.

parative study of Augustinianism and Baianism, which leads de Lubac to the conclusion that the idea of a system of pure nature and the ensuing dualism locking natural and supernatural in separate compartments begins in this chapter of theology's development. In the second segment de Lubac devotes himself to the problem of the impeccability of angelic spirits, insofar as the solutions offered contributed, he thinks, to the formalized notion of pure nature and the weakening of the traditional meaning of the desire for God. The following section of *Surnaturel* delves into the origins of the word "supernatural." It was the fourth and final section of *Surnaturel*, a series of historical notes and a discussion of the so-called natural desire for the beatific vision, that triggered strong reactions and made its author the central figure in a storm of controversy.

The magnitude of the opposition raised against de Lubac was unexpected. H. Rondet, B. De Solages, and H. Bouillard hastened to his defense; others followed eventually. But they were outnumbered by G. de Broglie, C. Boyer, J. de Blic, L. Renwart, R. Garrigou-Lagrange, P. Donnelly, A. Perego, M. Labourdette and many others.[4] *Surnaturel* came to incarnate everything the defenders of orthodoxy felt should be resisted in the "nouvelle théologie." While the debate raged, de Lubac retained a professional and courteous tone, his self-defence never descending to sheer polemic or bitter personal aspersion. What precisely was the position of de Lubac on the gratuity of grace that it brewed such a furor?

I. *A Transcendence That Is Immanent*

The human spirit is a natural desire for God. Human beings desire God long before they come explicitly to love God. In fact, human existence is itself a striving to liberate and actualize that desire. Yet human persons do not desire God as the animal its prey. Rather, human persons hunger for God as One freely making a gift of Godself. Can we, therefore, speak of an exigency in humans for God? The only exigency is that God be free in bestowing Self-communication and that humans be free in surrendering to the divine Self-donation. Persons can no more find

---

[4]For excellent coverage of the literature occasioned by *Surnaturel*, cf. the work of P. Donnelly cited above, ch. 2, note 2.

happiness in a personal relationship that they can seize or demand than they want a fulfillment that is forced upon them.

Is this to say that human desire for God is thinned down to a mere velleity, since it is inefficacious? To the contrary: the desire for God is the most absolute of desires. Although human beings cannot of themselves and without grace bring this desire to fulfillment and possess as their own the gratuitous divine Self-gift, it is not for all that a conditional desire.[5] To desire a gift as a gift is surely not to postulate an exigency or a right. The desire in question is essentially humble. The human spirit finds itself in a waiting posture. For it aspires to God's grace; it does not demand it. The natural desire of the finite spirit is hobbled by a radical inability to elicit its term. It is, therefore, inefficacious. It can only be hopeful expectancy of a gift. God, however, will not renege on completing a tendency freely willed by God-self. The desire is also, therefore, absolute, unconditioned and unfrustrable on God's part. Consequently there is no question of simple velleity. An end is not less absolutely sought because it is of higher value and more difficult to attain. There is the paradox. Humanity hungers for God; but for God as God can only be, i.e., as Love, freely giving Godself.

Now all this is so because humans can really demand nothing from God. There is no law or tendency so essential in human nature that it must be satisfied, in any hypothesis. To think otherwise is to offend the sovereign independence of the Creator. The difficulty is that we are often hampered by a rather puerile understanding whereby we put created being on a par with uncreated being. Laboring under this crude oversimplification we tend to see creation itself as purely extrinsic to our being, affecting only our origin, but not touching our essence; we tend to see humans related to God as any creature might be related to another creature exterior to itself. We imagine two equals facing one another and we reason that any essential desire in one begets in the other a corresponding obligation to sate that desire. Thus the latter is thrown into a state of dependence upon and obligation to the former. But the latter in the question at hand is God. Seeing immediately that the divine sovereignty must be salvaged, one sets about watering down the desire for God by saying that if it is truly a desire to see God, it is not absolute. Indeed, if we do not oblit-

---

[5]In ch. 10 of *The Mystery of the Supernatural* de Lubac delineates his understanding of the question concerning a desire that is absolute, but inefficacious.

erate it altogether, it is reduced to mere velleity. God's wisdom may be insulted, but our contrived solution has saved God's liberty and any exigency has been neatly eliminated.

Moreover, one might ask whether we should be as troubled as we are by this matter of exigency, for it seems to be little more than a phantom of the imagination. Had we given closer attention to Creator-creature relations we would not have fallen victim to the specious solutions and explanations offered for the problems raised by the nature-grace relationship. Surely the Creator could not have brought us into existence without being cognizant of the full import of the creative act and the exigencies it would launch, and to which we could lay claim.[6] If then our nature is weighted with a desire to see God, it can only be because God finalizes us in the vision of Godself and plants in us this desire. The desire is God's summons. God is the source of our desire as well as its term.[7]

More precisely, God's Self-gift to humans cannot be explained simply in terms of a gift made by one person to another, an analogy dear to the heart of those dependent on the pure nature hypothesis. A closer examination of the act of creation bears this out. I do not preexist my own coming into being, as a subject waiting to receive being from the Creator. Nor in creating me does God provide a gift extrinsic to myself. Rather God offers a gift wholly intrinsic to me: God gives me to myself. Similarly, the endowment of a supernatural finality, an interior gift, does not find its analogue in the human gift of a human donor. To say "I", or "I exist", or "I have a finality" is to implicitly affirm the same reality in each instance. The three are patient of no time gap. Our syntax, however, is too weak to bear the weight of the truth affirmed. I appear to precede my being, and my being my finality, as though my being were already defined without my finality.[8]

Certainly God can in no way be constrained to give me being, nor a supernatural finality. Further, since the historical cannot be equated with the ontological, existence does not necessarily imply a supernatural finality. Consequently, we may distinguish from our vantage point two moments of gratuity, a double divine gift, a double divine freedom. Creation is not a necessary consequence

---

[6] "Deus non debet aliquid alicui nisi Sibi." Thomas Aquinas, *ST*, *I*, 25, 5, ad 2.

[7] *Surnaturel*, 486–487.

[8] H. de Lubac, "Le mystère du surnaturel," *Recherches de Science Religieuse* 36(1949) 101.

of anything; neither is humanity's supernatural finality a *sequela creationis*. Both are free contingencies. This is the truth reiterated by *Humani Generis*. But in actuality, for God to create is to assign a given finality. To exist is to be definitively finalized. Essences void of any finality are at best mere abstractions. To actually exist in the present order is to be pointed to one finality, and that a supernatural one. In fact, it is not the supernatural that is explained by nature but vice versa. Just as we cannot conceive of some subject in existence prior to creation, neither can we envisage a concrete nature in existence prior to or without its supernatural finalization. God has willed us to be because God has willed us to be with Godself.[9]

In this light the problem of exigency is, claims de Lubac, a pseudo-problem.[10] De Lubac would maintain that our understanding of exigence drives a wedge between two things that cannot be separated. We posit first a desire for God, *then* a call to the supernatural. Between desire and call the "monstre de l'exigence" forces its way in. But if a desire for union with God is in human nature, it is not humanity's doing. Its ongoing and perhaps anonymous source is God. Still it can rightly be called "natural," situated as it is in the depths of human nature. Further, to suppose a nature that could realize its own exigencies is as absurd as to suppose a liberty that could win its own merits. In crowning our merits, God crowns God's gifts, and in fulfilling our desire, answers God's own summons. Hence, on no grounds, either moral or natural, can we lay any claim against God. There is no room for confusing the natural and the supernatural or for so explicating nature and the immanence of its desire as to compromise the transcendence of grace.

Implied throughout, then, is the fact that once we begin to discuss humanity's end, its beginning must also be brought into the picture. God is the human being's finality, but also the continuing source of all that the human being is. If this simple but pro-

---

[9]A. Pegis, "Nature and Spirit: Some Reflections on the Problem of the End of Man," *Proc. American Catholic Philosophical Assoc.* 23(1949) 79, summarized well de Lubac's point. The real question is not whether God *could* create, but whether God *would* create humanity for anything but union with Godself. Human finalization in grace is not an event that could just as easily not have happened. Yet no exigence for the supernatural is implied, "for the divine generosity does not presuppose receivers, it prepares them. God's most perfect gift comes first. It is not nature, therefore, which requires grace; it is rather grace which, as a gift of the divine life, given with a love which is as unconditional as it is perfect, calls into being spiritual creatures to receive it."

[10]*Surnaturel*, 486–487; 489, note 1.

found truth is kept in mind, there will be no need to carve the heart out of our desire for God so as to make of it a hollow velleity. As God's own gift it in no way militates against the divine liberty. The measure of our desire for God is the measure of our dependence upon God. In a word, not only is the natural, innate desire itself a free gift, but the completion of this appetite by a communication of the vision of God remains absolutely free.[11] Our own consciousness verifies as much. Transposed to the level of consciousness, the desire assumes the garb of duty rather than need or demand. To give oneself to it is not to render it less burdensome, for to want its fulfillment is to inflict a certain death on oneself.[12] So deeply rooted in us is the desire for God, that it is identified with our very being. God's call is *constitutive*. Humanity's finality, expressed in this desire, is inscribed upon its being. Yet paradoxically we are not our own. It is our nature to find ourselves only in the other, to become aware of ourselves in becoming aware that we are beings who are bound to the Other. Hence we cannot affirm that God is bound to give Godself to us simply because we desire it. Rather, because God wills to give Godself, we are bound to desire God, even prior to realizing that we can possess God only because God has freely initiated the possibility of possession. The more one analyzes this desire, the less it appears an exigency. More and more it manifests itself as a divine right, a divine exigency placed upon us.[13]

Now examining the matter more closely, one might say that when we desire something necessarily and absolutely, we are marked by an exigency for the desired reality. The temptation is to say this of the vision of God. Nonetheless, one ought immediately to draw a qualification. We do not demand it simply because it pleases us to demand it, but rather, because we are incapable of doing otherwise. It imposes itself upon us, even when we run from it. One can in no way divest oneself of the desire. In this perspective our whole understanding of any exigency changes. If we are permeated by an exigency for God, it is a given of the human spirit, and not at all dictated by the spirit's initiative. What we are confronted with is an exigency essential to us,

[11] Ibid., 469.

[12] *The Mystery of the Supernatural*, 36–39.

[13] De Lubac feels that his perspective on "exigence" should make it as free of misunderstanding as are the Thomist expressions "capere Deum" and "capax Dei." *Surnaturel*, 489, note 2 and 436.

one truly immanent, yet no more natural in its origin than in its term. More than a whim or caprice, and never colored by the tones of demand or claim, it dominates our being. Thus it is quite the opposite of what we first imagined it to be. We do not command by reason of its existence; we obey. Through acquiescence to it nature obeys the basic ontological orientation implanted in it by the Creator. Humans are made for God's grace and will never be able to extinguish the desire for God that burns deep in the heart. The term of the desire is not of our choosing. It obliges us to freely realize the ideal it calls us to.[14]

It should be clarified at this point that a rational knowledge of this desire outside the realm of faith does not prove that we are called to the beatific vision and made for that end. It is only through revelation that we become reflexively aware of the true nature of this spontaneous desire. When God reveals Godself to us God also reveals us to ourselves. The natural appetite for God does not as such, therefore, fall under the grasp of empirical psychology, nor can it be deduced by the philosopher from purely rational premises. Only when the intrinsic possibility of the beatific vision has been admitted by faith does the argument founded on the impossibility for a natural appetite to be vain attain its full impact. At most natural reason can recognize a radical aptitude for ultimate or supernatural beatitude, but this does not entail knowledge of the nature of that beatitude, nor the fact of our summons to it.[15]

From all this it follows, says de Lubac, that the integrity of the supernatural is safeguarded without appeal to the relatively modern hypothesis of pure nature, which is neither the only nor the best means of assuring the dignity of nature and the transcendence of grace.[16] Beatitude is service, vision is adoration, liberty

---

[14] De Lubac views the desire for God as absolute, though inefficacious, and as natural in the sense that it is constitutive of humanity, though not as an accident superadded to the human essence, which would be definable without it. On the other hand, the desire is, considering its source and term, supernatural.

[15] *The Mystery of the Supernatural*, ch. 11.

[16] On de Lubac's contention that the hypothesis of pure nature is of relatively recent origin, cf. *The Mystery of the Supernatural*, chs. 1, 2, 4. De Lubac is aware of the definitive character of Alfaro's work on this problem, though he does not seem to agree with Alfaro that Aquinas provided the principles needed for the formulation of the pure nature hypothesis, even though Thomas himself never explicitly avowed such a hypothesis. See also J. Alfaro, "La gratuidad de la vision intuitiva de la essencia divina y la possibilidad del estado de naturaliza pura segun los theologos anteriores a Cayetano," *Gregorianum* 31(1950) 251-252.

is dependence. To define humanity's supernatural end as beatitude, vision, liberty is to delineate but one aspect of it, viz., the anthropocentric. But the limitations of such a view are seen when we recall that God created the world for God's own glory. Humankind receives the world from the Creator's hands that it might bring it back to God and this it does in surrendering itself to God. But this self-surrender achieves its highest perfection only in the supernatural order. Herein lies the theocentric aspect and it is in this perspective that humans must view their destiny and seek solutions to any problems that destiny may pose. Thus, if it is maintained that human beings must have some natural beatitude as their end, since immanent orientation to or desire for the vision of God seems to postulate an exigency in them, one can only reply that the desire is the Creator's doing and human beings cannot escape a jealous God. "Totum exigit te, qui fecit te."[17]

In conclusion, all this should serve to set the problem rightside up. It is not a question of rights or exigencies that we have relative to God, but the converse. Realizing the anthropocentric and theocentric aspects of reality are inseparably wed, we are bound to see that the intelligent creature can have but one finality, and that supernatural. Historical analysis shows that the tradition has repeatedly upheld this truth. There is simply no question of an exigency in human nature. The supernatural is too large to be caught in the web of such categories as right, exigency, or justice, categories which are so important and central in the hypothesis of pure nature, but which have no place in the existential relations between God and humans. No limitations can be set upon the sovereign independence of God who gives Godself freely. Love alone can explain such a gift.

Here, then, is de Lubac's position insofar as it is tied to the theory of a natural desire for God, a desire that postulates in human beings an innate openness to a finality disproportionate to their poor power of attainment. De Lubac has tried to show that the absoluteness of such a desire in no way compromises the gratuity of its term.[18]

[17] Augustine, Sermo 25; see also In Ps 103, Sermo 4 n.2: "Non exigo participationem sapientiae meae ab eis quae non feci ad imaginem meam; sed ubi feci, inde exigo, et usum eius rei postulo, quam donavi."

[18] De Lubac contends that the principle "Desiderium naturale non potest esse nisi rei quae naturaliter haberi potest" is not of universal application. On the openness of the human spirit, cf. *The Mystery of the Supernatural*, chs. 6 and 7.

II. *An Attack on the Hypothesis of Pure Nature*

It has been noted that de Lubac refuses to appeal to the hypothesis of pure nature to explain the gratuity of grace. His opposition to that construct is not merely that it is of relatively recent theological vintage.[19] More important, he does not think it viable as a hypothesis to explicate the transcendence of grace in such a way that its immanence is equally affirmed. Its deficiency as a conceptual tool lies in the fact that what must be explained is the gratuity of grace relative to concrete graced human nature, not to some nebulous hypothetical nature that remains in the imaginary world of sheer possibility. Concentration on pure nature distracts us from showing gratuity in *this* order. In fact the hypothesis creates problems by throwing into jeopardy the very gratuity it purports to defend. In other words, the hypothesis does not do what it promises to do. The problem of gratuity reappears the moment one thinks it is solved. The hypothesis of pure nature should, thinks de Lubac, be condemned to Sheol.

To begin with it is extremely difficult to flesh out this "pure nature" and make it anything more than a great unknown quantity for which we have no precise content. History shows that theologians have tended to project into this abstraction those attributes, qualities, and privileges attached to historical human nature in its relation to God, thereby compromising the unique character of the supernatural, which fast became little more than a shadow of "pure nature." Faith, prayer, the virtues, grace, the remission of sin by infused charity, divine friendship, even revelation, and a certain natural beatitude in the vision of God, all these are found in the imagined state of "pure nature."[20] Nothing remains peculiar to the supernatural but its name, for the order of "pure nature" and historical, graced nature are juxtaposed and set in total harmony. De Lubac thinks his critics are the ones who have jettisoned the gratuity of grace. They are the ones who set up a "fatal homogeneity" between nature and grace.[21] Such

---

[19]De Lubac's early historical study led him to locate the origin of the "pure nature" hypothesis in Cajetan's misrepresentation of Thomas and in the reaction against Baius and Jansen. *Surnaturel*, 15–183. P. Smulders, "De Oorsprong van de theorie der Zuivere Natuur, vergeten Meesters der Leuvense School," *Brijdragen* 10(1949) 105–127, considers Ruard Tapper the first great exponent of the theory of pure nature.

[20]Cf. "Le mystère du surnaturel," 88–90 and *The Mystery of the Supernatural*, 50–55.

[21]H. Bouillard, "L'Intention fondamentale de M. Blondel et la théologie," *Recherches de Science Religieuse* 36(1949) 321–402.

nominalistic theologizing is a disservice to the transcendence of grace. The difference between the possibility and the actuality becomes one simply of degree. The sad progeny of this rationalistic thinking is the extrinsicism and dualism that have for so long worked havoc in the theology of grace.[22]

Furthermore, to buttress the gratuity of the supernatural it will not do to say that our present humanity in another order might have been constituted with another finality. The unwarranted assumption here is that our present humanity would be verifiable in another order, would be the same as it is now. To postulate another order, however, is to postulate another humanity, more concretely, a totally different "me."

> Entre cet homme qui, par hypothèse, n'est pas destiné a voir Dieu et l'homme que je suis en réalité, entre ce futurible et cet existant, il n'y a encore qu'une identité tout ideale, tout abstraite, sans passage réel de l'un a l'autre. Peut-être même est-ce là dejà trop conceder. Car la différence entre l'un et l'autre n'affecte pas seulement l'individualité; elle ne peut manquer d'affecter la nature même. Qu'y aurait-il donc moyen de conclure, à partir de la situation du premier, au sujet de la gratuité du don fait au second, à l'homme que je suis? Cependant, repétons-le, c'est uniquement par rapport à moi, par rapport à nous tous, a cette nature qui est nôtre, a cette humanité réelle dont nous sommes les membres, que se pose en fin de compte, et que doit être résolue cette question de la gratuité.[23]

It is within the context of the real, existential order that we must seek an explanation for the gratuity of grace.[24] It is here that the modern hypothesis of pure nature breaks down; not because it is false in postulating the possibility of another order, but because it fails to adequately explain the real relationship of grace to the existing order. It does not demonstrate that I could have another finality, one fully natural, but merely that in another, hypotheti-

---

[22]De Lubac notes that this dualism eventually tends to overvalue the hypothesis of pure nature so that it becomes a reality. The purely hypothetical conditions become a real state prior to justification. A heuristic device becomes an ontological reality. De Lubac attributes this position to Suarez and to P. Donnelly. Cf. *The Mystery of the Supernatural*, 89-90.

[23]*Le Mystère du Surnaturel* (Paris: Aubier, 1965), 87. Because of the importance of this passage, the original French text is cited. English translation, *The Mystery of the Supernatural*, 77-78.

[24]Throughout his work de Lubac insisted that the concern of mainline theology (Augustine, Thomas, Scotus, and others), even during the period when pure nature held sway, has been the real, existing world, not purely possible essences.

cal economy, another being, other than myself, could be so finalized. And this is irrelevant to our problem. The radical extrinsicism
of the hypothesis fails to understand that the finality of the intelligent creature is an ontological reality, affecting its whole being,
and hence not changeable without entailing structural changes.[25]
The false premise under which the hypothesis labors is that a finality cannot be freely inscribed in an actual being were not a
different finality realizable for this exact same being from the start.
God could arbitrarily change finalities with impunity, as one might
change caps on a bottle.

De Lubac, therefore, sees the pure nature theory as a cancer-
ous growth on the tree of theological development, a theological
fiction inadequate to the task for which it was designed. Moreover, not only is it insufficient, it is unnecessary. Gratuity can,
he feels, be explained as he himself explains it in treating of the
human person's natural desire for God. To refuse to see nature
as a self-sufficient, closed system with its own finality, to insist
that humans have only a supernatural end, is not to affirm they
can achieve this end of themselves. Rather, it is only in this way
that the immanent transcendence of grace and a true harmonizing of nature and grace can be had. When the natural is viewed
as a closed system, the human being is split in two, and the supernatural becomes an artificial and irrelevant imposition devoid of
its own unique character.

III. *Reflections on de Lubac's* Surnaturel

It would be going too far afield to evaluate all the premises undergirding de Lubac's final position. Has he been guilty of a facile
concordism between Augustine and Thomas? Is his eye too selective in its study of Thomistic texts? Are his historical analyses
vastly oversimplified? There is no easy or generally agreed upon
answer to all of these questions. Here the scope of our study re-
stricts us to an evaluation of de Lubac's conclusions concerning
the gratuity of grace.[26]

[25]The interior attraction exercised by the end determines humanity's essence and definition. We may impose a variety of accidental ends on the things around us without
changing their inner structure. The creative causality of God is quite different. God's
choice of the creature's finality determines its essence. Cf. "Le mystère du Surnaturel,"
94-95.

[26]For a measured critique of *Surnaturel* in its own time, cf. L. Malevez, "L'esprit
et le désir de Dieu," *Nouvelle Revue Théologique* 69(1947) 3-31.

De Lubac has brought out well the natural desire of the intellect to embrace being, which ultimately means to embrace God. This being so, its ultimate fulfillment can only be the direct knowledge that is the life of the Trinity itself. And he seems correct in affirming that only the believer can affirm the natural desire for what it is. The philosopher must live in paradox. De Lubac's position is grounded in the rejection of that static essentialism which precludes any natural aspiration to grace and glory, and in the repudiation of rationalistic conceptualism which cuts off the possibility of our being tormented by paradoxes that only faith can fathom.

The weakness of the essentialistic tendency is its conception of finite natures as prior to world orders. God sees world orders only derivatively; only after seeing the possibility of finite natures. For a world order is an integrated complexus of natures, which must themselves be known first before unity can be imposed upon their multiplicity. There are, for the essentialist, two elements to a world order: the necessary, the exigencies of finite essences, and the contingent, their individual and collective finality, which may or may not be present, since it calls for a free decision of God over and above the exigencies of nature. It is just this essentialism that impedes acknowledgment of a natural desire to see God. It is one of de Lubac's contributions to have insisted that world order has priority over finite natures. It is only insofar as God knows the possibility of many world orders that the structures and natures that compose them are known. It is really the finite nature that is the derivative possibility; and it is what it is because of the freely chosen economy in which it is situated.

De Lubac's natural desire, even if one rejects it on other grounds, also served to point up the limitations of a closed conceptualism which follows hard on the heels of essentialism. Conceptualism sees things too neatly and too handily ties all essences into tidy bundles, perfectly matching all powers and their operations, desires and their objects by the bonds of necessity and exact proportion, with no loose strands that might end in paradox. In the world of closed conceptualism nature is seen within the strict limits of species, finality is measured rigorously within potencies specified by the active capacities of nature, and beatitude is limited to what is naturally attainable since every natural desire implies a determined natural exigency.

The disproportion between nature and grace thus necessarily rules out any natural desire for a supernatural end. De Lubac's theology would replace all of this with an open intellectualism which is much slower to see necessity, or nature closed in on itself and its immediate world, especially where the intelligent being is concerned. Simply to posit the superiority of the supernatural may be fidelity to the tradition. But what still remains to be reckoned with is the paradox which the created spirit finds in itself, viz., that being finite it tends to the infinite which it cannot attain of itself. So there is the natural desire to know issuing in growth and perfection of understanding; but paradoxically, finite knowing is infinitely open, and can be completed only in the vision of God, the unattainable term of human desire. The darkness of paradox becomes light if one is willing to journey from Athens to Jerusalem. Herein lies de Lubac's opposition to those who reduce the human being to the level of a "natural object." The limits of a human being's active capacities cannot be measured by the finality open to its own attainment. In this erroneous view a plant, e.g., is considered to have certain capacities proper to it. It is finite, has a finite end. It is the same with humans. If human nature is ordered to grace, something must be added to it and it can in no way, not even in desire, be already part of human nature. For then grace would be due and its gratuity violated. Thus a narrow conceptualism with its univocal mentality raises an insoluble problem where there is paradox. Historical human nature's end does elude its native powers of achievement. But it does have a natural desire for its end. True, something is added: the grace to achieve. But nature is for grace. There is no question of God, the tiresome intruder on humanity's peace, coming to assign a fresh end for it.[27]

Now we turn to what is perhaps an ambiguity in de Lubac's thought. Neither clearly nor consistently does he distinguish historical human nature from human nature as such. De Lubac admits, and more clearly in *Le Mystère du Surnaturel* than in *Surnaturel*, that an order of pure nature is possible.[28] But by this he means one can conceive an order in which intelligent beings *essentially* different from ourselves would not be invited to share the Trinitarian life. But is it not also possible to conceive of human

[27]In "Duplex Hominis Beatitudo," *Recherches de Science Religieuse* 35(1948) 290–299, de Lubac argues that when Thomas speaks of a happiness proper to the human being (*ST, I-II*, 62, 1), he is not referring to humanity's last end in a hypothetical world of pure nature, but to a terrestrial happiness which is not ultimately satisfying. For Thomas, only the beatific vision as humanity's sole end is wholly satisfying.

[28]Cf. *The Mystery of the Supernatural*, 17f., 69f., 115f.

nature as such, a nature with all our essential attributes, without a definitive end, and capable of varying modes of realization? There seems no inherent contradiction. The call to graced existence is gratuitous. And once given it penetrates and transforms the dynamism of humanity. Without a doubt, the differences between historical nature and nature as such may be large. But is it necessary to postulate a total difference of equivocality? The notion of humanity as such may be marginal; still de Lubac never seems to attribute to it any heuristic worth in explicating the gratuity of the present world order. He thinks almost exclusively in terms of a concept of pure nature which would, to explicate the gratuity of grace, necessarily have to appeal to a change of ends, or a nature held in suspension, at least momentarily until an end were assigned.[29] Obviously neither option is viable.

Indeed it is this same line of argumentation that seems to militate against his own insistence on a double gratuity. De Lubac is correct in finding the gratuity of the supernatural in the fact that God decreed freely and primarily the end, and in view of that a nature capable of it (*capax Dei*). Nature exists for grace; not vice versa. God does not create a human nature, then decide as an afterthought to order it to a determinate end. Human being was created for and ordered to a single end from the beginning. This entails the double gratuity of creation and finality. But what de Lubac failed to weigh sufficiently is the possibility that humanity, de facto called into existence for grace, might have also been called to being for another destiny. His contention is that the two would differ as diverse *essences*.[30] Does this empty his assertion of a double gratuity of any real meaning? It would seem so. For it makes the ordination to grace part of the *constitution* of human nature as such. One might still speak of gratuity, but only insofar as it meant God is perfectly free in creating such a

[29]Ibid., 87–88. De Lubac appears to find little room for the notion of humanity as such. The alternatives he seems to envision are historical humanity or pure nature as a closed nature.

[30]De Lubac contends that a creature's finality affects it intrinsically and not merely extrinsically. To change the finality is to change the *identity* of the creature in question. The customary qualification has been that this is so only if the end to which the being is gratuitously ordered is radically new, wholly other than it would be were the creature not so gratuitously ordered. The human spirit as such is an openness to being, hence a conditioned desire for God. Thus ordination to beatific vision is not an organic, absolute change. It is the perfection and completion of a directedness already present. It actualizes humanity's most radical possibility. Cf. L. Malevez, "La gratuité du surnaturel," 683–684.

being at all. This, however, seems to erase de Lubac's double gratuity.

We have seen, moreover, that de Lubac tells us clearly that an intelligent being with a purely natural end is conceivable, but it would not be human being. There seems to be only one passage in his later work where he directly turns to the idea of a human being like ourselves not having the supernatural end we have.[31] But what he says here is not put forward as a "coherent hypothesis"; rather it is only "to illustrate the situation of created being in regard to God." We can imagine, he says, a being, a spirit like ourselves, to whom God had never chosen to lay open access to God's own divine life, yet carrying deep in its being, but unconsciously, an attraction to God similar to our own. But the speculation is abruptly halted. Such a being "would be forever moving around God without knowing it. . . but as we know from Christ, universal gyration is not the ultimate reality." It seems then that de Lubac was able to bring himself to the point of moving beyond pure nature as a closed system to a consideration of human nature as such. It is one thing to deny that humanity has a double finality and that it is a nature closed in on itself; it is something else to equate human nature as such with historical human nature.

Clearly there is an ambiguity that marks de Lubac's approach. It is crystallized in two passages. In one he tells us: "Après comme avant, nous pourrons continuer de dire que si Dieu l'avait voulu, il aurait pu ne pas *nous* donner l'être et que cet être qu'il *nous* a donné, il aurait pu ne point l'appeler à Le voir."[32] But just previous to this he had stated: ". . . elle [the hypothesis of pure nature] montre seulement, à supposer qu'elle soit fondée, que dans un autre univers un autre être que moi, possédant une nature analogue à la mienne, aurait eu cette destinée plus humble."[33]

Again, in an effort to bring out the immanence of grace de Lubac has appealed to the natural desire for God as the point

[31]Cf. *The Mystery of the Supernatural*, 267-269. See also 94.

[32]"Le mystère du Surnaturel," 104.

[33]Ibid., 94. The issue is complicated by the fact that twice in this article (pp. 101 and 105) de Lubac borders on admitting a distinction between nature as such and historical nature. He notes that ". . . dans son espèce, ma nature n'est que ce qu'elle est," and that nature has no claim upon grace. At the same time he sees grace as an ever-present reality in the history of humankind. This seems to be an opening to some hypothesis of pure nature, despite his broadsides against it. There is in these passages, then, the inkling of a nature that is logically prior to grace. Cf. W. Shepherd, *Man's Condition*, 77-78. Malevez, "Interiorité et gratuité," 64, note 18, exonerates de Lubac and argues that de Lubac is not a supporter of the X thesis explained above in ch. 1.

of insertion for grace. He seeks some immanent ontological link that orientates human being to its unique finality. If the beatific vision brings perfect happiness to humans, how is that beatitude not at least virtually present in every act of human appetency? De Lubac is willing to accept the idea of obediential potency. The intellectual being is capable of receiving from God any non-contradictory perfection. But the question is bigger. There must be the further insight that the elevation of humanity to the divine life is not contradictory precisely because the spiritual being is positively ordered by its nature to a universal knowledge of being. Only thus can a more positive rapport between nature and grace be established.[34]

And yet, without wanting to negate the natural desire so crucial to de Lubac's position, one might hope that it were further specified by him. He does tell us it is not biological, nor elicited, and that even the term "natural" does not fit it well.[35] Can it be grace? Or is it simply the natural appetite for the true and the good? Or is it a tertium quid? Perhaps de Lubac wants it to refer to the situation in which we find ourselves, a situation in which we find something attracting us which we cannot attain in this life. Nor is it clear that with all his efforts to remove any exigency in virtue of this desire that he has not placed an exigency in God, a moral necessity. If he affirms that grace is not necessarily given, does he escape having to affirm that it must be infallibly given? The problem stems from de Lubac's assertion that while the desire is present only because of the special gratuitous call of God, it is unfrustrable and *constitutive* of human nature.[36] De Lubac's reply to such a difficulty might well be that freedom and necessity coincide at infinity and can hardly be spoken of in regard to God in our finite language. Even if one is troubled by the *coincidentia oppositorum* one must hold both ends of the chain. The

[34]One must distinguish what humans seek universally and essentially, though not always with perfect awareness, from what they seek in particular decisions. In this matter of natural desire de Lubac shows the influence of M. Blondel whose phenomenology of action shows the insurmountable disproportion between the will's élan and the term of human activity. Cf. L. *'Action: Essai d'une Critique de la Vie et de la Pratique* (Paris: Alcan, 1893). Blondel viewed the supernatural as the inevitable completion of human action. It is absolutely necessary, yet absolutely unattainable by human resources alone. C. Boyer, "La Pensée de M. Blondel et la théologie," *Gregorianum* 16(1935) 485-503, thought Blondel destroyed the gratuity of grace. In defense of Blondel, cf. H. Bouillard, *Blondel et la Christianisme* (Paris: Edit. du Seuil, 1961).

[35]*The Mystery of the Supernatural*, 300-301.

[36]Cf. e.g., *Surnaturel*, 484, 492; *The Mystery of the Supernatural*, 70, 217.

apparent antinomy between the unlimited, dynamic tendency of the spiritual being and its powers of realization is matched by the apparent antinomy between divine fidelity and divine freedom. But the difficulty remains.

De Lubac's natural desire also faced a more traditional form of the same objection, which, however, was more patient of a solution. If the natural desire is an inclination implanted in nature, a tendency to its proper perfection, how can there be a natural desire for that supernatural completion which is grace and glory? Does this not destroy the gratuity of grace? If the intuitive knowledge of the divine essence falls within the natural volitional tendency, is there not an exigency established between its natural form, which it always follows, and the supernatural perfection to which it inclines? After all, a natural desire cannot be vain. Further, if participation in the divine life is humanity's ultimate end, why is it unable to attain it of itself?

De Lubac rightly approached this problem by insisting on the distinction between the order of finality and the order of realization. Simply to desire something apprehended as good (no matter how obscurely or unconsciously) pertains only to the goodness of the object, with no reference to the available means for procuring it. In any appetency abstraction is made not from the intrinsic possibility of a desired perfection but from our possibility of attaining it. If the intrinsic impossibility of the object does not press upon us, it can be desired naturally, regardless of our poverty of power to achieve it. Human finality must be conceived not as closed within the active powers of nature, but as reaching out in a sharing of the very dynamism of the mind. The dynamic notion of finality is well stated by Bernard Lonergan:

> It (finality) is not headed to some determined individual or species or genus of proportionate being. On the contrary, the essential meaning of finality is that it goes beyond such determinations. Potency heads to form, but it also heads beyond it to act; and it heads beyond act to coincidental manifolds of acts and through them to higher forms and higher coincidental manifolds of acts. Finality goes beyond the myriad individualities of the lowest genus to the fewer individualities of higher genera and it goes beyond those fewer individualities in perpetual cycles of change. Finality goes beyond lower genera and species to higher genera and species and, if it is halted at some

genus, the halt reveals not finality but the limitations which it
endeavors to transcend.[37]

At any rate, we must admit, in conclusion, that since de Lubac's
study, the state of the question as formulated in post-Tridentine
theology is no longer exactly as it was. Formerly the stress was
upon nature as primary in the divine intention and the approach
was from the natural to the supernatural. De Lubac's emphasis
on the divine sovereignty and the historical order reversed that
manner of addressing the problem. His effort to restrict his attention to the historical order, while not totally acceptable to all,
is, nonetheless, more an advantage than a disadvantage. A world
order without grace is, perhaps, a possibility for God; it involves,
according to some, no internal contradiction, though it may be
difficult to conceive positively and concretely just what an ungraced order would be like. However, we should not argue that
a concrete possibility is constituted by a finite nature and the fulfillment of its exigencies, and that since grace is not owed to any
creature and its exigencies, it follows that a finite nature without
grace is a possibility. The argument is valid only if one accepts
its essentialistic underpinnings, which cleave any world order in
two, one part necessary, the other contingent. Just as one can
uncap a bottle, so one can remove the supernatural from the existing order and the remainder is a possible world order. De Lubac
is, rightly, cold to such an approach. Concrete possibility is not
constituted by natures, their exigencies and satisfactions, but only
participated by them. A thinker of de Lubac's persuasion cannot
accept the assumptions of the essentialist view that the parts determine the whole, that created natures are prior to and determine world orders.

Finally, de Lubac was correct in unifying the order of creation
and the order of finality. Some mounted against him an argument from the special liberality of God in bestowing grace.[38] They
argued that if a world order without grace were not possible, God
would be free not twice, but once only: free to create, but neces-
sitated to call to grace. But God knows a twofold freedom, first
to create or not, then to grace or not. Against this we can only

[37]B. Lonergan, *Insight: A Study of Human Understanding*, rev. ed. (London: Longmans, Green, and Co., 1958), 447–448.
[38]Cf. P. Donnelly, "The Gratuity of the Beatific Vision," 393–394.

say that while admitting a double gratuity, creation and elevation, there seems no reason to posit two divine decrees, verifying
a freedom of exercise and of specification respectively. It seems
sufficient to affirm one divine will-act verifying both freedoms,
since there is only one reality willed, the one, concrete world order
and all it includes. God wills the existing economy by a single act.[39]
God could, perhaps, have willed another order in which there was
no divine Self-communication. Hence the effort to charge de Lubac with a failure to safeguard a double divine liberty, or double
gratuity, seems wide of the mark, based as it is on rather anthropomorphic and essentialistic orientations.[40]

We can only conclude, as does Lonergan, and as de Lubac does
also, that while a world order without grace may be a concrete
possibility, it should not be argued for on essentialistic grounds.
Even more important, it is not a central doctrine, but a "marginal theorem." Its demonstration from the gratuity of grace and
the special liberality of God in bestowing grace rests upon questionable suppositions. Post-Tridentine theology magnified the
theorem into a necessary and central doctrine. What Lonergan
wrote rings as true today as it did when the *Surnaturel* was a cause
célèbre: "The real issue does not lie in the possibility of a world
order without grace; the real issue, the one momentous in its consequences, lies between the essentialist and conceptualist tendency
and, on the other hand, the existential and intellectualist
tendency."[41]

[39]B. Lonergan, "The Natural Desire to See God," 42–43.

[40]"Le mystère du surnaturel," 104; *The Mystery of the Supernatural*, 105–108.

[41]"The Natural Desire to See God," 43.

4

The Interiority of the Invitation of Grace: Karl Rahner's Supernatural Existential

We come now to the theologian who in this century probably did the most to advance our understanding of the problem of nature and grace.[1] Rahner, here as elsewhere, hammered out new theological concepts and language. "Supernatural existential" has become a by-word to students of theology. It is the code word for a theological hypothesis which Rahner felt best explicates the relationship binding God and humans. With it Rahner strikes a middle ground between the position of de Lubac, which to some seems to compromise the transcendence of grace, and that of the "standard view" which compromised the immanence of grace. The existential is a crucial element in Rahner's theology, which, appearances notwithstanding, forms a coherent whole. Suffice it to say for now that the existential was not concocted by Rahner simply as an ad hoc solution to a very particularized mid-twentieth century theological debate. It grows out of his foundational theology and is woven into his theological synthesis. We shall return to this again.

[1]Rahner's entire theology is a theology of nature and grace. His most explicit works on the technical doctrine of nature and grace can be found in the following representative works. "Eine Antwort," *Orientierung* 14(1950) 141–145; "Concerning the Relationship between Nature and Grace," *Theological Investigations*, I (Baltimore: Helicon, 1961), 297–317; "Bemerkungen über des Naturgesetz und seine Erkennbarkeit," *Orientierung* 19(1955) 239–243; "Über das Verhältnis des Naturgesetzes zur übernaturlichen Gnadenordnung," *Orientierung* 20(1956) 8–11; "Nature and Grace," *Theological Investigations*, IV (Baltimore: Helicon, 1966), 165–188; "Existential, Übernaturliches," in J. Höfer and K. Rahner, eds., *Lexikon für Theologie und Kirche*, III (Freiburg: Herder, 1962), col. 1301. Other works will be cited as we proceed. Two excellent expositions and critiques of Rahner's thought are W. Shepherd, *Man's Condition: God and the World Process* (New York: Herder, 1969) and M. Taylor, *God is Love: A Study in the Theology of Karl Rahner* (Atlanta: Scholars Press, 1986).

I. *A Break With the "Standard View":*
Dualism and Extrinsicism

Karl Rahner's treatment of nature and grace is, like de Lubac's, largely an effort to overcome the extrinsicism alluded to earlier. In opposition to Michael du Bay (1513–1589), who refused to admit that God could not withhold from humans the gifts of original justice, in opposition also to Cornelius Jansen (1585–1638), who maintained the sole possible finality for intelligent beings is the direct vision of God, and in opposition to Juan Ripalda (1594–1648), who claimed that while the beatific vision is transcendent in the historical order, it could be wholly natural to intelligent creatures in another world order, there was a discernible over-reaction that came to be part and parcel of the "standard view" that was prevalent in post-Tridentine Scholastic theology.[2]

A cardinal point of the "standard view" is the assumption that grace lies beyond the pale of human experience. It is a datum of faith, but not of conscious experience. We never experience the difference supernatural elevation has made to our spiritual and moral activity.

> . . . Grace is a superstructure above man's conscious spiritual and moral life. . . . The relationship between nature and grace is thought of as two layers laid very carefully one on top of the other so that they interpenetrate as little as possible.[3]

Rahner finds the root of this extrinsicism in a particular interpretation of obediential potency. The life of grace is the ultimate fulfillment of human being, its sole divinely willed end. Yet nature, according to this standard interpretation, has in itself only a *potentia obedientialis* for the grace-life, which means that nature's orientation to grace is wholly negative and passive. The orientation to grace is reduced to a mere absence of contradiction in such an elevation. But Rahner does not think that the difficulties of extrinsicism are overcome merely by upgrading the *potentia obedientialis* so as to make it a conditioned desire to see God. For this alone could not impede a legitimate refusal of the supernatural by a nature already rounded off and complete in itself. Nature's proportionate end would not now become, by reason of the offer of the supernatural, a half-happiness. It would remain a true end,

[2]"Nature and Grace," 165–166.

[3]Ibid., 167.

a real beatitude. And nothing could oblige nature to renounce the end authentically proportioned to it.[4] Moreover, according to the "standard view" nothing can be detected that would mark off "pure nature" from humanity's present "fallen state." The latter differs from the former "*sicut spoliatus a nudo*"; as one who has lost one's clothes might differ from someone who had none to begin with. The absence of grace, according to the "standard view," is a deprivation only because there exists a divine decree commanding its possession, a decree violated by the introduction of sin into the world. In neither case, whether of fallen humanity or of humanity never called to grace, does the lack in itself make any real difference.[5]

Now Rahner's theology of nature and grace wants to overcome this extrinsicism, affirm that the two are related by more than the negativity of non-repugnance, and show that it is meaningful to say that nature is ordered to grace, all the while granting that grace is not due to nature, sinful or not.

> Being ordered to grace, and being directed to grace in such a way that without the actual gift of this grace it would all be meaningless, are not the same thing. . . . Even though a spirit (i.e., openness to God, freedom, and conscious and free self-possession) is essentially impossible without this transcendence, whose absolute fulfillment is grace, yet *this* fulfillment does not thereby become due. . . .[6]

For Rahner the human spirit has intelligibility in itself and is not simply a means, a phase in a process leading to the beatific vision. Though the human spirit is open to the supernatural and thus to ultimate self-transcendence, nonetheless spirit itself can be meaningful without grace. Absolute fulfillment by grace, therefore, answers to no exigency in the nature of spirit as such.

> We can fully understand man in his 'undefinable' essence if we see him as *potentia obedientialis* for the divine life; this is his

---

[4]"Eine Antwort," 142.

[5]"Nature and Grace," 167-168.

[6]Ibid., 186. Rahner's approach was from well within the mainstream. The Protestant treatment of nature and grace has traditionally stressed human sinfulness and the medicinal function of grace in restoring human nature to its original possibilities. Perhaps Protestant thought has not given sufficient attention to another aspect of grace, viz., grace as the free decision of God to enter into covenant friendship with humanity so that its gratuity extends beyond falleness. Cf. E. Te Selle, "The Problem of Nature and Grace," *Journal of Religion* 45(1965) 238-250.

> *nature.* His nature is such that its *absolute* fulfillment comes through grace, and so nature of itself must reckon with the *meaningful* possibility of remaining without absolute fulfillment.[7]

However, the dualistic anthropology born of a negativistic concept of obediential potency is not exorcised, as was noted above, merely by postulating an affinity to grace in the dynamic, positive openness that is natural to transcendent spirit.[8] Rahner, therefore, does not find the key to understanding supernaturalization in an examination merely of obediential potency. His problematic is not absorbed in finding a way "to get from nature to grace."[9] Rather, Rahner's labor is given to finding a way to steer clear of the ontological presuppositions begetting extrinsicism without compromising either the gratuity of grace or its immanence.

To begin with, the position that the human being's ordination to grace, prior to any grace-provoked response and justification, consists solely in a divine decree that remains wholly extrinsic is, to Rahner, unintelligible. In the totality of its concrete, historical quiddity the human being depends on the divine creative will not merely for what constitutes its nature, but also for that ultimate ontological constituent which makes of it the unique reality it is meant to be. Must not what God decrees for humanity be *eo ipso* an interior, ontological constituent of its concrete quiddity terminatively, even if it is not a constituent of its nature? For an ontology that grasps the fact that the total, historically conditioned quiddity is utterly dependent on God, "is not his binding disposition *eo ipso* not just a juridical decree of God, but precisely what man *is,* hence not just an imperative proceeding from God, but man's most inward depth?"[10] Because the Creator gives humanity a supernatural end (and this end is primary in the divine intention), human being (and its world) is by that very fact forever inwardly and structurally other than it would have been had it not been so finalized. In fact, human beings are other even

[7]"Nature and Grace," 186.

[8]The dynamic intellectualism that marks de Lubac's thought is more rigorously employed in Rahner's theology and is philosophically grounded in his *Spirit in the World* (New York: Herder, 1968), then worked into a foundational theology in *Hearers of the Word* (New York: Herder, 1968). See also G. Lindbeck, "The A Priori in St. Thomas' Theory of Knowledge," in R. Cushman & E. Grisilis, eds., *The Heritage of Christian Thought* (New York: Harper & Row, 1965), 41–63.

[9]"Concerning the Relationship between Nature and Grace," 302, note 1.

[10]Ibid., 302.

before they have reached this end even partially, by grace, or wholly, by glory. The point then is not to determine whether or not humanity's intrinsic orientation to grace is a constitutive element of human nature, but rather to determine how the divine call, terminating in human nature as it does, communicates to humans the reality of grace beyond the *ordo naturae*.

II. *The Unacceptability of the Position of the Anonymous "D"*

Rahner's critique of the position of the anonymous D, which held to an unconditional and unfrustrable reference of nature to grace, provides a foil against which his own position can more clearly be understood.[11] The difficulty with D's position as Rahner sees it, is this: is grace truly unexacted supposing an inner and unconditional reference to grace as a *constituent* of human nature so that humanity is unintelligible without it? Now the "nouvelle théologie" like all other theologies accepted the axiom that grace is absolutely gratuitous. But is the theorem of an unconditioned orientation to grace in virtue of *nature* as such compatible with the axiom? D regards this reference to grace as an intrinsic constituent of human nature so that the withholding of the term of this directedness would be contrary to God's wisdom and goodness.[12]

Rahner feels that such formulations negate the unexactedness of grace. For God, who created this immanent ordination to personal union with the Trinity, cannot, once the ordination is presupposed, simultaneously refuse to give this communion without offending against the very meaning of the creature and of the creative act itself. The granting of the end of this directedness is no longer free. Should the ordination not be detachable from the nature, its fulfillment would, from God's side, be exacted. And this is inadmissible. From the creature's side, a gift may not be regarded as unexacted when God's generosity must objectify itself by implanting in the very nature of the creature a definite disposition, so that under pain of losing its proper in-

[11] "D," "Ein Weg zur Bestimmung des Verhältnisses von Natur und Grade," *Orientierung* 14(1950) 138–141. See above, ch. 2, note 22. Rahner's critique of "D" is found in "Concerning the Relationship," 303–310. "D" cites as two of his important sources *Le Surnaturel* and "Le mystère du surnaturel," which led some to identify him, wrongly, as de Lubac.

[12] "Ein Weg," 138–139.

telligibility, nature must find in this gift its unique finality and sole possible fulfillment. God's wisdom would owe itself the completion of this disposition, since it has created this disposition in such a way that it demands its fulfillment. Owing it to Godself, God would owe it to us also. A right has been inscribed in the very absoluteness of the desire for God. Where an unconditioned disposition of nature precedes the gift, the gift itself can be thought of as unexacted only in the sense in which nature itself is, i.e., only in the sense that God's creation is free in the first place.

Now one might, as does D, take as one's starting point the nature of grace as God's Self-communication in love, and maintain that it must by necessity be unexacted. Such is the nature of love. Yet all this points up is that a disposition which would *inevitably* draw grace cannot be verified in human nature. And if it is, then it too must be unexacted. As a *natural* disposition it per force counters the gratuity of grace. For if the disposition *necessarily* belongs to nature, grace is unexacted precisely as a reality given in the same way nature is, and with it. Grace would be the most perfect of all the unexacted gifts; one essentially different from all other endowments from the aspect of their intrinsic worth, but not different from the point of view of their being unexacted. Hence a wholly natural disposition to grace could not but conflict with the gratuity of grace.

Indeed, if there is any such orientation, it belongs already to the unexacted supernatural order. Surely historical nature's finality is the prime object of God's creative decree. In view of it God designs concrete human quiddity.[13] If God calls humanity to a supernatural end, and if God wills it in such a way that human quiddity is to have for this end a positive, unconditional disposition, then God must give simultaneously with the end the disposition to it. But this does not mean the orientation must belong to the nature qua nature. Otherwise, God would be creating freely and unexactedly, but would not be creating a being for whom grace would be purely a gift of sheer divine liberality. D does not attend to this when he insists that the unbounded dynamism that is human nature is meaningless without grace, which is intrinsically necessary to it. The paradox of a natural desire for God as a link between nature and grace is understandable, even necessarily admissible, if the desire is equated with a certain openness

---

[13]This seems the view also of K. Barth in *Church Dogmatics* (Edinburgh: T. & T. Clark, 1956), III, part I, 230–237.

to the supernatural. And there is no need to interpret this openness in the overly negative way of mere non-repugnance. A desire, however, that is a natural, inamissible constituent (a *desiderium naturae*) in the strictest sense and inevitably calls for grace, even if only objectively, is an exigency that demands grace to escape meaninglessness. Such a desire is, in Rahner's mind, irreconcilable with the unexactedness of grace.

Rahner's hypothesis will, consequently, be situated between two diverse positions concerning the human ordination to grace. One situates it in nature, which is so orientated by an immanent, unconditional, and constitutive desire or disposition that it infallibly calls for grace. The other places the ordination to grace is a totally extrinsic but gratuitous divine decree, relative to which human nature is no more than "open" inasmuch as it is spirit naturally given to self-transcendence.[14] Steering between Scylla and Charybdis, Rahner will formulate his own hypothesis, the "supernatural existential," which we must now consider.

III. *The Supernatural Existential*

Rahner clearly and explicitly holds to the distinction between nature and grace. Though it may be difficult to precisely determine what nature is concretely, still it would not be lacking in meaning were it left to itself and ungraced. This distinction rightly understood, however, does not imply that nature is the historically prior member of the pair, grace being subsequent. If original sin is to be seen as a real deprivation and disorder, then historical human nature must be related to grace from the start. This is not to assert the human person is already justified, or not in need of justification. Again, the distinction does not imply that nature is related to grace as that which is humanly intrinsic to that which is extrinsic. Faith comes from hearing. But the hearer

---

[14]For Rahner, simply to view human openness, the obediential potency for grace, as more than a mere nonrepugnance, but as a yearning or velleity for God, is not sufficient. Rahner sees the openness as a conditioned orientation to grace, a natural existential. It is this transcendental orientation of humanity as such that provides the point of insertion for the supernatural existential of historical humanity. As we shall see, Rahner thinks there is no pure experience of this natural dynamism. ". . . One must guard against . . . identifying this unlimited dynamism of the spiritual nature in a simply apodictic way with that dynamism which we experience (or believe we experience) in the adventure of our concrete spiritual existence, because here the supernatural existential may already be at work." "Concerning the Relationship," 303, 315–316.

is one already related to and affected by grace. Preaching is grace calling to grace already there. Finally, nature is not a permanent substratum in a human being that is from time to time affected by grace. The transcendence of grace does not imply that it is rare and transient.[15] Rahner is further insistent that we must extricate ourselves from one of the cardinal presuppositions of extrinsicism, viz., that nature is the reality one experiences through introspection or self-reflection while grace is relegated to the realm of the unconscious. It was just this dichotomy which burdened us with a dualism that has dogged Christian existence for so long.[16] Religious acts which fell into the conscious sector of life were considered psychologically "natural" acts and not salvific. As a result, a corresponding series of "supernatural" acts, not falling under experiential awareness, was postulated as existing in the order of grace. Thus a distinct disservice was done to the integration of nature and grace.

To this point we have seen how nature and grace are not related, and what does not provide grounds for their distinction. More positively, for Rahner grace and nature are related as the *is-contingently* and the *must-be*, or the hypothetically necessary.[17] Creaturehood and contingency are coextensive. Yet granted creation as an order of grace, some elements in creatures then become hypothetically necessary. In historical humanity the hypothetically necessary factor demanded for realization of the adopted filiation that humanity is invited to live is nature.[18] Grace, on the other hand, is contingently verified in human being solely because of God's free decision to present Godself to humans as partner in a covenant of knowledge and love. Hence, while Rahner maintains it is extremely difficult through reflection to sharply delineate which of the data of conscious experience belong to human nature as such, and which to its historically graced condition, he nonetheless is not led to assert that limits are nonexistent.

The crux of the problem was seen by Rahner to lie precisely here. How am I to know that all I encounter in my existential self-experience actually falls within the bounds of "nature" and would exist in just this form were there for me no vocation to

---

[15]"Nature and Grace," 181–183.

[16]Ibid., 168.

[17]The terminology is that of C. Peter, "The Position of K. Rahner Regarding the Supernatural: a Comparative Study of Nature and Grace," *Proc. Catholic Theological Society of America* 20(1965) 85.

[18]"Nature and Grace," 185–186.

union with the Trinity? The possibility of experiencing grace and the possibility of experiencing grace as grace are two different things. Yet some elements in human experience must, it seems, be present if one is truly human. In fact, the more traditional definition of the human being as *animal rationale*, or the more recent definition, "created spirit in transcendence," are not without value.[19] Neither, Rahner tells us, is the method of introspection known as transcendental analysis without validity in designating certain experienced phenomena as belonging essentially to the realm of human nature, e.g., being-in-the-world, corporeality, sociality, self-transcendence. All such factors pertain to the hypothetically-must-be aspect of human being. To think that Rahner simply posits nature in the theological sense and then abandons it as a totally unknown quantity is to misread him.[20]

Yet for all that an exact and absolutely sure demarcation of nature as it historically exists in a graced world is surely impossible without revelation and at best extremely difficult with it. Reflection on the data of consciousness, no matter how refined, does not reach nature in a "chemically pure" condition, siphoned off from all else in concrete humanity.[21] Historical humanity is not, nor has it ever been, merely human, no more no less. As it stands in its concrete religio-moral relation to God, not all properties are verifiable as its own just because it is human. Historical human nature has ever been finalized supernaturally. Born into a world of sin, humanity is internally disproportioned in terms of capacity to attain participation in the Trinitarian life which is its *raison d'être*.[22] Such disproportion in no way negates this finality.

[19]"But do we know whether the subsistent object actually envisaged in terms of this formula would really be just such as we actually experience it, if this man were not called to eternal communion with the God of grace, were not exposed to that permanent dynamism of grace, and were not to feel its loss a mortal wound on account of being continuously ordained to it in his inmost depths?" "Concerning the Relationship," 327.

[20]Ibid., 317.

[21]For Rahner, "nature" is a fluid concept. But it is "a necessary and objectively justified one if one wishes to achieve reflexive consciousness of that unexactedness of grace which goes together with man's inner, unconditional orientation to it." Ibid., 315.

[22]Grace is a biblical and dogmatic concept. Nature is a theological concept for understanding the gratuity of grace. The distinction between the two was elaborated by the medievals. They held that humans are called to a perfection which cannot be the outcome of human striving alone, even in a sinless person. Sin renders grace medicinal; but grace, in Catholic thought, came to be viewed primarily as elevating. Thomas put it succinctly. Sinful humanity does not need grace *more* (*magis*) than it would apart from sin, since eternal life exceeds human capabilities. But as sinful, humanity does need grace *for more* (*ad plura*). *ST*, I, 95, 4, ad 1.

Rahner, therefore, is at odds with that ontological presupposition of extrinsicism that where grace has not yet laid hold of persons and justified them, their binding ordination to their supernatural finality can only consist in a divine decree that remains wholly external to them. Yet while granting that this ordination is not constitutive of human nature, it seems to Rahner that what God decrees for human nature must necessarily terminate in an intrinsic, ontological modification that becomes a constituent of human quiddity. Humanity and its finality "must not and cannot be conceived in such simple terms as the mutual order of a pot and its lid or of a biological organism and its fixed environment."[23] To reduce humanity's existential situation to something purely juridical or moral grounded in a divine decree is, to Rahner, the exercise of an unconscious nominalism.[24]

For Rahner, then, historical human being is a unity of nature and a supernatural existential.[25] And he terms nature in the theological sense the *Restbegriff*, the remainder when the unexacted supernatural modification that is prior to external grace, faith, and uncreated grace is mentally distinguished from the quiddity of historical humanity.[26] Further, this reality has a meaning and a possibility of existing even when the supernatural existential is thought of as lacking (for otherwise this existential would necessarily be demanded precisely by the postulated reality and it could only be unexacted with respect to a purely possible humanity).

This existential, employed by Rahner to explain the pain of loss (*poena damni*) experienced by the (possibly) damned who are wholly lacking in any other supernatural determination,[27] is then the term of the irrevocable divine decree calling humans to divine filiation. It begets in human beings immanent ordination to union with the triune God, even prior to their hearing the gospel

[23]"Concerning the Relationship," 317.

[24]Ibid., 312, note 1.

[25]The term "übernaturliche Existential" seems to occur for the first time in 1941 in "Zum theologischen Begriff der Konkupiszenz." Cf. "The Theological Concept of Concupiscentia," *Theological Investigations*, I, 374–382.

[26]"Concerning the Relationship," 313–315.

[27]J. Kenny, *The Supernatural* (Staten Island: Alba House, 1972), employed Rahner's existential to better explain original sin and justification, as did R. Pendergast, "The Supernatural Existential: Human Generation and Original Sin," *Downside Review* 82(1964) 1–24. E. Hellman, "Anonymous Christianity and the Missions," *Downside Review* 84(1966) 361–379 applied it to missiology. H. Duméry, "Notes," *Revue Philosophique de Louvain* 62(1964) 692–704 examined its implications for the relationship between philosophy and theology. Implications continue to be drawn.

proclaimed, prior to their justification, and despite their poverty without Christ to realize the personal union with God that is their end. For Rahner, therefore, added to the conditions necessary for the intelligibility of human nature as such (humanity in any order) there has always been in historical human nature something more. In addition to the basic existentials of humanity-as-such, which give shape to the concept of nature, humanity's concrete quiddity in the present economy is affected by a supernatural existential. Historical nature has never known a natural finality. Consequently, humans are, from the beginning, intrinsically other than they would have been if they had another finality. Any other view would equivalently frustrate the absolute finalizing divine decree. Thus ultimately, one is never able to encounter oneself "except in the region of God's supernatural loving will; he can never find the nature he wants in a chemically pure state, separated from its supernatural existential."[28] The divine will disposing of humanity must attain form within it as a real determination of its being, though not of its nature.

This brings us to a more direct consideration of gratuity. Rahner strongly insists on the gratuity of historical humanity's existential condition. The utter freedom of the creative act is realized in the fact that God could have had a different will for us. Therefore, God freely willed us to be "so." Correlatively, this freedom does not imply that God has not *precisely* willed us to be "so." Rather, our total consistency, coherence, structure and meaning draw their concrete reality from his creative act. "This 'so' is not something purely mental, external to what is willed, and without significance for its real consistency; it is a genuine existential, a mode of our own existence, without which we can indeed grasp ourselves as question, but never as the answer which it alone gives to the question which we are."[29] To grasp this more clearly, one must say something briefly of Rahner's anthropology. Rahner touches the heart of the matter when he says in his article on "Anthropology" in the *Lexikon für Theologie und Kirche*:

[28]"Concerning the Relationship," 315. It is important to note that Rahner's early writing focuses on the supernatural existential as an effect in human nature as a result of God's call. His later work focuses on the divine activity of calling and the situation God thereby effects in history. In his technical doctrine of nature and grace, Rahner, focuses on human quiddity and in his synthetic theology on the human situation. Cf. Shepherd, *Man's Condition*, 91–92.

[29]"Current Problems in Christology," *Theological Investigations*, I, 184.

> The Incarnation is rightly received and understood only if Christ's humanity is not merely—in the last analysis—the external instrument through which a God who remains invisible makes Himself known, but is exactly the same as what God Himself—while remaining God—becomes when He empties Himself into the non-divine. . . . But then man is in original definition the possible being-other-than-Himself of God's Self-surrender and the possible brother of Christ.[30]

This definition of humanity affords context for a fuller understanding of Rahner's existential and its unexactedness.

In Rahner's view we are existential beings only because through the incarnation God has freely willed Godself to be an existential being. God's humanness is not an item added on to God. It is God's very presence in the world.[31] The human Jesus is the visible form assumed by God in the Word's kenotic leap into time and space. Now to exist humanly is to exist in situations which weave together a personal history. Indeed, to exist humanly is to become a person. Human existence through being-in-a-situation, through being there (*Da-Sein*) is a coming-to-be, a self-realization. Obviously, God cannot come-to-be Godself. As God, God cannot exsist. Yet precisely through the incarnation, God does become an existential being, and this permits God to realize possible otherness, while at the same time freely willing the possibility that beings other than Godself can realize this otherness through participation in the divine capacity to be an existential being, and as such, willing a self-donation to humankind.[32]

The possibility of existing humanly is ultimately grounded in God's possibility of being other, in the possibility that Christ can exist. Only because God wills to be an existential being as a possibility through the incarnation, do human beings now *de facto* have the possibility to ex-sist in personal communion with the three divine persons. One must distinguish between an essential possibility and an existential possibility. Humanity's existential condition, involving as it does the mystery of divine love manifesting itself to humans through the mystery of grace, in view of which

---

[30]*Lexikon für Theologie und Kirche*, I, 626. Rahner considers Christology as the "end and beginning of anthropology." See "On the Theology of the Incarnation," *Theological Investigations*, IV, 117.

[31]On Rahner's understanding of God's presence and activity in the world and the difficulties it entails, cf. M. Taylor, *God is Love*, ch. 6.

[32]On the implications of the incarnation for the question of divine mutability in Rahner's theology, see M. Taylor, ibid., chs. 6, 7, 9.

all else is willed concretely and freely, must be unexacted. Rahner sees God's free love as effecting in human being what is the highest and inmost perfection it possesses. It does not lie on the fringe of human being, but in the deepest interior. But it is not thereby considered as emanating from or identified with the natural and the essentially necessary.

> Is it not precisely the essence of man to receive the unexpected as the inmost and to have the inmost as grace? But then the inmost love is not only the love of an aristocratic "gratuitousness from above" but that of a "gratuitousness from below," because precisely *man* himself, man as existential (hence very much from below) is meant to accept this love as unexacted by him, not owed to him.[33]

Far from being deducible from the nature of humanity, this perfection is grounded in the most unpredictable and freest occurrence in all reality, the incarnation, in which the Logos realizes itself outside the sphere of the divine. Moreover, the humanity of Jesus is not planned independently of and prior to the plan of the incarnation. Humanity is the ontological and existential result of the Word's self-emptying. The humanity of Jesus is God's Self-utterance, Self-dispossession. God expresses Godself through a *kenosis* that is an alienation. Now the human nature of all humans is the same as that of Jesus; and so historical, existential humanity must be defined as the potential expression of God's Self-kenosis. Humanity is the potential otherness of God's Self-emptying and the possible brother or sister of Christ. Indeed, we may even say that historical human quiddity is an obediential potency for hypostatic union and for the grace of Christ.[34] Ultimately the goal of historical humanity is to find its perfection as the otherness-in-being of God, either through the grace of union or through participation in the capital grace of Christ. This orientation and capacity is not simply a felicitous but adventitious suita-

[33]"Concerning the Relationship," 311–312.

[34]What is grasped "from above" can also be seen "from below" though this is possible only in the revealed light of the incarnation. Human being points beyond itself to the absolute mystery, not to seize it, but to be seized by it. The nature of human being is to be taken over, to step into the unknown in love and trust and so to realize itself most fully. Thus the incarnation is the supreme fulfillment of human being insofar as it is the nature of human being to find itself by giving itself away. This is an implication of Rahner's transcendental anthropology, which is the key to his methodology. Cf. "Theology and Anthropology," in T. Burke, ed., *The Word in History* (New York: Sheed and Ward, 1966), 1–23. See also A. Carr, *The Theological Method of Karl Rahner* (Missoula: Scholars Press, 1977).

bleness to God's incarnational plan. Rather, concrete nature is conceived as a condition for and in function of the divine Self-communication. Self-donation is God's fundamental intention. Derivative as hypothetically necessary for this is concrete human quiddity and finally, material creation as condition for humanity's possibility. The existential possibility of creation rests on God's capacity and desire to share divine life with us. Creatures, and more especially humans, are the grammar of God's potential Self-utterance.[35]

The theological worldview of Rahner thus can only allow that the real receptivity in humanity, its supernatural existential, which is the reflection in its being of its existential situation, is in no way founded upon a natural ordination, even as gratuitously created. Neither, on the other hand, is God's coming to humanity a coming that is met by a purely passive potency. Humans have a real congeniality for the love offered them. It sounds the deepest resonances within. For the divine will that humanity be graced is not an additional decree resulting in a Self-surrender so totally gratuitous as to admit of no prior principle of receptivity that would make humanity open and capable of a response. "Everything else exists so that this one thing might be: the eternal miracle of infinite love."[36] It is crucial in Rahner's perspective to see that in creating human being, God is creating a being called to sharing divine life and made capable of it; but a being also to whom God can so communicate Godself that divine love will be received as all love must essentially be received: as an unexacted bestowal calling for a totally free response.

> Hence He must create man just "so" that he can receive this Self-communication only as grace; thus He must not only give him an essence but also constitute him as a "nature" (as opposed to an unexacted supernatural). . . . The Self-communication simply *cannot* be other than unexacted, i.e., the Will to a "purely" unexacted Self-communication is not only a fact but a *necessity*: there is no essence of a creaturely kind which God could constitute for which this communica-

---

[35]Rahner's theology of grace bears a definite christological character. Creation is within the order of grace. Christ is more than mediator of grace to a sinful world. The world and humanity are pre-conditions of the divine Self-communication in Christ, which is primary in the divine intention. For the practical implications of Rahner's more Scotistic approach, cf. "The Order of Redemption within the Order of Creation," *Christian Commitment* (New York: Sheed & Ward, 1963), 38–74.

[36]"Concerning the Relationship," 310.

tion could be the normal, matter-of-course perfection to which it was compellingly disposed.[37]

In a word, God must so create humanity that not only is the offer of grace gratuitous from the point of view of the divine order (from above), but also on the human side (from below), so that humans can only accept it precisely as the always astounding wonder, the unexpected blessedness that is wholly unowed, whether they be sinners or not.[38] Grace for the creature is necessarily unnecessary.[39]

What more precisely is the supernatural existential? Rahner provides no clear and definite answer. It would seem consistent with his exposition to say that it is a positive modification, an inamissible, *a priori* constituent of the concrete quiddity of historical humanity. The existential is a reality in humanity in virtue of its situation and perdures independently of refusal or acceptance of the love God offers. It is itself already a grace, the finite term of the loving divine decree summoning humans to divine life and endowing them with an unconditional openness and orientation to the life of grace. In virtue of this existential humanity is not neutral with regard to God, but positively susceptible to willingly accepting as a gratuitous gift a reality not alien to it but striking a resounding chord in its most profound depths.

Previous to justification by sacramental or extra-sacramental grace the human person already stands under the salvific will of God as redeemed. This situation, which might be termed objective justification as distinct from its subjective acceptance, and which precedes and influences one's free self-determination, consists not merely in a divine intention but in a real, ontological determination of human being. Thus there is in everyone something supernatural, prior to any baptism or act of belief. There is something not proper to human nature as such but to all the children of Adam called to Christ. One is drawn to God by far more than logic or the attractiveness of the man Jesus. God "the answer" provokes a vital resilience in humanity "the question." One is oriented to say "yes" before doing so. To say "yes" to oneself is to become an "anonymous Christian." The anonymity gives

[37]Ibid., note 1.

[38]Ibid., 311, note 1.

[39]For a fuller exposition of the interrelationship between christology and anthropology in Rahner's theology, cf. W. Shepherd, *Man's Condition*, 120–150; 177–213 and M. Taylor, *God is Love*, chs. 4 and 6.

way to explicit Christianity when one expressly gives oneself to Christ and incarnates inner assent in external Christian symbols.[40]

Now the openness in question here is to the divine infinity. But it involves more than just openness to the created world which reveals God's infinity through the mirror of finite beings, thus opening persons to God as Creator and allowing them to approach God in a purely asymptotic fashion. For this is not yet openness to the infinity proper, to what is formally and uniquely divine, God's Trinitarian life. The *raison d'être* of human existence is the establishment of a knowledge-love relation with this tripersonal God. Now if we inquire into the existential basis for knowing and loving, and for rendering possible our being-in-this-situation, we find certain orientations in the human being. These orientations

> . . . are not particularized phenomena of human existence but the *a priori* conditions in order that human existence should exhibit particularized phenomena; and again they are not *a priori* conditions in the sense of ultimate propositional formulations, but the modalities of the ontological structure of human existence itself. . . . It should be clear that an 'existenzial' is an ontological and not a moral determination.[41]

In light of this, Rahner's point is that since our concern here is the very special human knowing and loving that establishes a unique and immediate relationship with the proper personal reality of each of the three divine persons who are present to all persons, the existential that grounds this situation is itself supernatural. Thus the supernatural existential is the foundation of an inner *existentiell* experience of what is historically revealed.

[40]On the basis of the supernatural existential Rahner worked out his notion of anonymous Christianity. Each and every human being is the recipient of God's constant offer of saving grace, which is decisively and reflexively realized in Christ and in the Church. Rahner's stress on the universality of grace allows Christianity to encounter both modern atheism and the non-Christian religions in a new way. Cf. K. Rahner, "Anonymous Christians," *Theological Investigations*, VI, (Baltimore: Helicon, 1969), 390-398; "Thoughts on the Possibility of Belief Today," *Theological Investigations*, V, 3-22; "Christianity and the non-Christian Religions," *Theological Investigations*, V (Baltimore: Helicon, 1966), 115-134; A. Röper, *The Anonymous Christian* (New York: Sheed & Ward, 1963); K. Riesenhuber, "Rahner's Anonymous Christian," *Theology Digest* 13(1965) 163-171. The notion has not been unopposed. See e.g., H. Küng, *On Being a Christian* (New York: Doubleday, 1976), 97-98, 126.

[41]C. Ernst, "Introduction," *Theological Investigations*, I, xvi. Rahner refers to "Existenzialien" as "Existentials."

When Rahner qualifies this existential as "supernatural" he does not remove it from the ontological realm. Rather the adjective bespeaks its unexactedness.

> If he were in a certain sense nothing but this *existential* and were this . . . simply his nature, i.e., were it in absolutely no way capable of being dissociated from what he is otherwise and from what he could understand himself to be, then he could certainly as a free agent always continue to behave contrary to this nature despite the divine Love; but he could not accept this Love as bestowed gratuitously and without exaction upon him. . . . Were he simply this *existential*, and were this his nature, then it would be unconditioned in its essence, i.e., once it has been given, the Love which is God would 'have to' be offered by God.[42]

The existential only permits grace to be free when it is itself undue and when, fulfilled by grace, it becomes aware of itself as supernatural and so unowed. Further, pre-conscious and gratuitous in relation to nature, the existential allows the grace relation offered to be actualized not as something alien to which one can offer no responding love, but as something to which one can freely and gladly assent. It is the pre-existent condition of the possibility of surrender to God's self-donation entailing no destruction of what one already is prior to surrender. God does not offer God-self in such a way that the acceptance prevents one from being fully human and completely oneself. The life of grace once entered into renders one fully human and far more so than one could ever desire.

Finally, it might be asked, if the supernatural existential is the always-present possibility of response at each moment of life to the divine offer of personal union, does it enter into consciousness? Rahner answers this query with a distinction between those data of consciousness apprehended reflexively as objects of consciousness, as other than the conscious subject, and those data of consciousness which are not included in consciousness as objects known, nor even experientially distinguished from the simultaneous data of consciousness (e.g., a natural formal object), but which serve as *a priori* mental horizons conditioning the very possibility of any knowing and loving.

---

[42]"Concerning the Relationship," 313–314.

The fact of being a datum for consciousness does not imply that the existential concerned is capable of being reflexively apprehended or indeed is apprehended as supernatural. Nor need it imply that the existential concerned is capable at least of being reflexively *distinguished* from other data of consciousness. . . . We are thus quite free to suppose the above mentioned existential also helps to structure man's spiritually conscious existence even if this does not take place in the manner in which *objects* of consciousness do it which are apprehended *as* supernatural and reflexively demarcated from others. Unexpressed impulses, basic dispositions and attitudes which escape total clarification by reflexion are of more comprehensive significance for the totality of our spiritual life in certain circumstances than what is objectively recognized and expressed.[43]

Summarily, the *a priori* possibility of perfection by grace in no way bespeaks an exigence for realization of this possibility. The human spirit directed to the totality of created being could be positively fulfilled if the Creator had revealed this totality to it at once or successively.[44] But as it is, God created in humanity the real possibility of ex-sisting in ontological union with the three divine Thou's, yet in contingency upon each one's wholly free, but ever-possible responding love. For one ought to be able to receive God's grace as someone having room, scope, and desire for it. "Thus he must have a real potency for it. . . . This potency is what is inmost and most authentic in him, the center and root of what he is absolutely. He must have it always . . . must . . . always remain what he was created as: the burning longing for God Himself in the immediacy of His own threefold life. The capacity for the God of Self-bestowing personal Love is the central and abiding *existential* of man as he really is."[45]

IV. *Reflections on Rahner's Existential*

In general, Rahner's hypothesis met a favorable reception by the theological community.[46] With de Lubac he attempted to extricate the theology of nature and grace from the building-block approach of extrinsicism which so dichotomized the two that their

[43]"The Theological Concept of Concupiscentia," 377–378.

[44]"Concerning the Relationship," 315–316.

[45]Ibid., 311–312.

[46]Ibid., 297, note 1.

rapport was not done justice, nor even the proper character of each. Like de Lubac, Rahner too is interested in the gratuity of grace as it concerns the concrete, historical order. And like de Lubac he sees humanity in this order other than what it would be in another order. The more existential approach of both theologians considers the possible only as it is related to the real, rather than the inverse, which marked the essentialistic foundations of the extrinsicist theology. Unlike the extrinsicist, Rahner refuses to see concrete nature as complete in itself, rounded off, open to full understanding, with grace granted over and above all this as an unsought and unnecessary gift.

But Rahner breaks with de Lubac and "D" because of their radical intrinsicism. Yet the break is not achieved by following the trail of those who simply thin down de Lubac's natural desire to a mere velleity. That way would only lead back to the "standard view." From his earliest writing one of the underlying motifs in Rahner's work has been the delineation of humanity as an obediential potency for grace. Still he never suggested that humans, simply by reason of their *nature*, are possessed of an exigency for personal union with the Trinitarian God. For Rahner, unlike de Lubac, does not deny the intelligibility and necessity of the notion of humanity-as-such. Unlike the extrinsicist, however, he places the notion in its proper framework since his first concern is the real, not the possible, the existent, not the essential. Hence even before *Humani Generis*, he took issue with those who interpreted human nature as necessarily endowed with an *a priori* dynamism that is an absolute, unconditioned desire for God.

Now de Lubac's view is attractive because it sees life under grace not as something secondary and adventitious, but as nature's only genuine fulfillment. Thus grace becomes truly relevant to humanity. And if grace can be seen as the completion of a tendency inherent in humanity that would otherwise go unsatisfied, it follows that humanity stands in total dependence on the divine freedom and love, and that the ultimate in human perfection must be received as a gift. Thus grace becomes truly indispensable to human being. Further, the data upon which a doctrine of natural desire can be built are not wanting. Human cognitive and affective life forever reaches out insatiably beyond the range of human capabilities. Hence, far from being sinful arrogance, it can be interpreted as a secret desire for the vision of God. The theory borrows even more conviction from history's stream of philosophies, ranging from Platonism to existentialism, that calls attention to human self-transcendence and disillusionment with the finite as ultimate.

Rahner's attack on "D", however, pointed up the serious dangers cloaked in the attractiveness of this theory. Grace, perhaps, is viewed more as an aid in the procurement of a reality already desired and called for in the constitutive depths of the self, more as a means whereby human potentialities are actualized than as a free and gracious coming of God that looks for a response. One is called to follow the deepest proclivity of one's nature as spirit, but the aspect of free response to freely given grace easily runs the risk of losing its due weight. For human response could easily be interpreted here as motivated by what humanity is (and must be) rather than by what God does. Ironically, the view of "D" and de Lubac, if too literally interpreted, becomes shackled by the very naturalism it wants badly to be free of, because humanity is conceived on the model of an incomplete being which necessarily tends towards a specific end which is the necessary actualization of its potencies and tendencies.

These latent shortcomings do not wholly disqualify the natural desire theory as a live theological option. But they do lead us to ask whether the Rahnerian hypothesis is perhaps more viable. If it does not seem satisfactory to posit a constitutive desire in nature as such, nor to view the grace-life as a second end superadded to humanity's natural finality, then the problem remains of finding the point of confluence between nature and grace, the point of insertion for grace. Rahner's solution to this problem gives even greater weight to humanity's existential and historical dimensions than does de Lubac's, though admittedly a strong orientation to the existential order was a worthwhile contribution in the latter's break with the essentialism of post-Tridentine theology. Perhaps Rahner's hypothesis can be better appreciated if we blend it with a biblical theme.

The model of covenant, calling into play the elements of history and decision, is helpful in highlighting certain features of grace that are perhaps more easily obscured in the employment of ontic categories and patterns.[47] The covenant as God's free decision looks to persons' free decision, since it addresses them in their own self-determination. Thus persons are endowed with self-

[47]Here we borrow a Barthian theme. Cf. *Church Dogmatics*, IV, Part I, 3–66. The covenant theme is used also by H. Bouillard, "L'Idée du surnaturel et la Mystère Chrétien," 153–166.

determination even in the realm of grace.[48] Not that they are thrown back on themselves. Each one is challenged to realize a determined possibility, to give oneself to a definite course through free decision. The grace-life is therefore twice removed from any "natural tendencies." It is contingent first on the wholly unowed divine initiative and them on free commitment. So it is that in Rahner's exposition the emphasis is not upon the inner life of the person following a naturally determined line of development. Persons are determined to indeterminacy, thrown into the task of self-determination. This is not to imply that once grace is offered the human posture is neutral or indifferent, as though choice may be purely arbitrary. Lack of natural determination is not warrant for an exhilarating freedom to create one's own ends. If a theonomy that obliterates human choice by overpowering divine action is unacceptable, so is an extreme autonomy that functions in a historical vacuum.

Hence it is that Rahner brings to bear the historicity of humanity, but in such a way that humans do not, even in their self-determination, stand indifferent in the face of grace. For freedom is already qualified from within by its being keyed to the wider situation. Self-determination is not realized *in vacuo*, but in conjunction with a certain understanding of one's self and one's situation. The introduction of the historical situation does not so much hem in freedom as focus on an element one must factor and in light of which freely determine oneself. Thus it seems closer to the truth that the problem of the conduct of life is not resolved by some *desiderium naturae* and that one in freedom must responsibly act in relation to one's situation and its possibilities, especially as these are brought to light by understanding as one experiences oneself in a given world.

The most significant queries about humanity, then, are answered by analyzing it, not so much as it is "in itself," but in its situation, flexible as it is to be found in a variety of situations. Humanity is never in a condition of pure indeterminism. It is always situated; always existing under certain circumstances, interpreting them and relating itself to them by decision or indecision. Humanity, in a word, is openness to a situation. Now, while there may be in human nature no explicit tendency to God of which one is immediately conscious as such, one is by no means closed to God. The gracious design of God having been communicated,

[48]Thomas Aquinas, *ST*, I-II, 113, 3c.

the situation no longer is what it was thought to be and it must affect humanity in such a way that it cannot legitimately assume toward it a neutral posture, for it is a more momentous situation than everyday situations, or certain limiting situations.

In this regard it is well to note that while contemporary thinkers stress human historicity, they differ in interpreting the total situation of humanity. The early Heidegger and his followers may have been concerned primarily with existing in unshakable autonomy in the face of the world, conventionality, and death. But in the I-Thou theorists the presence of and openness to persons is the crucial and constitutive element of human existence. To these strands of thought must be added the thinking of theologians like Rahner who want to view humans as standing always under the grace of the covenant God. Respond or not, the situation ever perdures. And it is central. There is, no doubt, a problem in seeing how this is so for those who have not heard the gospel. But for Rahner this is the human situation, even apart from anyone's hearing the gospel in a community of faith. Standing under grace is a supernatural existential, a consistent situatedness which affects the structure of human beings.

God's grace of covenant thus situates humans and in relation to this situation they must decide. Unlike situations originating merely in juxtaposition with an environment and assuming meaning only as falling under the light of a person's own relative horizons, this situation has no aspect that is foreign; it affects the person from the start, continually challenging to a free and appropriate response. The possibility of reply is always grounded in the prior, gratuitous situation-making decision of the covenant God. So Rahner affirms the radical distinction between nature and grace because the present human condition and the relationship to God can never be regarded as essential developments of human nature, nor realized by human capabilities alone. Grace, as God's historical Self-communication in covenant, establishes the possibility of a relation not implied in humanity as such. Rahner has done well in emphasizing historicity in our understanding of humanity and in viewing humanity as having a destiny shaped by free decision, not in absolute and pure autonomy, but in openness to a situation that has marked its being without being of humanity's own making.

In this connection it is interesting that Rahner's notion of human nature, theologically considered, is lacking in any refined determination, whereas in the history of Christian thought it has been understood from a variety of perspectives: in terms of fallenness, as sinful or natural; or, as in Augustine's thought at times, in terms of the state of original righteousness in which Adam was created;[49] or, less historically, in the context of some essentialist distinctions between nature and grace, as a set of clearly defined capacities and potentialities that are inalienable and perdure through all the circumstances of life and are distinct from the grace of God, which is another reality, and which makes possible actions beyond the scope of nature alone. In this last context it often happened that human nature was clearly defined with great certitude as to just what was "natural" and what "unnatural." Now to conceive of nature as distinct from grace is not necessarily to endorse any particular view of human nature, least of all one growing out of naturalistic assumptions. Nature and grace may not be theologized from any and all conceptions of humanity. But neither is it required that the theologian be restricted to one notion of nature. It seems then that there is much value in Rahner's consideration of nature as a *Restbegriff* that is not subject to easy definition. This, of course, is at odds with the "standard view" which Rahner criticizes, a view plagued by an objectivism that pushes grace out of the world where persons live and experience themselves. Grace comes to dwell in an objectified spiritual realm beyond the rim of human consciousness; it is an unconscious modality of the soul, an ontic state elevating one but discernible only to the eyes of faith. Grace and its effects are simply not data of the experiential order. Except in the rare case of the mystic, grace is an unconscious mystery.

The dubious assumption operative here, however, is that nature is what one consciously experiences of oneself without revelation. All else beyond that experience is considered supernatural. This is simplistic to say the least. It is, as Rahner has rightly maintained, not at all patent that what one attains by use of reflexive awareness is, and can only be, "natural." By what criteria are we to determine that what we experience is the product solely of nature? Rahner's approach to nature should liberate us from that essentialistic passion for clarity which so easily tags one experienced reality as "natural" and another inexperienced reality as "supernatural." Such formalistic considerations are traceable to

---

[49]Cf. e.g., Retractions I, 14, 7.

an effort to isolate human being from historicity and the existential situation which, in Rahner's view, creates an *existential* that permeates the very fiber of human being, making it impossible to experience nature at any time as hermetically sealed off from the influence of grace.[50] Certainly transcendental reflection may distinguish the contingent, empirical data found in human experiences from the structures of humanity's concrete quiddity which serve as *a priori* conditions of possibility for such experiences. One may, e.g., detect a longing for encounter with infinite being as so much part of the human drive to self-fulfillment as to consider it an essential dynamism of human nature. Nonetheless, for Rahner, the distinction between the dynamism of humanity as such and the desire for God experienced in historical humanity calls for criteria that only a theological anthropology can bring to bear. For the purely natural desire cannot now be experienced as such. It does not seem that on this score Rahner's "remainder" notion of nature leads to fideism. Philosophy can, by its own method, still provide valid understanding of human being. It is true that this might largely coincide with the theological notion of historical nature. Yet it is also possible that the philosopher's concept of human being would include more than the theologian's concept of nature (the *Restbegriff*), for the philosopher's definition would be based upon data permeated by the supernatural existential. It is impossible to bracket the supernatural element in any evaluation of the human phenomenon.

At this point it is worth noting that Rahner's existential preserves much of Blondel's insight that a phenomenology of action must ultimately confront the philosopher with the possibility of an encounter with God. There are hints of Rahner's existential in Blondel's "transnatural" or "immanent order." Blondel himself had already touched upon an unconditional desire and even Rahner's remainder notion of nature when he wrote of humanity's "état transnaturel":

> On ne peut que par une erreur indéniable raisonner comme si *l'état naturel* de l'incroyant, de l'ignorant, de l'apostat était l'état de "pure nature", cet état qui sans doute eût pu être, mais

---

[50]L. Malevez, "La Gratuité du surnaturel," 685–689, had reservations about what he considered Rahner's pessimistic attitude relative to our capacity to assign a definite "content" to human nature. On this same matter, cf. Rahner's "Reflections on the Experience of Grace," *Theological Investigations*, III (Baltimore: Helicon, 1967), 86–90.

qui n'est pas, qui n'a jamais été et dont nous ne pouvons même definir précisément les conditions réelles.[51]

Blondel's phenomenology of action achieves fuller impact in the light of the supernatural existential. Since human nature *de facto* is finalized supernaturally, a sound phenomenological analysis of its existential situation must reveal its drive to this transcendent end.

Rahner's existential also shows a marked affinity to the theory of E. Brisbois, who, in anticipation of Rahner, held that if humans are called to the beatific vision, human nature must be affected accordingly.[52] This, Brisbois tells us, calls for nature to possess a new disposition, a new exigency prior to every free will-act, prior even to faith and sanctifying grace or the external grace of preaching. This finalization creates in us a new "vouloir non deliberé" analogous to our natural tendency to good. Like Rahner, Brisbois maintained that humanity's supernatural finalization must affect its ontological structure, bringing into existence an inclination that is itself gratuitous and supernatural.[53]

Earlier we noted that Rahner himself is not very explicit as to the nature of the supernatural existential. This lack of clarity may be unfortunate, but will it do to simply equate this Heideggerian category with the Aristotelean category of accident?[54] Or to reduce it to the natural desire to see God while qualifying it as nonconstitutive?[55] Since the framework in which the term is employed was fashioned mainly by Heidegger, perhaps it is best to leave it at that with no effort to translate it into terms congenial to the

---

[51]Le Semaine Sociale de Bordeaux, *Annales de Philosophie Chrétienne*, Dec., 1939, 268; *Letter on Apologetics*, 283–284. Bouillard, "L'Intention fondamentale," 343–347, claims that Blondel analyzed humanity in a supernatural context and had no desire to concoct a system of nature independent of grace.

[52]E. Brisbois, "Le Désir de voir Dieu et la métaphysique du vouloir selon St. Thomas," *Nouvelle Revue Théologique* 63(1936) 978–989; 1089–1113.

[53]H. de Lubac, *The Mystery of the Supernatural*, 240, note 63.

[54]L. Malevez, "La gratuité du surnaturel," 579, 685.

[55]Ibid., 667–668. Malevez, while seeming to equate Rahner's existential with a desire for God, realizes that it is non-constitutive. Malevez also wants to qualify any such desire as absolutely absolute for humankind collectively and as relatively absolute for the sinner not yet justified. Whether Rahner's blanket approval of Malevez's qualifications (cf. "Concerning the Relationship," 297–298, note 1) covers this emendation is not clear. Malevez is saying the desire is conditioned for the individual by the need for the gift of sanctifying grace and its free acceptance. Only with personal grace would the desire for completion in the vision of God become absolutely absolute. But is there a confusion of psychological and ontological orders here?

Scholastic mind.[56] But let us try briefly, and at some risk of over-simplifying, to describe the meaning of an existential in its original context. This should, in addition, further clarify the stress Rahner has placed on human historicity.

For Heidegger *Dasein* is unique. Things, being much alike, are given to classification. But the human being as an existential being defies classification. The distinctively human dimension is always marked by *Jemeinigkeit*; existence is always my own, unique, proper, individual existence. Still this does not rule out an analysis of *Dasein*. In this regard the distinction between *existenzielle* and *existenzial* possibilities is important. The concrete, practical possibilities of the individual *Dasein* are the *existenzielle* possibilities. These are the contingent variables of human facticity, the concrete possibilities whereby one makes oneself a person. But there are horizons to Dasein's *existenzielle* possibilities, boundaries within which every existence situates itself. These broad possibilities are *existenzial* possibilities.

Now the investigation of these latter possibilities is an existenzial analytic of *Dasein*. This analytic is not an attempt to describe universal properties of *Dasein*, an impossibility since *Dasein* is not a mere object, but an ex-sistence. Rather it is an attempt to sight the horizons of possibility within whose range the *existenzielle* possibilities of every human *Dasein* must fall. Thus an *existenzial* denotes one of the broad fundamental possibilities of Dasein's being, possibilities antecedent to any free human decision. The *existenzial* basis that makes possible our *existenzielle* existence is discovered only by a phenomenological analysis of the latent orientations concealed within existence. Thus when Rahner refers to the supernatural *existential*, his reference is not to a particular phenomenon but to an *a priori* condition of possibility for particularized phenomena, a modality of the ontological structure of human existence as concretely unfolded before us in an economy where God has freely willed to have us become covenant partners.

---

[56]Rahner himself claims the existential is a perduring condition of the finite spiritual person, which, as an ontological predetermination, makes possible a definite kind of personal behavior. The existential under discussion is supernatural insofar as it directs one to a supernatural finality and is unowed. It is an *existential* rather than an *existentiell* in that it does not result from free personal action, but serves as its transcendental condition. "Über das Verhältnis Naturgesetzes," 9–10. See, too, G. McCool, "The Philosophy of the Human Person in Karl Rahner's Theology," *Theological Studies* 22(1961) 547.

Further, according to Heidegger, the traditional metaphysics that attempted to ground the ultimate explanation of reality in a reality transcendent to the phenomenological world is no longer viable.[57] We cannot proceed as though the nature of reality conforms to a prior plan fixed by a reality beyond experience. If the transcendent exists, it is beyond verifiable ontological reality. Thus any attempt to find "essences" by a philosophical method other than phenomenological analysis is doomed. The only real avenue of discovery lies in a phenomenological analysis of the fundamental reality of the existence whereby things arrive at intelligibility and meaning through historical disposition of themselves in time. Finite being is the philosopher's concern and it reveals itself only progressively; hence the need for a phenomenological rather than a metaphysical analysis. Reality is on the move; therefore it is discernible only as unveiling itself in time. Finite beings do not, consequently, reveal themselves as endowed with a unified essence possessed once and for all. Thus the question "what is human being?" can receive something of an answer only by analyzing human being in the world. Its "essence" *is* its history and it is this history which is the philosopher's concern. Only the patterns of human consciousness achieved by phenomenology deserve to be considered as revealing the true structures of finite being.[58]

It is this non-theistic phenomenology that has been influential upon Rahner's anthropology. But needless to say, the data facing him as a believer, including the existential situation of humanity's need to be graced, has necessarily modified his analysis of human being. It is in this context, nonetheless, that Rahner's existential must be understood. This must suffice for now. We shall return again to this matter.

We see, then, that Rahner has substituted a much more existential theology for the post-Tridentine essentialistic and conceptualistic theology of nature and grace. We have already noted at the close of the preceding chapter that herein lies the crucial issue.[59] For the essentialist, essences exist in themselves, somewhat in the manner of the Platonic world of ideas. Thus if the essence of humanity is considered independently of existent human beings,

[57]T. Langan, *The Meaning of Heidegger* (New York: Columbia University, 1961), 11.

[58]Ibid., 143–152.

[59]On the reaction against essentialism in this period, cf. E. Gilson, *Being and Some Philosophers*, 2nd ed. (Toronto: Institute of Medieval Studies, 1952).

then humanity is vested with an intelligibility, apart from its actuality in the individuality of concrete persons, in some universal idea of the spiritual intellect. Very subtly an essence begins to be endowed with a minimal being "irrespective of the fact that it is not actualized in any known subject or in any existing thing."[60] As for God, the divine mind sees the myriad of possible essences and can make of a given series of essences a world order. As Lonergan has well put it, for the essentialist, Plato's ideas are in the divine mind as Noah's animals are in the ark.[61] Thus essence is the basic building block to which all else is relative. A world order is derivative of some combination of possible finite essences that God chooses to endow with being. It is not surprising that this philosophical orientation feels it can precisely define humanity apart from any existential situation. In consequence, all non-essential qualities conferred by God are products of a divine second-guessing, wholly extrinsic to the fixed natural order and therefore easily labeled super-natural, or preternatural. These metaphysical presuppositions are not without their psychological implications, as we have seen in Rahner's view on experiential consciousness of nature and grace. Obviously de Lubac's surnaturel and Rahner's existential could never find a home in the world of the essentialist.

The error of the essentialist lies in a failure to see that essences cannot be grasped apart from their existence. Neither is intelligible without the other. One arrives at the possible only through the real. This seems true even where the Creator is concerned. God knows potency only in relation to act, the undetermined through the determined. Possibles that were or are or will be are known by God through their rapport with the actuality of existence.[62] Pure possibles which never were nor will be are known only in relation to God's practical knowledge of the actually chosen order. Only thus can the intelligibility of essences be retained as dependent on existence. Pure possibles, therefore, presuppose a relation to the existence-endowing creative will of God insofar as they continue eternally to offer themselves to the divine refusal. It is in this offering that the possible finds whatever virtual determination it comes to possess in human understanding.

[60]Ibid., 74–75.

[61]"The Natural Desire to See God," 35.

[62]Thomas Aquinas, *ST*, I, 14, 9; *De Veritate* 3, 6.

It follows that the intelligibility of beings is not found in moving from the possible to the real, but the inverse. To define essences apart from their relation to actual existence violates the priority of existence which is one of the tenets of the Thomism the "pure nature" theorists claimed to be following.[63] Our knowledge of reality is more than a complex of abstract concepts. It is a unity of concepts whereby we define and judgments whereby we reach the act of being itself. True understanding is realized only in regard to the existent, which in turn is adequately perceived only against the horizon of a total world order, which itself is the direct, primary object of the divine will and in function of which all other structures are derivative.[64] Obviously Rahner has stressed the historicity of the supernatural, the primacy of the supernatural world order, from which all else, including the quiddity of humanity, is derivative, and the need to maintain one's consideration of possible worlds and natures as a secondary and dependent reference. A purely natural order becomes intelligible only if related to and derived from the existential supernatural order. Considering humanity's historical situation, Rahner finds postulating the possibility of another world order useful to better understand the graciousness of God's purpose in the present state. Rahner moves only from the real to the possible, unlike the extrinsicist, and postulates pure nature only as a remainder once one prescinds from the actual supernatural order that could have not been. Yet in moving through the real to the possible, the realm of pure nature, he does so without a nuanced delineation of the possible. Contrary to de Lubac, however, Rahner sees no reason to circumscribe the possible by the actual, especially since, it seems, possibilities can be deduced as conditions for the intelligibility of the actual.

In conclusion, Rahner's position is an attempt to steer a middle course between the extrinsicism of the "standard view" and the intrinsicism of de Lubac. In a later work de Lubac seems to refer to Rahner in such a way as to leave one with the impression that the existential is the equivalent of his own surnaturel.[65] Rahner, however, will not admit of an absolute desire that is constitutive of nature. True, de Lubac has well accented the gratuity of the supernatural in its intrinsic grandeur as compared to all the Crea-

---

[63]Thomas Aquinas, *ST*, I, 14, 3; H. Bouillard, "L' Intention fondamentale," 378-379.

[64]B. Lonergan, "The Natural Desire to See God," 36.

[65]*The Mystery of the Supernatural*, 275-276.

114 The Interiority of the Invitation of Grace

tor's gifts which are also gratuitous. But for Rahner, this *absolute* gratuity from above must be translated in terms of a *relative* gratuity from below as well (i.e., relative to historical human nature) if the full gratuity of grace is to be adequately thought through. This is done only if human nature as-such is considered conceivable without grace. But unfortunately it is precisely at this point that de Lubac's theory proves incompatible with Rahner's view. There is no small irony in this, since it was especially with regard to relative gratuity that de Lubac thought his theory most solid. De Lubac, unfortunately, seems ultimately to reduce the gratuity of grace to that of creation. God's love is always gratuitous. But for Rahner the real gratuity of grace must be seen in the light of God's revealed love and call to salvation in Christ.

Rahner's treatment, like most treatments of the problem in the Catholic tradition, is systematic and concerned with the ontological and psychological aspects of the problematic. In the biblical view, God is seen as turning to sinful people to make them responding covenant partners. Protestant discussion of the nature-grace antinomy has tended to make this the whole picture.[66] Bultmannians, e.g., view the Christian life as an "authentic existence" toward which one naturally inclines, but cannot realize, because of sinful nature, until liberated by the grace of Christ coming in the kerygma. In line with a tradition going back to Aquinas Rahner theologized on the premise that grace is not exhausted by its medicinal function. God is gracious not only to humanity as sinful, but to humanity as humanity. Even apart from sin it is pure grace that one is summoned to a relationship with God which is in no way an inherent possibility of one's own, but is made possible only by God's Self-communication and all it entails for the ontological structure of and its psychological resonance in human beings.

We shall return to Rahner in our concluding chapter, which will develop in greater detail Rahner's understanding of grace as horizon. There we shall also consider some of the negative criticism that has more recently been lodged against his technical doctrine of nature and grace and against his entire theological project's basic assumptions. For now, following the historical trajectory of our problem, we must turn to more immediate reactions to Rahner's technical doctrine of nature and grace.

[66]H. Urs von Balthasar, "Deux notes sur K. Barth," *Recherches de Science Religieuse* 35(1948) 92–111.

5

The Absolute Gratuity of Grace:
Hans Urs von Balthasar's Gratuity
"From Above"

We have already noted the generally favorable reaction that greeted Rahner's revisionary existential. In this and the following chapters we treat of reactions not wholly in accord with Rahner's explanation of the nature-grace dialectic. The significance of the positions now briefly to be exposed and evaluated can to some extent be measured by the stature of the theologians concerned: Hans Urs von Balthasar, Edward Schillebeeckx, and Juan Alfaro. The latter two theologians will be the subject of our study in the following chapter while the present chapter will be wholly devoted to a consideration of von Balthasar's position, which is more fully developed than that of the other two.

I. Gratuity "From Above"

Von Balthasar's fundamental observations, which were not made by way of offering a definitive solution to the nature-grace problem, are found in a chapter of his work on Karl Barth.[1] In agreement with Rahner and de Lubac, von Balthasar wants us to recall at the very outset the divine intention that was primary in the act of creation. God has created humanity for intimate personal union with Godself. It is this destiny that explains humanity

[1]H. Urs von Balthasar, *Karl Barth: Darstellung und Deutung Seiner Theologie* (Cologne: J. Hegner, 1951) 278–335. An abridged English translation is available under the title *The Theology of Karl Barth* (New York: Doubleday, 1972). For von Balthasar's anthropology, see *A Theological Anthropology* (New York: Sheed & Ward, 1967).

and gives it meaning. Its dignity, truth, and unity are that of a being orientated in its most profound depths to the possession of God.

Such a destination is, von Balthasar insists, totally gratuitous. Yet a gratuitous gift can never be defined solely in *absolute* terms, in itself or "out there." Rather, its gratuity must be seen in relation to its beneficiary. Hence the existing order of things, which is a graced order, must by necessity call into play the correlative concept of nature. Without this correlate it is inconceivable. "Grace is grace for a nature and to a nature; logically, if not chronologically, grace always presupposes a nature."[2] What the word of God reveals to us is a concrete human being whose nature is faced toward God. Nature may be distinct from this orientation, but never separated from it. Further, nature constitutes in the indivisible unity of humanity's concrete essence, a relatively independent sphere which is a necessary presupposition of grace, though it is never simply derived from the latter as one of its forms of expressions. On the other hand, any derivation of grace from the demands or needs of nature so that grace appears an epiphenomenon of nature is unacceptable, as is any reduction of nature to a form of grace, or any destruction of nature by grace.

But, notes von Balthasar, the concept of nature as distinct from grace is little more than an abstract and formal mental construct. Abstract, because in fact there is only graced nature. Nature can be without grace properly speaking. But it does not by virtue of this cease to be called by God to personal union with Godself. Nature is never reduced to a condition of pure nature, for its insertion in the supernatural order is ever-present. There is no reason to equate the possession of grace with constitution in the order of grace. Sin eliminates the former, but never the latter. Moreover, the absence of grace in the sinful humanity of this economy is not comparable to its absence in the humanity of pure nature. Only in the first case is there a true privation of what ought to be. This fact—that grace ought always to be actually possessed—is precisely what constitutes the supernatural order in which humanity finds itself situated.

However the concept of nature as distinct from grace is also a formal notion, for the real content of this notion is hardly definable for us. The notion itself, born of abstraction, designates a reality that completely eludes our experience. It is impossible

[2]*Karl Barth: Darstellung*, 291.

to know from our experience what traits belong to nature as such and what to nature by reason of its insertion in a supernatural economy. To what extent would pure nature be hampered by ignorance, concupiscence, resistance to good? Would it know sickness and death and if so, what kind of death? Would society, marriage, the state be found in this abstract condition of nature? What would nature's relationship be to its silent, non-revealing God? Would there be a need for prayer? Would there be an afterlife, a resurrection, a final beatitude? All these intriguing questions relative to pure nature must be left unanswered.[3]

Von Balthasar goes on to expressly deny the possibility of constructing a purely natural theology. This for two reasons: (1) the only relation to God we have been given to know is that which our concrete nature presently enjoys, one that involves our being forever situated in a supernatural world order, which even sin cannot put an end to; (2) theology without a doubt is formulated in the light of reason, but not at all by abstract reason, a pure reason that is segregated from the influence of grace and of what Rahner calls the supernatural existential; rather, from the first dawn of its awakening ours is a reason involved in the theology of belief or unbelief.[4] Von Balthasar does not mean to deny the possibility of a rational knowledge of God endowed with certitude. His point is that such knowledge, both in its point of departure (our experience) and in its means (reason), is under the influence of elements which do not derive from abstract nature.[5]

Nowhere in our world, then, is there a humanity that is merely a nature.[6] Thus the concrete concept of nature, grounded in a reality that is implicated in the history of salvation, must be our essential or predominant concept (*der Beherrschende*).[7] The formal, abstract notion of nature can be little more than an auxiliary concept (*Hilfsbegriff*). Its function is limited to protecting the notion of grace and to expressing the sub-structure, the subjectivity in which grace is gratuitously inserted. To enunciate its content, let it suffice to say that it denotes one's creaturely condition as a knowing and free subject composed of spirit and matter; that

[3]Ibid., 294.

[4]Ibid., 291

[5]H. Urs von Balthasar, *Science, Religion, and Christianity* (Westminster: Newman, 1958), 61-77.

[6]*Karl Barth: Darstellung*, 298.

[7]Ibid., 300.

it designates a sphere that is relatively consistent and intelligible; that it grounds the sphere of culture, of personal relations, of sexuality.[8] But von Balthasar hastens to add a qualifier. We can never exactly circumscribe this abstract nature in its own proper and isolated reality; we can never draw a clear-cut distinction between it and grace, which penetrates it to the core and leaves its mark on all the registers of nature.

Does von Balthasar go so far as to maintain that the gratuity of grace can be explicated without affirming the possibility of pure nature, as did de Lubac and the anonymous "D"? Like Rahner before him, he has told us that abstract nature is not easily knowable in itself, shorn of the supernatural existential. But does he think it necessary, in order to safeguard the gratuity of grace, to admit for this pure and hardly definable nature the absolute possibility of real existence? Does he side with Rahner in asserting this possibility, or with de Lubac in negating it? At first glance von Balthasar apparently rejects this possibility. The gratuity of grace, he maintains, does not suffice to ground the idea that nature could actually exist in a pure condition without its present supernatural finality.[9] At times von Balthasar gives the impression that a definition of gratuity "from above" suffices to guarantee the transcendence of grace. His reference seems to be to the *absolute* gratuity of grace in terms of its intrinsic excellence, its character as an uncreated gift, which distinguishes it from all other gifts conferred in creation. This alone assures it a distinct and proper gratuity so as to satisfy the demands of Christian dogma. From this point of view there is no need to provide warranty for the gratuity of grace by appeal to a nature that hypothetically could exist without it.

Nonetheless, von Balthasar does not let the matter rest there. For while he sees the gratuity of the supernatural order substantially defined in terms of its unique excellence, thus conceived absolutely, he nevertheless admits that gratuity cannot but be conceived *relatively*. In other words, the gratuity of the super-

---

[8]Ibid., 301, 311.

[9]"Is it possible and meaningful to assert that the meaning of the whole creation ultimately rests on God's will to bestow his grace (all the rest is so this one thing can be), to explain the innermost essence of man in terms of this meaning-content (*Sinn*) and yet at the same time to make an attempt in all seriousness to subtract precisely the ultimate source of meaning (*Letztsinngebenden*)? How is it possible to subtract the innermost center?" Ibid., 310–311. See Rahner's reply to von Balthasar in "Concerning the Relationship," 311–312, n.1.

natural must also be seen in reference to an abstract nature, relative to which it is gratuitous. The view of gratuity "from above" must be complemented by a view "from below." It is precisely here that von Balthasar sets sail on a rather novel course.

Von Balthasar acknowledges that from a certain viewpoint, and at a particular level of thought, one must agree that this abstract nature, the beneficiary of the grace-gift, is absolutely possible and capable of existing unendowed with grace. But from what viewpoint can this be seen? From the vantage point of humans, not of God. Humans see grace coming to them as the gift of a sovereignly free God. They then necessarily and without delay translate this gratuity into a meaningful reality by telling themselves "it could have been otherwise."[10] Thus humanity sees itself as called and elevated by God to the heights of divine friendship. In the burst of gratitude provoked by this revelation, how could creatures not confess their own unworthiness? Knowing that they are summoned to share in the divine life, they are painfully aware that their own right is to "the lowest place." They realize that, far from deserving the stature of God's friend, their proper status is that of creature and servant. And yet even these latter positions are the gift of divine love. "From the standpoint of a creaturely theology (*vom Standpunkt einer kreatürlichen Theologie*)" there is good reason not to abandon the concept of pure nature. Still, this in no way implies that we should give ourselves to the futile task of sketching its content.

When it comes to God's vantage point, on the other hand, we cannot say as much. Von Balthasar would ask: Is the content of the so-called "natural" so well delineated, so coherent and intelligible that it would suffice, even for God, to ground these elements in the possibility of existence? No affirmative answer can categorically be given to this query according to von Balthasar. Once we admit that in the divine intelligence and will it is the supernatural order that *de facto* has given meaning and intelligibility to human being, then we are no longer in a position to correctly judge whether outside the order of grace nature would continue to enjoy any intelligibility. Hence the way is closed to an out-and-out affirmation of its possibility. Eternally God has willed but one thing: to open the divine love and life to humans. This alone explains creation. Seeing reality in this perspective, one should immediately recognize that questions concerning the possibility

[10]*Karl Barth: Darstellung*, 312.

of an ungraced world are an exercise in futility. What is of no importance to God should be of no importance to us, not even as sustenance for our humility.[11] However, we cannot construct a theology that is purely theocentric, one that speaks of God solely as God is in Godself and from the divine viewpoint. A creaturely theology will always be necessary. Obviously such a theology, viewing things from the creature's angle, as it must, will express the revealed reality of grace by formulae that reflect the hazardous limitations of the human viewpoint. On this score our thought will have to remain in a state of tension. We will accept the possibility of a pure nature, without which abstraction, we would, from our point of view, betray the gratuity of grace. But we will also transcend this abstraction by moving on to a consideration of the order of grace which, as God tells us, is the only real order and therefore the only order absolutely endowed with intelligibility and possibility.

What von Balthasar seems to want to establish is simply this. In our human effort to rightly construe the gratuity of grace we naturally tend to transpose the problem to a level more readily understandable to us. As a result we imagine the divine creative will antecedently poised before two equally possible orders of essences, one the order of pure nature, the other of graced nature. Contemplating the existent order we then conclude: "It could have been otherwise." For von Balthasar this approach to the gratuity of grace is understandable, perhaps even necessary, but nonetheless very anthropomorphic in its grasp of the divine creative action and intention, and to that extent inadequate. It is, first, impossible to conceive of God as having to choose between two world orders. God's very nature precludes such ambivalence. For the situation so conceived would imply in God an indifference preliminary to the act of willing. This is wholly unacceptable. On the other hand, von Balthasar in no way wants to negate the sovereign freedom of God in creating humanity and finalizing it in the grace-life. The type of indifference or power of option (*potestas voluntatis ad opposita*) envisaged by the anthropomorphic approach is by no means requisite for a fully perfect liberty. It is, no doubt, a modality of liberty, but surely not identified with it.

---

[11]Ibid. Von Balthasar might cite Wittgenstein here: "Whereof one cannot speak, thereof one must be silent." *Tractatus* 7. Theology is authorized neither by faith nor by reason to speak in absolute terms of what God can or cannot do, of whether the idea of an intelligent nature without a supernatural orientation is self-contradictory or not.

God then does not choose, nor can God be thought of as choosing between two possible orders for the simple reason that possibles do not have in God some kind of ideal existence which precedes their real existence. Briefly, God does not first excogitate essences, or world orders and then create one of them by choice. Rather God creates a world order in the very act of conceiving it. Only then, in the light of the actual, is ideal or possible existence thinkable. The possible always stands in reference to the actual.

II. *Six Theses on Nature and Grace*

At a later date von Balthasar provided a thesis-like recapitulation and further refinement of his observations on nature and grace, though without changing his basic position.[12] Six areas are lightly touched upon: (1) the theological concept of nature; (2) the importance of the nature-grace distinction; (3) the essence and nature of humanity; (4) the gratuity of grace; (5) the hypothesis of a graceless world; (6) the natural desire for God.

Von Balthasar readily assumes the distinction between human nature and the gratuitous revelation of and participation in the inner life of God. Nonetheless his nature-grace duality is not to be hastily identified with other pairings employed by theology such as creation and covenant, the creature called to grace and the creature actually receiving revelation, *homo peccator* and *homo iustus*. A simple identification cannot be made because in each of the three pairs the first member, situated as it is within a Christian economy, is itself already graced, bearing within it the influences and determinations of grace. Consequently the first polarity in each instance cannot be tagged as "nature."[13]

Indeed, von Balthasar seems to feel that theology has a special competence to forge a concept of nature. For theology alone weighs the data of revelation and the supernatural, and hence

---

[12]"Der Begriff der Natur in der Theologie," *Zeitschrift für Katholische Theologie* 75(1953) 452–464. This was a reply to E. Gutwenger's "Natur und Übernatur," which appeared earlier that year in the same journal (82–97). Von Balthasar is loathe to situate his understanding of nature and grace within any system. His approach is openended. Fides quaerens is not intellectus inveniens. Grace and nature cannot be reduced to one level of being. For von Balthasar, this is not a case for agnosticism but a recognition of the limitations that necessarily hem in theology.

[13]Ibid., 452–453.

qualifies more than philosophy to formulate the complementary concept, nature. Theologically viewed, nature bears two distinctive characteristics. It refers to humanity's creaturely make-up as the presupposed otherness from God, or to that which is over against God-revealing. God does not speak to Godself, but to another. Nature points, secondly, to that abiding reality in humanity, that constant which remains throughout all historical states— innocence, sinfulness, justification, glorification. In this connection von Balthasar endorses Rahner's differentiation between "pure nature", which is neither graced nor called, and the concrete human quiddity marked with a supernatural existential prior to any other gift of grace. The divine decree must realize itself in the creature's interiorly being-this-way. This supernaturally polarized humanity is the only one existing, and it alone can be the object of the philosopher's study. Theology, however, has the capacity to prescind from nature's supernatural modality and to formulate an abstract, remainder-concept after the existential has been bracketed. What remains is subjectivity, spirit in transcendence.

The distinction between nature and grace is, for von Balthasar, plainly necessary. It is necessary, first, for the intelligibility of grace and revelation. For nature denotes the subjectivity that is other than God and the possible recipient of and respondent to divine Self-manifestation and donation. The distinction is also necessary to point up the gratuity of grace, for divinizing grace can in no hypothesis be owed or merited. The notion of merited grace is both contradictory and heretical. It is the theological concept of nature that wards off any attempt to make grace simply interchangeable with nature. Concrete, historical nature, however, has, from the start, an absolute and necessary relation to grace. To be summoned to vision is to be graced, and it does not occur only *after* humanity is humanity. The supernatural existential ordering humanity to intimate union with God simply flows from and expresses the inner logic of the divine creative and summoning decree.[14]

Von Balthasar turns next to the idea, nature, and essence of humanity, reminding us that the conceptualization of these must evidence an awareness of human being's true finality, its call to participation in divine life through incorporation in Christ. The Aristotelean notion that nature is essence considered as the dy-

---

[14]Ibid, 454.

namic base of human operations cannot give humanity's revealed finality its due weight, for human nature with its finalization in grace does not fall within the framework of deeds and results that cannot range beyond the edges of this world. Again, the conceptual frameworks of philosophy are for von Balthasar too weak to bear the weight of revealed reality. Unlike the great thinkers of the patristic and Scholastic eras, whose focal point was existential human nature ordered to a supernatural finality, later thought, leaning on a philosophy wholly divorced from theology, overextends itself in establishing analogies between the essence of humanity and non-human substances. This is conducive to an over-facile equalization of nature and essence. What must be remembered is that nature's ordination to grace and its consequent inclination to it entail a modification (the supernatural existential) that precedes the gift of grace. Rather than simply equating nature and essence where humanity is concerned, von Balthasar considers the essence of historical humanity to be a grace-modified nature, and to include something more than a nature pure and simple. If essence is what a human being is, then in addition to nature it must include the supernatural existential that follows hard upon the fact of creation in Christ.[15]

Only through an appeal to the existential, von Balthasar feels, can the difficulty of extrinsicism be overcome. He can agree with Malevez that the existential is a reality modifying humanity, and with Rahner that it is what is inmost and a necessary, ontological constituent of humanity's concrete being, without belonging to its nature.[16] The paradox is so rich that comparisons with other structures of nature and finality are impossible. That nature is *always* essence observed to be a dynamic principle may ring true in philosophy. But the *always* finds its exception in the case of historical human nature which is ordered to a unique ultimate end. And so von Balthasar will not pour new wine into old skins.

In his observations on the gratuity of grace von Balthasar champions divine freedom. From start to finish the human/divine relationship is marked by the fact that grace is unmerited by any creature. This is true in any hypothesis, even in an economy where God has irrevocably called creatures to grace and where creation is in function of this call. That we now may and must demand

[15]Ibid., 455–456.

[16]L. Malevez, "La gratuité du surnaturel," 685, maintained that the existential is an accident directly modifying the human essence rather than its faculties.

this grace in prayer in no way erases this truth. What von Balthasar wants especially to highlight is that the gratuity of grace resides primarily in its own inmost essence and not in an extrinsic bond with the realm of nature over against it.[17]

In the historical order grace can be understood only if one grasps two of its characteristics. First, it is necessary for historical humanity since it has been decreed and promised. Secondly, it is always presented as a free gift from the sovereignly free God. To properly perceive and appreciate both qualities, it must be borne in mind that grace is not just like any other thing in the human inventory of things. Its absoluteness or necessity, therefore, ought not to be confused with the necessity one finds in nature. For while it is eternally necessary, it is at the same time eternally free, always the fresh, new, contingent miracle of divine love. The trait of necessity leads us to the realization that we cannot view the order of grace as something accidental, an additional and optional accessory to an already finished nature. As a free divine contingency, on the other hand, grace is seen to be unowed, and unlike other contingencies, basically impervious to human comprehension.

At this point von Balthasar seeks light from the analogy of human lovers. The first meeting of two persons that will with time mature into deep, lasting love is an event that later is viewed by them as a breathtaking stroke of luck and yet as an eternally predestined encounter written in the stars, or mythically determined by fate long before they come to be. Necessity and freedom complement and elucidate one another. Prayer knows the same dialectic. One praying knows he or she has been created precisely to become the recipient of the divine favor of grace. But for all that, the grace received remains an unowed miracle of divine largesse.

Von Balthasar concludes by noting again that the necessary-free paradox of grace is without comparison with any other contingent necessity known to us. The gratuity of grace is of a wholly different cloth. In this perspective, he feels, to pose the question "what would have happened if . . .?" is in no way demanded by revelation and indeed is to veer from the lighted way of "faith seeking understanding" and to set oneself upon the dark path of rationalistic philosophizing. Notions such as necessity, freedom, exigency have an entirely different value in the prayer of the saint

---

[17]"Der Begriff der Natur," 457.

than they do in the thought of the philosopher. And it is to the saint that the theologian should turn.[18]

Von Balthasar next proceeds to reflect upon a double query. Is a world possible in which God would have created intelligent beings not called to the life of grace? Does such a possibility follow *necessarily* from the gratuity of grace in the present economy? The first is a question of pure and simple possibility; the second, one of *necessary* possibility. One might conceivably on hypothetical grounds answer affirmatively to the first without thereby wanting to answer affirmatively to the second. For to affirm that the present graced order necessarily demands the possibility of an ungraced order is to equivalently affirm a necessary possibility, i.e., a possibility as necessary as the actually existing order, which, insofar as it exists, cannot not be, and which demands as condition for its being-as-it-is, the possibility of its being-other-than-it-is.

To begin with, it surely does lie within the divine omnipotence to create eternally and differently. No doubt a myriad of worthwhile possibilities lies open to God's creativity. But what all this means specifically lies beyond human ken. The distinction between God's ordered power (God can do what divine wisdom does not forbid) and God's absolute power (God can do whatever is non-contradictory) is a dangerous abstraction. So too is the rank assertion that a certain compatibility of notes (*non-repugnantia in terminis*) grounds intrinsic possibility. In the first place, whatever is possible for God in some hypothesis must be in conformity with divine wisdom, which is beyond human comprehension. Moreover, how can we know a given conception entails no contradictions unless we see the elements considered coherent and possible harmonized in real and actual compatibility? Moreover, created realities do not come tumbling out of the Creator's hand at random and in isolation, one from the other. Each is part of a set, a whole, a universe, an order. To postulate possibility for a particular thing one must grasp the master plan that sees all particularities locked together in order and interdependence. But this panorama lies beyond human vision. Hence that the human mind sees no contradiction in an idea is a fragile criterion for affirming it to be necessarily realizable for God. One truly honors the divine omnipotence by leaving the contents of the possible to the divine discernment.[19]

[18]Ibid.

[19]Ibid., 458.

After this brief assessment, von Balthasar looks at the same problem from the viewpoint of Christian faith. Is the necessary possibility of an order of pure nature simply the negative formulation of the dogma of the gratuitous gift of Christ by God? It would not seem so. The negative formulation does not give full expression to the total content of the positive formula. It does not designate what it is that is not granted to pure nature. Moreover, the focus of the negative formula is upon what could have been, rather than what is. Consequently the negative formula is incapable of adequately articulating the distinctive quality that marks the gratuity of grace so that it is seen to be a special gratuity over and above the "unmerited" character that marks all the Creator's gifts. Hence von Balthasar will not admit the total equivalency of the positive and negative formulations of gratuity. The unique gratuity of grace, therefore, is not satisfactorily articulated by simply parroting a line from *Humani Generis*. What is crucial is to show that grace is gratuitous relative to the here-and-now, and not that it would have been gratuitous relative to some hypothetical might-have-been nature. In no way does the possibility of an order of pure nature explain the gratuity of grace. In this light it is difficult to see how the encyclical's affirmation that it could have been otherwise *necessarily* follows hard on the heels of the gratuity of grace as a *necessary* possibility.[20] In approaching the two questions, one must always recognize the serious limitations that human speculation is saddled with. It is certainly questionable whether any *a priori* conjuring of possibilities can be fruitful as an act of philosophical or theological speculation. The imaginative invention and serious acceptance of possibilities whose inner consistency cannot be verified seems a senseless undertaking. Dreams of what God could or might have done are of little use. The game is an exercise in anthropomorphism. In fact the whole thing needs turning around. The world itself is not possible before it exists. Its possibility is given, even in God Himself, only following the creative act that brought it to existence. Possibility is the retrojection of actuality.[21]

---

[20]Ibid., 458–459.

[21]Following the lead of Malevez, "La gratuité du surnaturel," 585f., von Balthasar enlists the aid of A. Sertillanges, *Le Christianisme et les Philosophes* (Paris: Aubier, 1939), I, 274f: "On sait que pour H. Bergson, le possible est postérieur au réel, et non pas antérieur. [Cette thèse est] parfaitement thomiste en ce qui concerne les faits contingents, puisque ceux-ci n'ont pas de verité *ante eventum*, pas d'intelligibilité, donc nulle possibilité objective. L'univers n'est pas possible avant d'exister. Sa possibilité

Lastly, von Balthasar discusses briefly the problem of the natural appetite for the beatific vision. He treats of this last because (1) the prior questions, fundamental to its discussion, should not be prejudiced by it; (2) a true perspective on the problem of the *appetitus naturalis* is impeded by the fact that the issue has been formulated in terms of Greek philosophy (the pitfalls of which were noted earlier) and the application of which can end in a *petitio principii*; (3) there is difficulty in designating the central elements of humanity's historical essence, endowed as it presently is with an existential ordering it to the vision of God.

If we keep in mind that historical humanity is forever finalized in the vision of God so that this orientation affects its very being, speculation about a purely *natural* desire loses both its urgency and its feasibility. The whole problematic is rooted in an idea of nature we cannot hold. But again, von Balthasar does not want to appear wholly agnostic about human nature. One can certainly analyze the processes of judgement and will, their transcendental conditions of possibility, and certain empirical factors in human existence. Here the philosopher is at home. If, however, one attempts the type of analysis of the human spirit that Blondel undertakes in his *L'Action*, then the precise content of nature becomes more nebulous and the line of demarcation between theological nature and essence more difficult to draw. Von Balthasar's agnosticism does not touch historical essence, but the boundaries

n'est acquise, en Dieu même, que postérieurement a l'acte qui le crée, et cette possibilité n'est que la projection en arrière de son existence. [Pour Thomas] le monde ne préexiste pas réellement sous forme d'idées, même divines. Ce que préexiste, c'est Dieu, simplement, et ce qu'on appelle idées n'est que la projection en Dieu, par notre intelligence à nous, des objects du temps et des acquisitions du temps. Ces acquisitions du temps, qui sont la création même, sont donc bien un gain véritable, et croissant; elles ne sont nullement une diminution, une réduction, si ce n'est par rapport à Dieu; mais cela qui le contesterait? Le réel n'est pas une ombre, mais une lumière grandissante jusqu'à ce que soit complet le nombre des 'elus' et achevé 'l'enfantement' universel dont parle l'Apôtre. Le 'parfait' ne precède pas; on y marche. Le monde n'est pas tout fait d'avance et seulement manifesté; il se fait. Il n'est possible, encore une fois, que par projection en arrière, après avoir existé. Quand donc Thomas écrit que Dieu a tout créé *per intellectum*, il ne faut pas comprendre, quoi qu'il en soit des apparences verbales inévitables, que Dieu conçoit d'abord, puis qu'il crée, comme un fabricateur humain; mais bien que le crée émane de lui en lui empruntant son intelligibilité aussi bien que son être. L'intelligibilité, reportée en Dieu après coup, engendre la possibilité; ce n'est pas las possibilité qui engendre l'être. Le langage correct est de dire que Dieu est un infini de *possibilité*, et non qu'il y a en lui une infinité de *possibles*. La possibilité qui est en Dieu, c'est Dieu, et il n'y en a pas d'autre, si ce n'est pour les *rudiores* dont parle Cajetan (In q.14, a.5, n.11). En ce qui nous concerne nous-mêmes c'est notre existence en Dieu qui fonde notre possibilité, au lieu que ce soit notre possibilité en Dieu qui fonde notre existence. Et notre existence en Dieu, c'est Dieu, comme Thomas le repète fréquemment.''

between it and abstract nature. This latter should really, he feels, be of no serious concern to the philosopher or theologian. The theologian's true field of study is the real, not the possible; the theologian studies the actual world with its tensions between creation and covenant, fall and redemption, old and new covenants. For it is they that are of concern to God, not some hypothetical entity.[22]

If one wants to ask whether the supernatural existential adds a *desiderium naturale* or simply elevates the exocentricity of the human spirit, von Balthasar will opt for the latter alternative. He sees the intelligent being so structured precisely that it might be elevated without violation of its inner consistency. Any other explanation simply projects Platonic longing into the structure of human being as finalized in the order of grace.

Von Balthasar thinks, then, that he has situated the problematic properly. It is of no decisive import whether certain debatable passages in Thomas Aquinas are interpreted as philosophical or as theological texts. For they were penned at a time when, unlike our own, philosophy and theology were not divorced, indeed, a time when Rahner's distinction between nature and the existential would have carried less weight. Of even less importance is the determination whether the concept of pure nature originates with Cajetan (1469–1534) or traces its lineage further back. What is more significant is that with Cajetan two fundamentally different modes of thought, philosophical and theological, cross paths, with the result that pure nature becomes a construct employed by both. Cajetan was unaware of the dualism thus embraced and the radical disparity yawning between "a pure Aristotelean concept of nature" and the theological notion of nature which is the correlate of a gratuity transcending nature.[23] Von Balthasar's effort was spent on making it clear that these two paths do not lead to the same reality.[24]

III. *Reflections on von Balthasar's Nuanced Gratuity*

Obviously von Balthasar's thought is akin to that of de Lubac and Rahner in that his focus is the concrete, historical order. An

[22]"Der Begriff der Natur," 460.

[23]J. Ternus, "Natur-Übernatur in der Vortridentinischen Theologie Seit Thomas von Aquin," *Scholastik* 28(1953) 399–404.

[24]"Der Begriff der Natur," 461.

even stronger kinship with Rahner appears in his forthright acceptance of the supernatural existential on the grounds that the divine creating and finalizing decree realizes itself in the ontological realm. Further, his contrast between nature and essence reechoes Rahner's differentiation between nature and quiddity. For both theologians historical humanity is more than a nude nature; it is graced even prior to justification. For even stronger reasons than de Lubac, von Balthasar refuses to consider humanity as simply another "natural object." And again, like Rahner, von Balthasar sees nature as a practically indefinable residual due to permeation by the existential. The theological notion of nature is had only by mentally abstracting the supernatural components in historical humanity.

Beyond all this any similarity between von Balthasar and Rahner is perhaps more apparent than real. A closer analysis can only lead us to conclude that von Balthasar has, perhaps, greater affinity to de Lubac and the anonymous "D."[25] Von Balthasar does explicitly acknowledge a distinction between nature and grace. Nature is the logical antecedent and presupposition of grace. Grace is in no way constitutive of nature, he tells us. If, however, one were to press into service here the Chalcedonian *"inconfuse et inseparabiliter"*, one has the impression that von Balthasar's stress would fall heavily upon the latter. For he seems to see the distinction as an intellectual abstraction having minimal relevance in the concrete and minimizing the mutual compenetration and existential unity of the pair. For von Balthasar it is not only difficult, but perhaps impossible, to distinguish between the necessary constituents of human nature and its always-present, gratuitous historical determination in the order of finality. The distinction then is not to be belabored.[26] In fact, one suspects that von Balthasar is striving hard to eschew a putative lingering dualism and extrinsicism in Rahner. Thus he seems to shy away from identifying the existential as an accident affecting the essence (Malevez) or as an added ontological constituent (Rahner.).

It is this all-out effort to forcefully bring home the awesome unity binding nature and grace that leads von Balthasar to a ne-

---

[25]Rahner seems to think of von Balthasar as sharing the views of de Lubac. Cf. "Concerning the Relationship," 304, note 1.

[26]It is interesting to find de Lubac reminding us: "Les realités le plus séparables ne sont pourtant pas forcément celles qui se distinguent le plus fortement entre elles. L'union et la differentiation sont bien plutôt deux choses qui croissent de pair." "Le Mystère du surnaturel," 87.

gation, or at least a strong skepticism, concerning the possibility of an order of pure nature, or a concept of humanity-as-such. He does not see the possibility of another world order as following *necessarily* from the dogma of gratuity in the present order. On the other hand, Rahner does not hesitate to maintain that the gratuity of grace does justify the theological conclusion that humanity could have been created otherwise. Though another order has never factually obtained for us, Rahner does see the possibility as a necessary though secondary, even if negative way, of formulating the gratuity of grace.

The Swiss theologian, as we have seen, based his position on philosophical and theological grounds. First, the mere fact that we see no internal inconsistency in the characteristics of the hypothetical creature under consideration does not at all argue to its being intrinsically possible for God. For a thing must be consistent and coherent not only in itself, but also with all other things in the order being postulated as possible. Now to assert the intrinsic coherence of any such imagined creature is, to von Balthasar's way of thinking, to assert more than our fallible and myopic vision can warrant. Consequently, we cannot simply affirm the possibility of an intelligent being who is not called to grace. Secondly, the negative formulation of gratuity (that the present order need not be since reality could have been otherwise) is not the equal of the positive statement of gratuity, because the former fails to fully explicate the substance of the latter. Nor for that matter, says von Balthasar, should this negative formula concern us. We are, after all, interested in vindicating a gratuity relative to the actual here-and-now, not to a hypothetical could-have-been order.

These premises, which are not without validity, led von Balthasar to stress an "aristocratic gratuity from above"; the absolute gratuity of grace is a gratuity derived from the intrinsic worth and excellence of the gift itself.[27] Nonetheless he was shrewd enough to see that such a gratuity becomes meaningful only if he can relativize it and translate it into a formula that tells him "it could have been otherwise." But this is a readily understandable, but hardly excusable anthropomorphic projection, a perspective that is wholly human. And we have no assurance it gets to the truth of the matter. We have no basis to postulate that as far as God is concerned it truly might have been otherwise, as

---

[27]K. Rahner, "Concerning the Relationship," 311–312.

though prior to creation, in a state of deliberation and counsel, the Creator was confronted with two (or more) live options. Moreover, von Balthasar finds the supernatural existential so central and inmost to historical humanity that one appears unable to envision nature without it. In other words, since the existential is what is inmost and central, it cannot be disregarded in favor of a possible pure nature or a concept of nature-as-such. It is not possible to extract this inmost element, indeed the very element in view of which all else in human nature is devised, without finding oneself left with a meaningless residual.[28] By now it should be evident that von Balthasar, as we stated, has steered a course that has placed him wide of Rahner and located him in a position proximate to, if not identical with that of de Lubac and "D."

Now von Balthasar's intense effort to make pure nature a secondary concern is laudable. In this he would find agreement with all those others (e.g., Rahner, Lonergan, Malevez, de Lubac) who want to pass from the real to the possible and make pure nature a marginal theorem. They too are interested in avoiding the weaknesses inherent in the essentialistic approach. But some might be unwilling to admit that one can achieve these aims only at the cost of negating the possibility, in fact the necessary possibility, of another world order.

In the first place, it is difficult to see how von Balthasar can contest the possibility of God's creating humanity in another world order (from the divine viewpoint), and at the same time acknowledge such a possibility "from the standpoint of creaturely theology." He seems not to take seriously our creaturely standpoint; he asks us to see things through the divine eyes. But the human angle of vision is all we have. Even in attempting to see things as God does, it remains always our seeing. We cannot transcend human modalities of thought and expression. And they will ever remain finite and limited, hence colored by the anthropomorphic. We may demand that philosophers and theologians continually sharpen, refine, and purify their concepts, judgments, and formulae. But to demand more is to abandon our cause to the agnostic, or to call for a complete moratorium on all God-talk.[29] More specifically, von Balthasar insists there is no

---

[28]*Karl Barth: Darstellung*, 310–311.

[29]Von Balthasar calls upon theologians to pay closer attention to biblical categories ("Der Begriff der Natur," 460). But what could be more anthropomorphic? If "God revealing" cannot avoid anthropomorphism, how much less can we?

ideal existence of possibles in God, so that the Creator would stand before these possibles indifferent or undetermined prior to the divine creative decree. Fair enough. To hold otherwise is to yield to a crass anthropomorphic view. But some might hesitate to agree when von Balthasar goes on to maintain that pure nature is not a possibility *absolutely* speaking, from God's side, but is, at most, only *relatively* so, from our view of things, a view which is not to be taken seriously.

In referring to an ungraced world as having a possibility of existence, one does not mean it is contemplated by God objectively, in a kind of ideal existence prior to its actualization. In God there is only God, no division between subject and object, no essence or order opposed to or distinct from the divine understanding itself. There is no boxful of possibles not strictly identical with the absolute divine existence itself. The assertion, therefore, that God decreed a graced order rather than an ungraced one in no way implies there is in the divine will a passage from indecision to decision, from indetermination to determination. What then is meant by referring to something as possible? Simply this. Divine being can be participated in an infinite variety. Its imitability by creatures is bounded only by the contradictory. In a word, God's creative genius far and away exceeds the terms upon which it confers actual existence. It seems, consequently, full justice is not done the divine creative power if its realization is narrowly confined to the *de facto* order of creation.

How do we know God's creativity includes an ungraced order among its *virtualities*?[30] Some might answer that the tradition affirms a gratuitous supernaturality immanent to the present economy. This gratuity cannot be defined solely "from above" in absolute terms, i.e., by reason of the intrinsic transcendence of the gift bestowed. It must also be defined "from below", or

---

[30]Malevez, "La gratuité du surnaturel," 674, drew an analogy from the writer's creativity. Hamlet has no reality till Shakespeare conceives him and births him in an idea. The idea of Hamlet is his possibility. Yet it does not precede or engender but accompanies or even follows his actuality. Nonetheless, prior to Hamlet's actuality, Shakespeare carried him *virtually* in his own being. Moreover, Hamlet does not exhaust the author's creativity, which surpasses all its actual creations. It is this creative power that warrants our speaking of possibilities. Not that they have an *ideal* existence in Shakespeare's mind; nor that he stands before their array and must choose. What is significant here is the virtuosity, the unlimited scope of the artist's genius. Possibility is spoken of primarily in terms of a given actualization of the creator's genius. It can also refer to what is virtually included in the creative genius, viz., the pure possible that never was nor will be.

relatively. If grace is grace, humanity can hold it only as grace, as unowed and unmerited; creation can lay no claim to it. Grace is lavished upon a creation that could be intelligible without it. Consequently, it will seem to some more reasonable to maintain that an ungraced human order is possible, and not simply from a human way of looking at things, but from the divine vantage point as well. Among the virtualities of the divine creative power there is room for a humanity uncalled to the graced horizon we know.

From this it follows that it may be difficult for some to concur in von Balthasar's rejection of the necessary possibility of an ungraced order as the complementary negative formulation of the dogma of gratuity. True, as he points out, the positive and negative formulations are neither equal nor identical. But they are complementary. They are related as concave and convex, and highlight different aspects of gratuity. The positive expresses the absolute facet; the negative, the relative. *Humani Generis* thought it necessary to defend the negative formula with its focus on the necessary possibility of another order as a valid and needed expression of gratuity.[31] Again, it is true that what is of no concern to God should be of no concern to us. At least it should not be our primary and direct concern. What is not but could have been concerns us only to the extent that it can sharpen our appreciation of and concern for what is. We shall return later to this matter of the double formulation. Similarly, it follows that some will not accept von Balthasar's contention that it is not possible to subtract the existential from historical nature without finding oneself left with an unintelligible remainder, since he sees, and rightly so, the existential as that which is deepest and inmost in humanity. But the paradox of divine love is operative here. Only if it is given freely, not by any essential necessity, is the divine love the inmost and that for which all else is given. Precisely because this love is effective of what is deepest and inmost, it is most unexpected. Does von Balthasar, like de Lubac, fall victim to the naturalism he wants desperately to elude when he assumes the inmost and most personal is at the same time the most inamissible and irremovable? His narrowed view of gratuity "from above" does not attend sufficiently to the view of gratuity "from below." Hu-

---

[31] Von Balthasar feels he has complied with the teaching of *Humani Generis* insofar as he has not made an outright denial of the pure possibility of another world but only of the necessary possibility of another world. The latter, he thinks, is not demanded by the doctrine of the gratuity of grace.

manity as humanity must receive the unexpected, the inmost, as grace, unowed and unexacted. This means a concept of human nature as-such seems to some inescapable. And what has been said about gratuity holds not only for the divine Self-gift, but also for humanity's ordination to it, for it is far more than the natural and conditioned possibility of the obediential potency, as von Balthasar himself admits.[32]

In conclusion, the verdict of some was that von Balthasar has not fully satisfied the demands of the gratuity of grace. His agnosticism, if not denial, concerning a possible graceless world and a concept of human nature-as-such implies that grace may very well be necessary to human being, which cannot be human without it. Appeals to the absolute gratuity of grace "from above" do not seem sufficient to extricate him from the problem that ensues from pursuing the tack he has chosen. As it was with de Lubac and "D", so it seems to be with von Balthasar. Briefly, no special gratuity over and above that of creation can be claimed for grace. The ordination to grace seemed part and parcel of the human constitution as such.[33] It may be that the genesis of von Balthasar's position lies in his basic distrust of human intellect and his generally aesthetic and mystical approach to theology, which is not wholly indefensible, and which, in fact, provides a healthy antidote to excessive rationalism. In an age of theological pluralism there is a place for such an approach.

---

[32]"Der Begriff der Natur," 460.

[33]Gutwenger's "Natur und Übernatur: Gedanken zu von Balthasar's Werk über die Bartsche Theologie," cited above in note 12, had attacked von Balthasar's tenuous conception of human nature. In his remarks on von Balthasar's response, "Der Begriff der Natur," 461–462, Gutwenger charges the former with making human nature a *substantia supernaturalis*.

6

Grace as Intersubjective Relationship: The Personalism of Juan Alfaro and Edward Schillebeeckx

The supernatural existential came to know a fairly wide acceptance in Catholic theological circles. There were, however, voices of dissent. We have seen von Balthasar's endorsement of the existential, an endorsement, nonetheless, which carries with it modifications of Rahner's thought, and to that extent entails an element of dissent. In the present chapter our exposition and evaluation bear upon two other theologians who seem to register some unwillingness to accept the existential, Juan Alfaro and Edward Schillebeeckx. Unfortunately, both Alfaro and Schillebeeckx enter oblique disclaimers insofar as their thought on the existential is drawn from essays whose chief interest lie elsewhere. The dissent is more openly and forcefully expressed by Schillebeeckx, and in both cases it may be more apparent than real, as we shall see.

Juan Alfaro was prolific and profound on the theology of grace.[1] The focal point of our considerations here is Alfaro's attempt to reformulate the nature-grace pair as a person-grace duality. In so doing Alfaro indirectly touches upon the supernatural existential, and in a way that would seemingly find its Rahnerian understanding unacceptable.[2]

Alfaro aims to show that it is possible to explain the transcendence and immanence of grace and its inner structure from a per-

---

[1] We have already cited (ch. 2, n. 2 and ch. 3, n. 16) *Lo Natural y lo Sobrenatural*; "La Gratuitad de la vision intuitiva"; "Transcendencia y immanencia de lo sobrenatural." See too his "Natur und Grade," in *Lexikon für Theologie und Kirche*, VII, 830–835 and his "Natura Pura," in the same volume of the *Lexikon*, 809–810.

[2] Cf. "Persona y gracia," *Gregorianum* 41(1950) 5–29.

sonalistic perspective. His starting point is the paradox posed by the fact that the human being is a finite spirit, a recurrent theme in Alfaro's writing. As a finite cognitive being the human person is incapable of pure self-awareness devoid of any objective content. One can consciously possess oneself only in reaching toward something beyond the self. The same holds for the person as an affective being. In free decisions one never comes to possess oneself as something absolute, for freedom must always realize itself within the *a priori* horizon of an absolute value that is neither the self nor its decision. The process of self-determination is an effort to achieve inner completion but this is in vain unless one tends at the same time toward an absolute which is the directing norm of free decision.[3]

Now because the human being is spirit, it is open to the unlimited horizon of being. It is capable of transcending anything finite. Human intellect and will can rest definitively only in the perception of ultimate being and the possession of absolute value. Short of this one must indefinitely expand the frontiers of cognitive and affective life and enjoy a happiness only in movement. Precisely because human being is open to the infinite as its ultimate goal, it is *capax Dei* and the *imago Dei*. Yet, finite as it is, direct union with the infinite forever eludes humanity. Here is the paradox of the human. Its structure is finite; its orientation is to the infinite. Its active powers are limited; its aspirations unlimited. Human being cannot grasp the infinite; yet it cannot help but reach for it. Human life lives out of the dramatic tension of attraction to the infinite and awareness of its absence due to the human inability to make it its own. In the turmoil of this tension is found humanity's openness to grace. The divinization of the person in the beatific vision is the ultimate perfection of all its striving as spirit. In this one sees the immanence of grace, for it is the fulfillment of the deepest human yearning. Nevertheless, because the human person is a *finite* spirit, it stands open to the vision of God only as a *grace*. Desire becomes fulfillment only when God offers the free gift of Godself. And in this one sees the gratuity and transcendence of grace. Only God's love resolves the paradox embedded in the splendor and misery that is humanity.[4]

[3]Ibid., 5.
[4]Ibid., 7.

I. Gratia Supponit Personam:
Grace as Interpersonal Bond

It must be noted, Alfaro tells us, that the definitive perfection of persons is not realized in a subject-object relationship, but only in an I-Thou personal union. Alfaro borrows a page from de Lubac in affirming that persons would not be happy with an absolute they could master and appropriate as they do finite things. Rather, fulfillment lies in immediate union with an infinite Thou, which is realized only as a grace, because of the eminently personal attitude of love that impels God to impart Godself to humanity. All of this necessarily presupposes that human being is itself personal being. Human beings are open to grace because they are persons.[5] Since the human being's final perfection is a person-to-Person union with God, the formula "created person" more aptly expresses humanity's openness to grace than does "finite spirit." *Gratia supponit personam*. This is not to negate but to complement the axiom *gratia supponit naturam*. The preliminary condition for the possibility of grace is, no doubt, the existence of the human being as a rational, finite being who is open to the absolute, to the unlimited horizon of being. This is what is meant by "nature" as expressing the human capacity to be graced. Nevertheless, the human being is not open to the infinite as an impersonal object, but as free, personal being who gives the divine Self in a gratuitous act of love. While grace presupposes nature, it also presupposes the human being is a person, for it presupposes the human being is capable of being addressed in its personal freedom and called by God to engage in a dialogue of love, person to Person. To assert that grace presupposes human being as personal means it presupposes the human is a being capable of giving itself freely to another, a being capable of achieving self-possession in the free choice of self-donation in response to the gratuitous Self-donation of the infinite Person. The category of person is not opposed to that of "rational nature"; it includes and presupposes it.

For God, then, grace is a personal Self-giving. The effect of grace in humanity is an interior summons to immediate personal union with God. Due to grace humanity's dynamic tendency toward being is effectively given a new directedness. Its orientation now is to the infinite being as a Person communicating Godself. The spontaneous, non-deliberate attraction born of grace in the human person is not an attraction to an object, but to a Person; an attraction whereby humanity now tends to God with a certain connaturality. And the term of this tending is now obscurely present to human consciousness, for grace awakens a living experience of a personal I-Thou relationship with the Absolute, an experience of ourselves as children of God.[6]

The inner operation of grace and the experience it begets are elements of concrete, historical human existence. So it is that historical humanity finds itself permanently situated in a graced economy. "One can, in this sense, speak of a supernatural existential in man." But it is most important to add, Alfaro goes on, that the psychological aspect that is characteristic of the supernatural in humanity is eminently personal. It is the call of the Personal Absolute Who, operating within, is inviting humans to a personal I-Thou relation. By reason of this grace a person becomes capable of opting for entry into this Person-to-person union. Having made self-determination possible, grace leads the human person to a unique form of self-possession and is consequently seen to be perfective of human beings as persons, for it brings them to the highest possible expression of personal existence. Grace resolves into a deeper paradox, the paradox that humanity is: a human being is most fully self-possessed when it offers itself totally to the infinite Person. The vital cycle of grace unfolds itself in personalistic fashion: its origin lies in the personal attitude of God Who initiates the whole process, its immediate term is an inclination in humanity toward personal union with God, and its end is humanity's free personal surrender of itself to the God of grace. Alfaro thinks the absolutely supernatural character of such friendship with God is evident, since the elevation of a created person to personal intimacy with the transcendent one can be explained solely by God's free and gratuitous condescension.[7]

In this same line of thought Alfaro insists that the beatific vision, the consummation of God's Self-offering, must not be con-

[6]Ibid, 10, 12.

[7]Alfaro found difficulty with Rahner's effort to articulate a theology of grace in terms of quasi-formal causality (actuatio creata per actum increatum). Cf. Rahner's "Some Implications of the Scholastic Concept of Uncreated Grace," *Theological Investigations*, I, 319–346. For Alfaro, the inadequacy of such a hypothesis lies in its employment of categories equally or even more applicable to non-personal realities and in its failure to weigh sufficiently the personal self-giving entailed in the grace-

ceived as contemplation of an infinite object. To do so is to rob it of its deepest meaning. Rather, it is the effective culmination of God's desire to lead humans to participation in the very personal life process of the three divine Thou's. Human beings are given union with and therefore a personal relation to each of the divine Persons. The vital activity involved, an unchangeable act of loving knowledge, transcends the potentiality and mobility that mark created personality. It is a gratuitous and supernatural sharing in the divine eternity that brings about the inward unification of consciousness that the finite person could never attain by itself.[8] For this reason the grace of vision resolves the paradox that is humanity and lifts the duality that burdens the finite spirit. Longing for the infinite being, which humanity cannot fulfill, is finally sated. The duality of affective striving after one's own personal good and the absolute value yields now to unity. The tension between the basic drive for self-possession through self-awareness and the need always to tend to an extra-subjective term (the radical subject-object clash in the cognitive life of the finite knower) is conquered. When the human spirit achieves immediate union with God, Who is subsistent Self-awareness, it becomes wholly transparent to itself, for when God, Who is "intimior intimo meo," fully reveals Godself to glorified persons, human consciousness becomes fully lucid to itself. Hence Alfaro conceives of the beatific vision as a divinizing fulfillment of the person as person, i.e., as a being that strives for self-possession through self-awareness achieved in self-giving. This latter element must not be overlooked. While the grace-life is primarily God's total personal giving of Self, it necessarily includes and renders possible the human person's total personal self-possession through the giving of itself in return.

At this point Alfaro adds a crucial qualification. To explain the transcendence and immanence of grace the category of "person" is not sufficient. Surely one can theologize the life of grace only in terms of its being a Person-to-person relation. But it is also true that this communion can only be understood as founded upon the free condescension of the uncreated Person to the created

relationship. There is the further difficulty, not alluded to by Alfaro, that in the Aristotelean framework, act (or form) is limited by the potency it determines. For Rahner, this is not so in the case of the *gratia unionis* or of the *gratia inhabitationis*. The hypothesis is hard pressed to explain much if the analogy used is so radically qualified. We shall return to these problems in chapter 8.

[8]"Persona y gracia," 15; see also "Transcendencia y immanencia," 39–50.

person. Between the two there is only an analogy. Thus the union between them is a grace only insofar as it is seen as purely the gift of God to humanity. The transcendence of God, precisely as Person, and the transcendental dependence of the human person relative to the divine Person is presupposed for the possibility of grace. The key elements here are personality and creatureliness. No doubt, it is impossible to understand the created person without appeal to the ontological categories of "finitude" and "creatureliness." On the other hand, the personal structure of the human is not stated if one confines consideration to ontic categories. The hallmark of the human is openness to someone other than itself—an absolute Someone—and the capacity to arrive at self-possession by free decision before this absolute. One must, then, bring both the ontic and psychological elements of human personality to bear upon the theology of grace.[9]

Because grace transcends the created person, there can be no immanent, automatic, and necessary development from humanity's creation to its elevation to divine friendship. That the uncreated Person makes the created person a covenant partner can be due only to the fully gracious divine initiative. Nothing in God necessitates, nothing in humanity demands such intimacy. Humanity in its nature, with its created spirituality non-divinized, would not be absurd. God could create without calling to immediate personal union. The grace of personal union that culminates in vision is possible for humanity only as a sheer gift of the divine liberty. The ultimate in self-awareness and self-possession flowing from the vision of the uncreated Person is a fullness beyond human power. In this perspective, according to Alfaro, it becomes clear than one can theologically explain the absolute gratuity of grace down to its last corollary with the schema "uncreated-created person."

The same is true of the immanence of grace.[10] Human being is open to grace because it is personal being, i.e., finite spirit open to the Infinite not as an object to be seized, but as a free being Who lovingly communicates the divine Self. Grace presupposes the existence of the human being as an intellectual creature who can be called by God to an I-Thou relation. It presupposes human being as personal being and it is grace that perfects humans as persons insofar as it infinitely expands their capacity for self-

[9]Ibid., 20.

[10]Ibid., 17.

awareness and self-possession through full and free self-giving. As participated being, consciousness and being are not identical in the finite person. The created person cannot in virtue of itself achieve pure self-awareness. A human person can come to some possession of itself in giving itself to another finite spiritual being, but is not, on its own, capable of an I-Thou relation with God. This friendly intimacy can only be pure grace.

In summary, Alfaro maintains a human is a person insofar as it is capable of receiving as a pure gift elevation to an I-Thou relationship with God and insofar as it can realize the fullness of personal existence through immediate union with the uncreated Persons of the Trinity. Factually, humanity has effectively been called by God to a personal perfection surpassing human powers, a perfection that transforms humans through direct personal encounter with God and brings them to a self-awareness and self-possession otherwise impossible.

An uncreated Person is subsistent I-Thou relatedness to another consubstantial uncreated Thou. The creature-person on the other hand, can be raised to a relation with the Other, the divine Thou, but the relation is not subsistent. It is a reality only because grace actualizes what was merely possibility. For the human person is not pure self-consciousness, but finite consciousness, sundered by a centripetal drive to self-possession and a centrifugal pull toward a transcendent infinite. The human person is not an actual relation to a divine Thou, but simply (yet splendidly) the capacity for such a relation, a relation to a transcendent Thou, not a consubstantial Thou. Grace thus connotes the crowning consummation of a human as person because it involves the perfecting of the human as being-spirit (*"espiritualidad"*) and as being-to-another (*"alteridad"*) and consequently brings to definitive development self-possession and self-donation. For in the beatific vision the human spirit shares the divine spirit-life and comes to a self-possession far exceeding its creaturehood. The human person shares the divine relatedness to Another, and thereby comes to encounter God in an I-Thou bond that permits its own to-anotherness to transcend its creaturely scope.[11]

Alfaro concludes with a consideration of the relation between person and grace in Christ.[12] Obviously, since Christ is not a created person (as the term is used in classical Christology), the

[11]Ibid., 21–22.
[12]Ibid., 23–29.

relationship between person and grace in him cannot be in every respect paradigmatic for that relationship in the created person. Alfaro's observations on the grace of union and on uncreated and created grace in Christ are brief and conventional, and geared simply to highlighting the fact that the Father's love for the man Jesus extends through him to all humanity. Indeed, the ultimate ground of our adopted filiation is the incarnation. God is our Father because God is Christ's Father. The personal aspect of uncreated grace in us is rooted in the Father's personal gift of Self to the Son. Herein lies the Christological character of all grace: it is a sharing in the created grace of Christ which flows from his uncreated grace.[13] The filiation of Jesus renders intelligible adopted filiation. This is so, Alfaro informs us, not only here and now, but in the very fullness of grace, the beatific vision, which bears a distinctive Christological character. It is in and through the glorified humanity of Jesus that glorified humans come to the intuitive vision of God.[14] God forever gives Godself in the eternal incarnation of the Word. Through union with the glorious Christ, humans come to know immediately the intimate intra-Trinitarian life. In this immediate personal encounter the fullness of one's personhood is realized.

II. *Reflections on Alfaro's Personalism*

What someone says is easily repeated. How someone intends it is not easily detected. Interpreting Alfaro's understanding of the supernatural existential is hazardous because he has so little to say about it directly. In the work under study his effort has not been to explore at length the relationship between nature and grace so much as to present grace as a personalizing force. It is at the risk of some eisegesis, therefore, that we undertake a brief reflection on Alfaro's position.

Alfaro seems to see humanity as always having been situated in a supernatural economy. The possibility of divinization through personal union with God has always been offered. If grace presup-

[13]One of the features of mid-twentieth century Catholic theology was the restoration of the Christic and Trinitarian dimensions of grace. See, e.g., H. Bouillard, "L'Idée de surnaturel et le mystère Chrétien," 153–166 and K. Rahner, "Some Implications of the Scholastic Concept of Uncreated Grace," 319–346.

[14]Cf. J. Alfaro, "Cristo glorioso, revelador del Padre," *Gregorianum* 39(1958) 222–271. See also K. Rahner, "The Eternal Significance of the Humanity of Jesus for our Relationship with God," *Theological Investigations*, III, 35–46.

poses nature, the converse is equally true. For Alfaro God's Self-communication is the ultimate foundation of the world and humanity. In this sense one can speak of a supernatural existential ("en este sentido es lícito hablar de un sobrenatural existencial en el hombre").[15] Alfaro does not clearly speak of an existential in the sense of a grace distinct not only from nature, but distinct also from illuminating actual and sanctifying grace as drawing humanity and enabling it to accept God's offer. In this he perhaps appears to part company with Rahner.

Moreover, what seems primarily to concern Alfaro is the need to give due stress to the personal and psychological dimension of the supernatural in human existence. "Pero es preciso añadir que la coloración psíquica característica del elemento sobrenatural en la existencia humana es eminentemente personal."[16] This in no way negates the ontic aspects of grace. It appears that for Alfaro the supernatural existential is not to be viewed so much in terms of an ontological modification of nature but rather in terms of its being the personal call of the Absolute Who is summoning humanity from within to personal union with God's own Self. The divine decree that constitutes the present economy as a graced one effects more than a juridical situation. God's word does not return empty to God. God's *dābhar* always has its real term. And in this case, it is the actual and/or habitual grace transforming humanity's dynamic tendency toward being and endowing it with a new, spontaneous, and indeliberate orientation to infinite personal being.

Alfaro's point seems to be that the only supernatural existential we can speak of is an historical relationship of all persons to God through the grace of Christ. In Rahner's perspective the existential sometimes is presented as implying an ontological disposition prior to any so-called actual and/or habitual grace and inseparable from the quiddity of historical humanity, though not inseparable from humanity as such. Obviously, for both theologians historical humanity is different from humanity as such. Rahner establishes the difference in a historical situation that is concretized in an ontological modification; Alfaro, in a historical condition that is verified in a personal and psychological element. Rahner could hardly fault this. Despite the apparent difference of opinion neither Rahner nor Alfaro sees historical

---

[15]"Persona y gracia," 10.
[16]Ibid.

humanity to be humanity-as-such without any further determination. The seeming divergence between Alfaro and Rahner seems to reduce to a variation in focus, the former focusing on the divine summons, the latter, especially in his early works, on the effect in humanity of the summons.

As for the gratuity of grace we have seen that to Alfaro's mind, that too must be viewed in terms of grace as a personalizing reality. Like de Lubac and Rahner, Alfaro has rendered pure nature marginal; the transcendence of grace is referred primarily to the present, historical world order. Though it could have been otherwise, according to Alfaro, what-is rather than what-might-have-been is the focal point. Still, what is of interest in Alfaro's exposition is his attempt to see the gratuity of grace not so much in terms of the exigencies and powers of human nature, but rather in terms of the process of personalization. For Alfaro nature-grace is less apt than person-Person or person-Grace to explicate the mystery of the divine/human relationship. Grace divinizes.[17] It opens the way to the possibility of a human participating in the divine spirit-life. It does this by binding persons in personal union to each of the three divine Thou's. Hence it invites the human person to a fullness of personal existence that infinitely transcends whatever level of personalization one could aspire to and attain if left to oneself.

Finally, Alfaro leaves us with questions for which he provides no elaborated answers. In light of the above, how does he see the infant related to the supernatural economy? And what of the adult who spurns the divine offer of personal communion? In the absence of the interpersonal relationship due to uncreated grace, sanctifying grace, and, perhaps, the grace that is Rahner's existential how are they related to the supernatural order? Is the relation in these cases analogously constituted by sin, by the privation of a due perfection? This certainly seems not to be the only alternative. Nor would Alfaro simply say they fall beyond the pale of God's salvific will and the world order that enacts it. In the following section of our investigation we shall encounter in Edward Schillebeeckx a position very similar to that taken by Alfaro, but the lines will be more clearly drawn.

---

[17]On the various interpretations given to the traditional axiom "gratia supponit naturam," cf. B. Stoeckle, *Gratia Supponit Naturam: Geschichte und Analyse eines theologischen Axioms* (Rome: Gregorian, 1962).

III. *A Retrieval from Aquinas:*
Max Seckler and the Instinct of Faith

In 1961 Max Seckler presented still another approach to the modern problematic of nature and grace in terms of the Thomistic *instinctus fidei*.[18] In an incisive critical review of Seckler's work, E. Schillebeeckx openly rejected the supernatural existential of Rahner and von Balthasar. Underlying Seckler's work, as Schillebeeckx perceived it, is the problematic tackled by Rahner and von Balthasar.[19] For Seckler's genetic analysis of the *instinctus fidei* and the non-conceptual aspect of the act of faith according to St. Thomas is really asking, this time in the context of the theology of faith: Is there place for a "medium" between nature and grace? Seckler understands Rahner and von Balthasar to propose the supernatural existential precisely as a mediating reality in order to put to rest the difficulties surrounding the immanence of grace and human response to it. To properly understand and appreciate Schillebeeckx's reservations about Rahner's existential at that time, it is necessary that we begin with a broad outline of Max Seckler's interesting analysis of the structure of faith according to Aquinas.

A. *Thomas Aquinas' Conception of Faith According to Seckler*

In the first part of his work Seckler sketches the history of the word "instinct" through its Greek, Roman, patristic, and Scholastic usages. Against this background its employment by Aquinas is analyzed.[20] Aquinas used the word in a wide variety of ways. Where humans are concerned he sometimes used it to refer to a dynamism of human nature (e.g., the instinct of the will) or to an effect of grace (e.g., the instinct in the gifts of the Spirit). Sometimes for Thomas *instinctus* has a psychological significance, sometimes an ontological significance. But the wide range of application is undergirded by a clear unity of meaning: *instinctus*

---

[18] M. Seckler, *Instinkt und Glaubenswille nach Thomas von Aquin* (Mainz: Matthias-Grunewald, 1961).

[19] E. Schillebeeckx, "Het niet-begrippelijke moment in de geloofsdaad volgens Thomas von Aquino," *Tijdschrift voor Theologie* 3(1963) 167–195. We are dependent throughout on the authorized French translation, "L'Instinct de la foi selon S. Thomas d' Aquin," *Revue des Sciences Philosophiques et Théologiques* 48(1964) 377–408. An English translation is available in *Revelation and Theology,* II (New York: Sheed & Ward, 1968), 30–75.

[20] *Instinkt*, 19–68.

is an active impulse apt to effect activity in a given sector of existence. This introductory semantic study leads into the second part of Seckler's investigation, where, in three sections, he analyzes the "instinct of faith", the grace inviting one to believe.[21] Seckler's area of concentration now becomes the *initium fidei*. How is the return to God, from Whom we came forth, effected? On this point Seckler detects a change of emphasis between Thomas' earlier and later writings. The young Thomas held that while ultimately it is God who moves us to believe, still the will to believe does not come about from a divine instinct, but through the mediation of one's appreciation of a value.

In other words, what initially moves one to believe is not the personal intervention of God, but the prospect of a value desired by the will in taking cognizance of the gospel message. There is no question here of interiorly experiencing a value due to the interior influence of grace when the Good News is heard. The message speaks to one, it calls, but emerges as a motive of belief only by way of appearing rationally justifiable. One can give the assent of faith only after argumentative thought. The value perceived must be verified if it is to become a motive of belief. Scope is thus afforded the voluntary character of faith. Once the gospel is heard it is up to one's free initiative to respond by belief or non-belief. According to Seckler, therefore, in Aquinas' early works there is no question of "actual grace" entering the process inaugurating the act of faith. The general dynamism of human life suffices for personal acceptance of the gospel message as a true human value or for its rejection as a non-value.[22]

At a later date (mid-point in the period during which he was writing the *Contra Gentiles*) three things appear which are not detected in Thomas' earlier work: (1) a stress on the divine initiative; (2) an *auxilium divinum* influencing the human will; (3) a more dynamic view of justification whereby the *motio divina* is now central rather than the *habitus fidei*. The transition is, according to Seckler, abrupt. Now there are numerous references to the Pelagians. And the notion of the instinctus is linked to the act of faith, a notion that played a part in the Church's documents condemning Semi-Pelagianism. In Thomas it plays the same role. Yet there is a difference. In Thomas the instinctus is fitted

---

[21]Ibid., 69–258.

[22]Only later, during his first period in Italy (1259–1260), did Aquinas come to know of the second council of Orange's stricture against "Semi-Pelagianism."

out with an ontological structure and an anthropological form it had not known before.[23] Hearing the gospel and appreciating the value it is pregnant with is seen by Thomas to be borne up by a "divine instinct that prompts us and moves us to believe." Moreover, the attraction (*tractio*) considered by Augustine on a psychological level, is now given by Aquinas an ontological significance. God draws a person by way of a recognized value. But it is not only the gospel as preached that radiates attraction, but an *instinctus interior* as well. God personally effects in one a sensitivity and an openness to the value perceived in the message heralded. This *instinctus interior* is for Aquinas an ontological and formal principle.[24]

Thomas now refutes any Semi-Pelagian tendency by appealing to the instinctus which he understands as a moving principle and as a divine instinct bringing happiness and making persons appreciative of a value. "Whoever believes has a sufficient motive to believe . . . is prompted to believe . . . especially by an inner instinct from God drawing him."[25] Seckler, however, remembering what Thomas taught in his earlier works, does not see in Thomas at this point a double motive for faith: the appreciation of value and the divine motion. The *instinctus fidei*, which is the starting point for the act of faith, is a dynamism of the human spirit itself.[26] But it is activated by the God of salvation. It is an instinct begetting an appreciation of the value in the gospel, an instinct bringing happiness,[27] because through it an objective guarantee is given the subjective experience of the person now inclined by God to what is objectively good as a value for oneself; it is a moving principle, because it is a divine power enabling the assent of faith as a fully human surrender.

But the instinctus itself as a moving principle is not, claims Seckler, an actual grace; rather, it is identified with human nature's inherent tendency to the absolute. Before one awakens to

---

[23]This broadened view of the instinctus derives from Thomas' increasing knowledge of the bible, Augustine, Aristoteleanism, Roman philosophy of law, and stoic ethics.

[24]Cf., e.g., *Super Evangelium Joannis*, ch. 6, lect 5.

[25]*ST*, II-II, 2,9, ad 3.

[26]*Instinkt*, 110–111. The instinct of faith is also an instinct of the Holy Spirit. See *Super Evangelium Joannis*, ch. 14, lect 6; *ST*, III, 36, 5; *In IV Sent.*, d. 13, q.1, a.2, sol. 1.

[27]Through encounter with Aristotle's *Liber de Bona Fortuna* (1259–1260), Thomas saw the divine instinct as bringing happiness, as a moving principle, as making one appreciate a value. *In X Ethics*, lect 14. See Seckler, *Instinkt*, 110–111.

this or that value one is already impelled by God toward the good. This élan, given to human nature in the act of creation, is, together with the proclamation of the gospel, sufficient to permit one freely to believe or not. The instinctus must be seen as an effect of God's on-going creative activity and as a constitutive element in human nature. Humanity is endowed with a primordial instinct, a "sympathy" for all that has value for it.[28]

Seckler proceeds next to an anthropological analysis of the *instinctus fidei*.[29] Through the intellect the primordial "sympathy" of instinct becomes conscious. Yet as a tendency or *forma* it is present prior to all actual willing and doing. Now the indispensable condition of all human action is the emergence of an object as a value. Every human act is thus grounded in an instinct of love, in the subject's being seized by values. Only what responds to a natural tendency is perceived as a value. Knowledge is embedded in this affective tendency. And through the representation of a value a person's natural tendential dynamism is rendered a conscious groping after value.[30]

Just as all human knowledge, originating from within and without, is marked by a universal intentional scope which is particularized through a multiplicity of contacts with the world, so too the interior instinct is a kind of "pre-evangelical climate" open to and addressed by the revelation of the gospel. By essence this interiority is intentionally geared to what comes from without. Put in contact with the evangelical message as a *bonum promissum* the *instinctus naturae* becomes an *instinctus fidei*. But the two are not identical. The latter involves two elements: the inner element of grace and the outer communication of the revealing Word.[31] For Seckler the inner grace of faith is a "formal openness to a determined sphere of reality." Like every *forma* this openness has its own proper tendency. But it must be explicated and, so to speak, objectively defined by what comes from the message heard.[32] The initially relatively undefined character of the grace of faith requires the *determinatio fidei*, which is had through

---

[28]This "sympathy" is not, according to Seckler, a datum of experience. It has no psychological value. Its significance is purely ontological, being "given with man's essential form" ("sie ist mit der Wesenform des Menschen gegeben"). *Instinkt*, 128–135.

[29]Ibid., 136–140.

[30]Ibid., 140–145.

[31]*ST*, II–II, 106, 1, ad 1 and ad 2.

[32]*Instinkt*, 153.

the explicit content of the gospel as proclaimed. External revelation "informs" the psychologically blind, groping instinct flowing from the "inclined heart." Inwardly illuminated in this way, "objective faith" is born in a free decision. "Believing is the informing of a tendency."[33] The saving power of the gospel is accepted as truth, but also as value; for believing is a judgment of assent enveloped in the appreciation of value ("*wertgeleitete Urteilsfallung*").[34] The rise of faith is situated in the heart (in affectione).[35]

The problem now arises: How relate the two Thomist assertions that we believe (1) on the authority of God revealing and (2) by the appreciation of a value? Seckler tells us the object of faith is saving truth, a life-value. Hence the value of what is testified to must play a part in our believing. On the other hand, the worth of what is testified to depends on the value of the witness. Moreover, in God the testifier and the testified are identical. Due to the *instinctus fidei* we recognize the outer message as a life-value, as the answer to the deepest tendency of our spirit, a tendency tracing back to God.[36] By the dynamism of the instinctus the will is brought within the sphere of influence of the value presented in the message preached. In its turn the will draws the intellect, till now toiling along the slow and stubborn path of argument and verification. On this basis one ultimately comes to risk believing or to refuse to do so. There is no question in this process of an affective intuition of faith's content. That is known only by hearing, though it is perceived as a value only because it corresponds to a tendency in the human spirit.

What, however, guarantees the objectivity of what is heard? The instinctus has no representational aspect. But the "light of faith", which, according to Seckler, is identical with the "habit of faith", is a principle of knowing in faith and makes something seen.[37] Yet according to some texts in Thomas, says Seckler, nothing is actually seen in this light.[38] What the *lumen* does is to make the truth of revelation an authentic knowledge of faith by showing this datum to be truly a value to whoever is confronted by

[33]Ibid., 155.

[34]Ibid.

[35]*De Veritate*, q. 14, a.2, ad 10.

[36]*Instinkt*, 156.

[37]Ibid., 158. See *ST*, II–II, 1, 4, ad 3; *In III Sent.*, d. 23, q.2, a.1, ad 4.

[38]See e.g., *In Boethium de Trinitate*, I, q.3, a.1, ad 4.

the message. In so doing it brings about the free act of faith.[39]
For Thomas the *lumen* guarantees not certainty grounded in evidence (*certitudo evidentiae*), but firmness in adhering (*firmitas adhaesionis*) to a non-evident truth. Thus a greater importance is attached to "tendency" than to "light." The *lumen* or *habitus fidei* provides a positive openness to revealed truth. Although as a *natural* tendency the inclination of this habit is in itself infallible, its explicitation and determination by what is presented from without is fallible. But most important of all, faith terminates in the saving reality of God's own Self, not in propositions (*enuntiabilia*) or judgments.[40] The light of faith is infallible insofar as by it the believer is orientated to the saving God. This is not so when the believer turns theologian and begins thematically to explicitate the encounter with God. Faith can survive amidst material errors concerning its articulation.

B. *The Instinct of Faith in the Dialectic of Nature and Grace*

With this background we come now to what is more immediately pertinent to us, Seckler's insertion of the *instinctus fidei* into the nature-grace dialectic. Seckler refuses to see the natural and the supernatural laid side by side like two blocks, or divided into two levels, one built upon the other. Grace is not a superstructure. Rather, historical human nature is so constituted that the beatific vision is "natural" to it, though it transcends human powers of attainment, and is, to that extent, "supernatural."[41] Seckler now asks: Is there room for a medium between nature and grace? Is the *instinctus fidei* nature or grace? The proximate background to this problem is, of course , de Lubac's *Le Surnaturel*, the difficulties of which Rahner and von Balthasar tried to overcome by affirming the supernatural existential, which is neither human nature as such nor sanctifying grace.

Seckler's own view comes to this. When God's universal, continuing creative activity touches humanity, which, by its very nature as spirit is open to grace, it is "converted" into a special

---

[39]Seckler attaches, it seems, little importance to the lumen fidei. He is riveted to the *instinctus fidei*. The latter is a tendency, the former an illumination. Schillebeeckx asks the probing question: What is the meaning of a light that produces a tendency?

[40]*ST*, II–II, 1, 2, ad 2.

[41]"Quamvis homo naturaliter inclinetur in finem ultimum, non tamen potest naturaliter illum consequi, sed solum per gratiam." *In Boethium de Trinitate* I, q.2, a.4, ad 5.

creative activity (*motio specialis*) identical with the instinct of faith. The divine action moving one towards natural and supernatural values is in itself always the same. It is neither "natural" nor "supernatural", because in itself it is "hardly qualitatively definable."[42] It is defined by the inherent form (*forma inhaerens*) in which it acts, in this case, human nature. The ordination to grace that is constitutive of humanity as a spiritual being explains the fact that the divine creative activity (*motio divina*) becomes in the human an "instinct impelling and moving him to believe."[43] God's continuing creative activity, without which creaturely action is inconceivable, is thereby, in the spiritual being, an offer of grace (*gratia oblata*). Because of humanity's structure it can realize in its being a variety of participations in the one ongoing creative action of God. Hence the *motio divina* is variously termed a "natural instinct" (*appetitus naturae*), an "instinct drawing us to believe", or an "instinct of grace." That is why human nature, in the core of its spirituality, is from the outset a promise of grace. Concrete humanity is in itself "a call to grace", an instinct impelling us to faith. In a word, the *instinctus naturae* is concretely a *gratia operans et praeveniens*. In Seckler's opinion this explains why Thomas did not in his Semi-Pelagian polemic incorporate a new supernatural instinct into human nature, but simply analyzed more profoundly the dynamism of concrete, historical human nature. Clearly the *instinctus fidei* is not the state of grace; it is an invitation to justification. It is a divine help that moves human nature by stimulating it, but concretely this refers to nothing but "the transcendental movement of the creature towards the good, thanks to God." Hence it is not actual or sanctifying grace, but the "divine movement which established in human beings the inner dimension of return."[44]

God's continuing creative activity does not act upon a creature already constituted in a definitive state of existence. Rather, the entire evolutive manner of being of the creature is that of a being which God is in the process of creating. Further, the tendency toward the absolute is itself the divine call that draws one to believe and to surrender oneself to the Being Who can satisfy and fill one's natural openness. It is here that Seckler situates the "re-

---

[42]*Instinkt*, 192.

[43]Ibid., 191.

[44]". . . jene Beiwegung Gottes, die dem Menschen die innere Dimension der Rükkehr erstelt." Ibid., 178.

mote preparation for grace'' in Aquinas' later works.[45] In the instinct of nature is located the ontological law for the transcendence of nature itself. Precisely because of the inner orientation of nature toward the supernatural, there is no need for a new divine impulse to believe over and above the instinct of nature.[46]

The very essence of humanity, therefore, is, in theological perspective, a divine invitation to believe, which, upon the hearing of the gospel, is freely accepted or sinfully rejected. Apart from all *gratia media* as a middle term linking the natural and the supernatural, human nature is by its spirituality orientated towards the supernatural. This is clearly manifested in the natural desire. Aquinas did not look for the distinction between the natural and the supernatural, which safeguards the gratuity of grace, in a differentiation between abstract human nature and concrete, historical human nature (the course followed by Rahner and von Balthasar), but "through an ontology of primary and secondary causality relative to the creaturely spirit as an aptitude for transcendence.''[47] One could say as much even if humanity were not destined to divine life, following as it does from a transcendental analysis of the human spirit. But Seckler goes a step further. The human spirit undergoes no modification because of its *de facto* supernatural destiny. Concrete humanity's interior and primordial instinct becomes the vehicle of its divine destiny. Formally there is a distinction between humanity which can be called and humanity which is called ("Zwischen *berufbarem* und *berufenem* Menschen''), but not materially. The nature-grace antithesis is thus the creation-covenant correlation.[48]

In our concrete experience, consequently, it is impossible to determine what in the *instinctus interior* is natural and what supernatural. From its first moment human existence is called to grace. Correlative to the actual vocation in the present order there must exist on the human side some corresponding reality, something more in comparison with the natural capacity for grace and that is the factual reality of being called. Further, this reality must be a positive element in humanity's essential constitution and it *must*

[45]Ibid., 193-195.

[46]"Habere fidem non est in natura humana; sed in natura humana est ut mens hominis non repugnet interiori instinctui et exteriori veritatis praedicationi." *ST*, II-II, 10, 1, ad 1.

[47]". . . durch eine Ontologie der Erst und Zweitursächlichkeit mit Rücksicht auf das geschöpfliche Geistsein als Anlage für Transzendenz." *Instinkt*, 207.

[48]Ibid., 212.

be of grace without actually being grace.[49] Rahner and Von Balthasar posit the existential as being this reality. But Seckler finds it difficult to define this existential. Its function is to point up the obligating quality of this destiny while bringing out the fact that this concrete finality cannot be constitutive of humanity-as-such, but at most of concrete humanity. Thomas, however, looked elsewhere for a solution. To his way of thinking historical humanity is not at all structurally different from humanity possibly not called to grace. This vocation remains extrinsic. It is God's will that calls. And it is precisely through the external, saving will of God that the "good of nature" (*bonum naturae*) is endowed with a new meaning. It is now a negative disposition for the reception of grace. In this way humanity's supernatural vocation is interiorized without human nature being subjected to any modification.

In other words, the divine vocation is communicated not only exteriorly via revelation, but also inwardly. This interior vocation prepares the ontological reality (*instinctus naturae*) which disposes one to hear the gospel truth. It is not nature *qua* nature that serves as vehicle of the call to grace, but the ontological instinctus. The instinct is a gratuitous gift, yet it belongs to nature.[50] The real ontological finality of the instinct remains hidden until it is explicated by revelation. As sustained by God the Creator Who calls, this primordial dynamism of human nature is itself an offer of grace. The one divine movement, therefore, leading all creatures according to their proper nature home to their point of origin is, in the case of the human spirit, called "grace." Because historical humanity is sinful, what factually is proposed to the instinct is the offer of the grace of justification (*"die Recht- fertigungsgnade im Angebot"*).[51] This ontological instinct, which due to God's summons is concretely an *instinctus fidei*, is operative in a variety of psychological phenomena. One constantly and inescapably finds oneself confronted by the offer of grace. This is verified even in someone who has not yet encountered the mystery of Christ. The psychological phenomena rooted in the primordial instinct are basically of two kinds: (1) wonder, restlessness, anxiety, dissatisfaction with being captive to the finite, the ex-

[49]"Sie muss ein positives Wesenkonstitutiv des Menschen sein, gnadenhaft, ohne schon die Gnade zu sein." Ibid., 213–214.

[50]Ibid., 214–215.

[51]Ibid., 217–218.

perience of human weakness and insufficiency; (2) the experience of a transcendental orientation resulting from a real or supposed existential discovery of the absolute. These and similar experiences are repeated effects of human nature's primordial instinct, or concretely, effects of a divine instinct moving and impelling one to believe. There can be no question of a "special organ" in humanity providing it with a special "religious sensitivity." This instinct takes hold of the total person and reveals the sacral character of its being.

Seckler concludes by noting that God did not create in humans a will to believe and be saved. Rather the term of creation is a person whose disposition toward salvation is grounded in human nature itself. It is useless to ask whether the grace of faith affects the intellect or the will. It does not enter from without into a psychology already functioning. It is given in the very root of human being where all such distinctions are meaningless.[52] For Seckler "the instinct of nature is the promulgated will of God" calling humans to grace, the relationship of the human subject to itself as due-to-be and due-to-be-such.[53] Faith then is the completion of a tendency which exists prior to the hearing of the message, but which comes to be fully itself only on hearing the gospel. In virtue of this instinct the free being that a human being is is a condition of being called; one is, in one's own being, an offer of grace which one must freely substantiate for oneself. Humanity's primordial instinct is, according to Seckler, what Thomas considers the effective and sufficient interior cause of faith and salvation.[54] The will to believe is *not* a decision brought about by an actual grace enabling one to assent to a number of propositions. It is the ethical translation, concretized in the free acceptance of a message, of an ontological law. The *instinctus fidei* is not the privileged possession of only those who actually believe; it is the vehicle of the divine mercy, which addresses all alike.

[52]"Gott schafft nicht am Menschen den Willen zu Glaube und Heil, sondern er schuf einen Menschen, dem die Gewilltheit zum Weg des Heils in die Wiege seiner Natur gelegt ist. Deshalb ist es eine müssige Sache, zu fragen, ob die Glaubensgnade im Verstand oder in Willen ansetzes. Sie tritt nicht von aussen in eine bereits funktionierende psychologie ein, sondern sie wird in jener Wurzel des menschlichen Seins gegeben, in der Unterscheidungen sinnlos werden." Ibid., 261.

[53]"Der Instinkt der Natur ist Promulgieter Wille Gottes . . . die Relation des Subjecktes zu sich selbst als Sein-Sollendem und So-Sein-Sollendem." Ibid, 264.

[54]"Dieser Instinkt ist nach Thomas die wirksame und ausreichende innere Ursache für Glaube und Heil." Ibid., 261.

IV. *The Real Situation of Humanity: Schillebeeckx's Critique of Seckler*

Schillebeeckx conceded that Seckler's genetic elucidation of the *instinctus* in the writing of Thomas, an elucidation achieved by employing the methodology of form criticism, is unimpeachable and a distinctly new approach, one unknown to Thomist circles heretofore. What is also novel, according to Schillebeeckx, is Seckler's integration of the *instinctus fidei* into Aquinas' global view of the relationship between nature and supernature. Seckler hoped to make certain elements that had been implicit in Thomas stand forth more boldly. It is precisely this explicitation of what is implicit in Aquinas that raised a number of questions for Schillebeeckx.[55]

A. *The Novelty of Seckler's Analysis*

That a modern problematic (launched by Maréchal, de Finance, de Lubac, and Heidegger, etc.), one that Thomas never explicitly grappled with in his own time, is now set squarely before the Thomistic texts which must answer for their author, is not a wholly illegitimate procedure. Obviously there is always the hazard of eisegesis. Nonetheless, to theologize is to theologize with others. Our concern is not simply with what Thomas taught. Our concern is with a unique reality that occupied Thomas and some centuries later confronts us too. True historical study is not simply an effort to produce a xerox copy of the thought of a theologian long dead. It is also an effort to think through with the theologian the questions he or she provoked. One cannot, therefore, deny Seckler his right, after analyzing Thomas' explicit affirmations, to explicitate what he perceives as implicit in the tests of Thomas.

But does Seckler succeed in putting his finger on what is implicit in Thomas? Despite a fine historical investigation, Seckler ultimately failed, according to Schillebeeckx, to appreciate Thomas as *Doctor Gratiae*. Situating the failure is a delicate task. Seckler recognizes the *instinctus naturae* and the *instinctus fidei* as materially identical though formally distinct. For he admits a formal distinction between one's openness to being addressed by God (*capacitas gratiae*) and one's effective destination or actual vocation to the life of grace. The natural *ordo ad gratiam* is not

---

[55]"L'Instinct," 395. H. Lavalette was of the opinion that Schillebeeckx did not properly understand Seckler. Cf. "Bulletin de Théologie Dogmatique," *Récherches de Science Religieuse* 54 (1966) 143-155.

as such an *ordinatio ad gratiam*.[56] Here Seckler is on safe ground. On the other hand, the formal distinction notwithstanding, Seckler maintains this *ordo* is in fact an *ordinatio*, a real destination, purely by reason of God's salvific will and without any intrinsic change in humanity. Humanity's positive but passive openness to grace belongs to the essence of the human as such. But in and of itself this is not yet a call to the supernatural. Seckler admits this. The actual call is concretely contained in God's creative act. That is why Seckler concludes that concretely the *ordo naturae ad gratiam*, the *instinctus naturae*, is an *instinctus fidei*. Materially nothing is changed, though the human spirit's natural openness to the absolute is by the act of creation not only an openness to grace, which is essential to humanity, but even more, a concrete gift of grace already prompting us to believe. Thus "nature" is concretely a gift of grace, not because of its being created, but because of its being created by the God *of salvation*.

What appeals to Schillebeeckx in this solution is Seckler's refusal to locate humanity's condition of being called to grace in an intermediary that bridges nature and grace as Rahner and von Balthasar do in their efforts to extricate de Lubac's *surnaturel* from the difficulties in which it was mired. Schillebeeckx feels a linking reality of this sort is unintelligible and of no real value. It simply transfers the problem to another locale; to the relationship between nature and this intermediary, which is not natural and still is not sanctifying grace. But with this modicum of agreement Schillebeeckx and Seckler go their separate ways. Schillebeeckx cannot follow Seckler all the way in the latter's exegesis of Thomas, nor *secundum rei veritatem*.[57] Schillebeeckx is of the opinion that Seckler and the proponents of the supernatural existential are wide of the mark due to an illusory perspective; i.e., that the sinner remains called and continues to live in the supernatural order. Therein lies the reason why Rahner and von Balthasar postulate in nature, as term of God's saving call, a reality that is equally present in saint and sinner, viz., the existential as a medium between nature and grace. Seckler, sharing the same false perspective, lets human nature simply be nature and considers nature concretely to be the term of God's saving destination.

Nevertheless Seckler has seen something important. It is true that in the Thomistic framework the *instinctus naturae* does reach

[56]"L'Instinct," 396.
[57]Ibid., 397–398.

out for the absolute good and therefore for the beatific vision, though it cannot realize this under its own power. Moreover, humanity's actual orientation to God in Godself does not occur mechanically, but in a free act.[58] Further, only through the mediation of a concrete representation of God as a value is the *instinctus naturae*, according to Thomas, orientated to God. Does this, asks Schillebeeckx, mean that wedding the *instinctus* to a representation of the gospel as a value suffices to endow the *instinctus naturae* with the significance of the *instinctus fidei*? An affirmative reply cannot be found in the implicit thought of Aquinas. He was too strongly convinced, says Schillebeeckx, that no matter how open to grace humanity is, of itself it cannot take a single step in the direction of being graced. The human spirit may in itself be an appeal for and openness to grace, but in Thomas' view, this does not make it a real offer of grace, as Seckler would have it. All it means is that should grace be offered, it will not be as a foreign body (*Fremdkorper*) forcibly injected into human life, but something very meaningful for us. Indeed only the gift of grace affords life its fully *personal* meaning. For Thomas there may be glimmers of the supernatural in the basic human condition; but they are on a distantly visible horizon.

According to Schillebeeckx, Aquinas did not even ask explicitly whether the natural desire for God in historical nature is an effect of the covenant God's saving will. This is a modern question, especially since the time of Baius. If we do pose this question to Thomas, he will tell us concrete human nature was created only for the personal union that is beatific vision. This does not mean, claims Schillebeeckx, that the *instinctus naturae* is therefore a concrete offer of grace. Humanity's radical powerlessness in the sphere of grace imposes an insurmountable barrier. Human being as spirit is of itself neither an offer nor a promise of grace. It is simply a possibility of being graced. Thomas then would make a clear-cut distinction between a desire for God based on the *instinctus naturae* and the offer of grace properly speaking, which enables us in a wholly new way to make our first step toward God.[59]

Schillebeeckx makes an incisive criticism of Seckler when he notes that while the act of creation and the act of vocation are

[58]De Veritate, q.28, a.4, ad 2. "Illud ad quod homo trahitur, aliquo modo ad liberum arbitrium pertinet."

[59]The *instinctus naturae*, through reflection on our conscious being-in-the-world, is explicitated as an orientation to God. Schillebeeckx thinks the distinction he is under-

one decree in God, this does not bring us any closer to solving the problem as to *how* the divine action or movement is accomplished in humans. But it cannot follow that the *instinctus naturae* is concretely an *instinctus fidei.* Schillebeeckx affirms a distinction between a human's natural finalization (as person or spirit) toward personal communion with God and its real destination. Finalization is fundamentally contained in the divine act creative of a spiritual being; destination is a salvific act, and therefore an offer of grace. Do not, asks Schillebeeckx, Seckler's "naturalizing" tendencies on the one hand, and Rahner's and von Balthasar's recourse to an existential distinct from nature and grace on the other hand, lose sight of one simple fact? And that is that in human persons the term of their real destination to the supernatural is sanctifying grace itself. The term is the person's *really being situated in a supernatural order* whether this be by way of acceptance (i.e., through sanctifying grace and real intersubjective union with God) or by way of rejection (i.e., through the real condition of sinfulness).

Why then look for another reality, a bridging element like the supernatural existential? Or why appeal to a rash solution that would identify the offer of grace with human nature, which is only an inefficacious appeal for grace? As a reality in the human being destination to grace can only be the effect of God's saving will, viz., admission to friendship with God, or for one not in the state of grace, one's real condition as sinner. In God there is no distinction between a project and its execution. God's summons is effective and constitutive of an alliance between Godself and humanity. A reality in humankind that would be neither nature nor grace, nor historical nature, but the term of God's covenant decree and prologue, at least with logical priority, to grace, is unacceptable to Schillebeeckx. The thesis that humanity's factually being called to grace is, as a reality in humanity, "of grace without actually being grace" is the fundamental flaw in Seckler's exposition, the same flaw in the position of Rahner and von Balthasar.[60]

Human openness to God does not suddenly become in virtue of an extrinsic divine decree a concrete offer of grace. God's sav-

scoring is clearly drawn by Thomas. Cf. *In Epistolam II ad Cor.*, ch. 5, lect 2 where Thomas distinguishes between God as *auctor desiderii naturalis* and as *auctor desiderii supernaturalis.* The latter is not grounded in the instinct of nature, but only in the granting of the Holy Spirit.

[60]"L'Instinct," 399–400.

ing will is God offering Godself. Through this offer a person is made capable of accepting the offer and of striking covenant. In the person the real offer of sanctifying grace is not only formally, but materially as well, something completely different from spiritual openness to the absolute, even though this "completely different" is geared to that openness. Outside of revelation, admits Schillebeeckx, one has no conscious awareness in experience, thematically or reflexively, of a difference between what concretely derives from one's transcendental openness of spirit (*instinctus naturae*) and what from God's grace-filled invitation (*instinctus fidei*). To identify the two and salvage something of a distinction simply by noting the Creator is a covenant God seems to Schillebeeckx a serious failure to grasp the transcendence of grace.

B. *Seckler's Appeal to God's Continuing Creation*

Seckler claimed that the *instinctus naturae* becomes concretely an *instinctus fidei* due to God's continuous act of creation. In this he might enlist the authority of Aquinas who did equate the *exitus* of created beings with the natural order and their *reditus* with the order of grace.[61] And God's activity leading creatures back to Godself is none other than God's ongoing creative action. Seckler insists this continuing creative activity whereby God leads creatures to their ultimate destiny (*conversio*) makes of the *instinctus naturae* an *instinctus fidei*. But, observes Schillebeeckx, Seckler forgets that Thomas did not confront the modern problematic that arises here since in his time the gratuity of grace was not in question. Seckler sees continuing creation itself as the grace of *conversio* and *reditus*. Created spirit is, according to Seckler, a tendency toward self-transcendence; God's continuing creation grounds this self-transcendence. This is incomprehensible to Schillebeeckx who can only see that through God's continual creation what one becomes aware of is precisely one's incapability of self-transcendence by one's own efforts. Actual self-transcendence cannot be explained by the *instinctus naturae*.[62]

True, God's saving will, the work of sanctification, is a divine act and always a *creatio ex nihilo*. The conferment of grace is creative and an aspect of continuing creation. God does draw humanity to intimate friendship and since this movement is creative, God

[61]In I Sent., d. 14, q. 2, a. 2; d. 15, q. 4, a. 1.

[62]"L'Instinct," 400–401.

remains in this Creator, and humanity in its acceptance remains creature, all of which puts a distance between the two. But sanctification is more than creation. And the sanctified human is more than merely a human. He or she is a child of God. "The fullness of human life is superhuman; it is a divine life in a human subject." If we wish, Schillebeeckx continues, to stress the immanence of grace as the fulfillment of human existence, then all the more should we emphasize that this fulfillment is an achievement transcending our human condition. The essence of Christianity is self-transcendence through grace. In this self-transcendence we find the best of our own selves as an additional gift. Existentially bound in unity, nature and grace are nonetheless distinct.

In creation God establishes the creature as a value in itself and unto itself. In sanctification God makes the gift of Godself to human creatures. Sanctification is a creative act whereby a human is drawn into interpersonal relationship with God. The initiative in this process, even its first stages, can never be materially identical with the dynamism of the human spirit. Rather the human being, who is transcendental openness, is personally taken hold of by God Who reveals Godself inwardly and outwardly. This God achieves through a creative action that permits us to experience in ourselves, however confusedly, the divine invitation in the message preached to us. Schillebeeckx, therefore, cannot endorse Seckler's view that God's unique continuing creative activity is determined by the spiritual being of the human and formed into a saving activity, the gratuitous character of which is absorbed into the gratuity of freedom that characterizes God's creative action.[63]

While God's invitation to grace is distinct from the dynamism of our spirit, it is neither an extrinsic reality nor a physical impulse. Rather we are addressed by Someone who is the ground of our being, "intimior intimo meo." Yet the experience of God as God is the exclusive definition of the beatific vision. Hence any immediate intuition of God's testimony concerning Godself must be totally rejected as the basis of faith. God's testimony is experienced in ourselves. We experience grace when we experience our own existence, because in our freedom we are confronted with the God of grace, with the divine redemptive will in its concern for us. Ultimately our experience is only of ourselves personally

[63]Ibid., 401–402.

addressed and graced by God; only in faith are we now united with God. Since God's word is identical with Godself, it is not experienced in itself, but only as a reality in our lives. This is why we cannot, apart from revelation, clearly distinguish grace from nature. In all its dimensions grace permeates all levels of our life in the world. Reflexively we know that nature is not grace, and a distinct experience of grace as grace is not lived out existentially in our day-to-day world. Were this all that Seckler wanted to affirm, Schillebeeckx could heartily agree with him. In fact, Seckler, in the opinion of Schillebeeckx, was on the verge of opening a door that would have given far better access to the mystery of grace than that opened by Rahner and von Balthasar. But what Seckler unfortunately wanted to affirm is the concrete identity of the *instinctus naturae* and the *instinctus fidei*. To this, Thomistic spirituality, rooted in the primacy and gratuity of grace, while strongly committed to the fact that *gratia supponit naturam*, can only reply with a resounding *non possumus*.[64]

C. *The Ambivalence of the Instinctus Interior*

Perhaps the fundamental error of Seckler is his seeming unawareness that the *instinctus interior* has for Thomas a neutral meaning, covers a wide range, and is applicable to the lowest and highest interior forms, natural and supernatural alike. Only context can specify its concrete meaning. The dynamism of the human spirit and the *instinctus fidei* are termed an *instinctus interior*. But semantic ties do not warrant identification of the two. Seckler confuses the term's unity of meaning with its field of application. The term *instinctus interior divinus* in Thomas always refers to the unique divine creative action. This activity is purely creative when concerned with preserving "nature" in being (*creatio continua*), but it is the activity of gracing when concerned with bringing into being or preserving the life of grace. Unfortunately, Seckler's study of *instinctus* was not matched by research into the term *lumen*. If it had been, thinks Schillebeeckx, he would have seen the basic difference between the *instinctus naturae* and the *instinctus fidei* and would not have interpreted the beginning of faith in a very unbiblical way. The term *lumen* points to the transcendence of grace, while *instinctus divinus* refers generically

[64]Ibid., 402–403.

to the divine action as conserving either nature (*lumen naturale*) or the life of grace (*lumen infusum*).[65]

In this connection Seckler forgets that the *forma inhaerens* that is of concern relative to the instinct of faith is not the *forma humana* but a new forma, viz., the light of faith. The divine creative activity is called *instinctus interior* in regard to all creaturely activity, natural or supernatural. It is specified as actual grace when it directly offers the new *lumen infusum* and as a natural *motio divina* insofar as it offers a *lumen naturale* (*natura humana*). The term *instinctus interior* merely signifies God's ongoing creative work as such. Of itself it does not indicate whether the divine action is terminated in natural or supernatural life. Thus the *instinctus fidei* is a divine creative act (*instinctus interior*) engaged in the work of sanctification (*infusio luminis fidei vel gratiae* or its conservation). On the other hand, the *instinctus naturae* is an *instinctus divinus* concerned with the divine creative activity engaged in continuing creation (*gubernatio*).[66] According to Schillebeeckx, Seckler does not understand that in the process leading to the act of faith (*conversio*) the *instinctus fidei* is an inward instinct which gratuitously bestows a new light, brings happiness, and at the same time prompts and enables one to freely accept the offer of justification. To reduce this offer of grace to the *instinctus naturae*, even if nature is being viewed theologically, i.e., as created by a saving God, and not philosophically, is to undermine the biblical notion of divine agape.

Humanity is a constitutive but powerless need for grace. Without grace human life is meaningless. However, humanity itself can never be an offer of grace, the *instinctus fidei*. Only in the warmth of God's redeeming love does human life become a concrete offer of grace. Only in this way too do we concretely become an offer of grace for one another. God's saving will is operative everywhere. It can be rejected but never escaped. Yet the miracle that is grace can never be identified with the desolate limits of our finitude. Seckler sounded a true note when he called our humanity a "pre-evangelical climate" of the *initium fidei*.[67]

Finally, Schillebeeckx contends that the full force of Aquinas' view will emerge and be of value for contemporary theologizing

---

[65]Schillebeeckx thinks there are irrefutable texts in his support. Cf., e.g., *In Boethium de Trinitate*, I, q. 1, a. 1 and ad 1, ad 2, ad 6, ad 7.

[66]"L'Instinct," 404.

[67]Ibid., 405–406.

only if disengaged from the philosophy of "nature" with which it was so closely interwoven in the Thomistic synthesis. Yet Seckler has left Thomas' view firmly attached to this physical and "naturalist" framework, for he seems, says Schillebeeckx, to identify the invitation to believe with Aristotle's *naturalis appetitus boni*. Indeed, he has embedded it even more deeply in this mindset by calling Aquinas' *desiderium naturale videndi Deum* a purely ontological and blind dynamism. A better direction to follow would be that of the openness of the knowing, free person confronted with a mystery that presents itself personally and to which one cannot surrender unless by the power of the living God. But not so for Seckler. He chose to search out a solution in the direction of the blind dynamism of the spirit, which permeates all, the intellect included, through which it rises to consciousness.

V. *Reflections on Schillebeeckx's Critique*

In Schillebeeckx's review of Seckler's work we find a trenchant criticism leveled against the supernatural existential.[68] A harmonious blending of transcendence (humanity has no right to grace) and immanence (humanity finds its completion in grace, to which it is interiorly directed) appears to be safeguarded through an appeal to the existential. But is this really so? Schillebeeckx thinks the problem with all its encumbent difficulties has merely been shifted. The problem has been the relation of nature to grace. Now it revolves about the relationship of nature to the supernatural existential.

Do human beings have a natural openness or nonrepugnance to the existential? If one appeals to the obediential potency, then the question becomes: why is the obediential potency itself not sufficient to serve as an opening for grace and to obviate the problem to extrinsicism? Why the intermediate step, the existential? What is it about this intervening element that with it nature has an affinity to being graced, without it little more than a nonrepugance? If grace would be, were it not for the existential, a foreign body, why is the grace of the existential itself not an intrusion? Why is there no need for a disposition for the disposition the supernatural existential is supposed to be? How can it be maintained that the existential provides human nature with a

[68] T. Motherway, "Supernatural Existential," *Chicago Studies* 4(1965) 79–103, took a position similar to Schillebeeckx's.

tendency to grace it would not otherwise have, when proponents of the existential plead a rather complete ignorance of nature to begin with? It would seem that Schillebeeckx, like Rahner, von Balthasar, and even Seckler, situates the term of God's creating and saving decree in the realm of the real rather than of the purely juridical. But finding the existential unacceptable, Schillebeeckx must assert that in humanity the real term of real destination to the supernatural order can only be humanity's *real situation* in that order, which is realized through an acceptance or a rejection that places one in a condition of union with God through sanctifying grace or of sinfulness.

It should be noted, however, that Rahner asserts that he has not postulated the existential to eludicate the many difficulties surrounding the obediential potency, nor to explain why nature has an affinity for grace. If this were his starting point, one could more forcefully claim his hypothesis has merely relocated the problem. Rahner's starting point is his position that the immanent divine decree must be defined *ad extra* by the real term it posits. If God's creation is at the same time a saving decree calling people to union with Godself, this destination must be translated into a real effect in the depth of human being.[69] The existential is simply an expression of the inner logic of the creative-salvific decree and not a contrived explanation of the nature-grace dialectic.

Schillebeeckx is aware of Rahner's contention but does not find it convincing. The contention is that God's decree marks the being-this-way of the creature, hence places an existential in the human before the gifts of created and uncreated grace are granted. But is this conclusive? The decision of God to call humans is a decision to give them the grace-life as their ultimate end. Is not the created term of this summons grace and glory in their own reality? Why look to a bridging element, since God's constant call operating through actual and sanctifying grace provides the alignment and movement to humanity's goal that one needs to establish the immanence of grace?[70] Is Rahner's hypothesis not in violation of the economy that should govern all good theologizing by outlawing the introduction of superfluous factors that are neither proven nor necessary?

---

[69]K. Rahner, "Concerning the Relationship," 302, note 1; 308; 310.

[70]On sanctifying or habitual grace as moving and ordering persons to their finality, cf. *De Veritate*, q. 22, a. 8; In II Sent., d. 29, q. 1, a. 2.

While Schillebeeckx's hesitation is not without merit, his solution is not without its difficulties. Both Schillebeeckx and Alfaro in their highly personalistic approach tend to emphasize the personal call of God and the human's personal, free response opting for or against grace. They do not see God's call as postulating "new" ontological elements in humanity's constitution. It is in terms of personal acceptance or rejection of grace and the graces dispositive to and consequent upon these options, that Schillebeeckx sees historical humanity as different from humanity as-such. In this perspective, however, how is the infant, incapable of option, inserted into the supernatural economy? One, of course, might reply that infants, by virtue of original sin as the sin of the world, are implicated in a real situation of sinfulness and thereby related to the supernatural. But how does a negative factor like the absence of a positive reality on individual and social levels relate one to the supernatural order unless absence becomes *privation*, an interior contradiction, in relation to a more positive element in one's make-up? Does not the privation become more intelligible in terms of an immanent, positive orientation to the perfection that is wanting? In the case of an adult in a condition of sinfulness, are we not back to the point where one is related to the order of grace not by an immanent reality, but merely by the extrinsic, juridical decree of God? Yet it may be that Alfaro and Schillebeeckx would, in the case of the adult at least, locate the real term of the divine invitation in the ubiquitous presence of the *instinctus fidei*, that *gratia operans et praeveniens* constantly moving and prompting the surrender of faith and the justification that God holds out to all. Wherever we turn, Schillebeeckx tells us, God's grace is always there ahead of us, confronting us in everything so that the project of nonbelief is not an easy one to bring off.

This major divergence notwithstanding, there seem to be points of convergence between Schillebeeckx on the one hand and Rahner and von Balthasar on the other. All three insist on the distinction between nature and grace, although they are agreed that nature and grace may be distinct reflexively, they also assert that we are at a loss in our lived experience to determine what is natural and what supernatural. We experience grace in experiencing our humanity, for our consciousness is of a human life constantly addressed by God and informed by grace, whether this be the *instinctus fidei* or the supernatural existential. Only in the light of reflection upon revelation do we differentiate grace from nature. We have seen how the existential unity of the two led Rahner to affirm that nature is an almost unknowable residual (*Restbegriff*), and von Balthasar to negate pure nature as a necessary possibility. Schillebeeckx would probably not go as far as Rahner and von Balthasar, but he is one with them in the refusal to incarcerate grace in the depths of our being where the light of consciousness cannot break in.[71]

It is his stress on the consciousness of grace and his personalistic approach to faith as a free response that moves Schillebeeckx to eschew Seckler's "naturalizing" tendency. Seckler fails to extricate the Thomistic understanding of the *instinctus fidei* and his own understanding of the nature-grace problematic from a naturalistic framework. A similar naturalizing tendency was found in de Lubac. Both de Lubac and Seckler appear to make the offer of grace a constitutive element of human nature as such. Possibly for the same reason Schillebeeckx finds the theory of the existential unacceptable in that its accent appears ontic and does not pay sufficient attention to the psychological and the personal.

Seckler's preoccupation, it seems, is to present a very unified theology of grace. The multiplicity of graces we theologize about ought to converge in a principle of unity. And marking the passage from multiplicity to unity is one of the theologian's chief tasks. The return realized from such a labor is the elimination of an artificial divine interventionism. The creative action of God is unique; it is not numerically measured by its effects in us or in our world. God is not subject to chronology or enumeration. Creation and covenant are not two different and successive actions, the second perfecting the first. The divine generosity is not exercised through successive additions, but through the gradual unfolding of one indivisible decision to communicate itself. It is this that Seckler wants to underline.

Yet it is in the term of this indivisible creative act that distinctions, qualitative and temporal, must be made. There is something in humanity itself which moves us to distinguish the gratuitous gift of grace from the gratuitous gift of creation. One with a personalistic bent might find a hint of this distinction in an Augustinian maxim: "*Qui fecit te sine te, non te justificat sine te. Fecit nescientem, justificat volentem.*"[72] Divinization is dis-

---

[71]For a period effort to elaborate a phenomenology of grace based upon ordinary life situations, cf. R. Haughton, *The Transformation of Man* (New York: Sheed & Ward, 1968).

[72]Sermo 169, xi, 13.

tinguished from creation because it signals a transfiguration, a completion which unlike creation demands free personal response to the divine initiative. Should the gift of grace be rejected, human beings would not cease to be God's creatures. Always present *in* human beings because humanity is created in the divine image, God becomes present *to* human beings only through free conversion. It is this need for an option that warrants the distinction between the two gifts in a personalistic way. If divinization, that perfecting of the divine resemblance (*similitudo*) in humanity in which alone it finds personal fulfillment, is a new gift over and above our original likeness (*imago*) to God, it is partially because it comes to us by means of our free acceptance, which implies a before and an after. Schillebeeckx at this juncture could employ an insight from de Lubac. One does not possess from the first moment of existence the total perfection God destines one to. As a creature one cannot have it of oneself. And if it were given in one fell swoop, it would be an infliction rather than an accomplishment, something passively undergone rather than cooperatively emerging. There is always a chasm between what one is and what one ought to be, between what one is at point of origin and what one is meant to be in fulfillment, or, to use Irenaean terminology, between being *imago Dei* and *similitudo Dei*. It is in the intervening chasm that a person finds place for the exercise of freedom under grace. This seems to be the tenor of Schillebeeckx's emphasis. And he would further add, contrary to Seckler, that humanity does not have within itself, simply in virtue of its being, even the beginning of such an option. The gift of divinization and free acceptance of it are in us, but they are God's doing.

As the *imago Dei* humanity is destined to become the *similitudo Dei*. According to the gospel the force and necessity of the destination are such that full self-realization hinges upon its attainment. Failure in this regard does not result in the simple absence of a possible perfection, but in a positive privation, an internal inconsistency, a negation in the very heart of one's being. Indeed, rejection of the *similitudo* must perforce entail a weakening of the *imago*. Hence there is a singular urgency to the option that Alfaro and Schillebeeckx in their personalism have highlighted. It is this option, effected by grace, which at once personalistically distinguishes grace from nature and unites them together in an indissoluble relationship.

The question remains whether Rahner, while receptive to Schillebeeckx's view of the *instinctus fidei* and his stress on free response, does not better underscore the immanence of grace and humanity's necessary fulfillment in grace by positing in humanity an abiding orientation to union with God prior to justification or divinization. Does the Rahnerian existential more sharply bring into relief the correspondence between the logic of human existence and the logic of the Christian life. Seckler's aim seems to have been to show that correspondence also, the difference being that for Seckler this orientation, identified as it is with the *naturalis appetitus boni*, seems constitutive of human being as such, while for Rahner it is a grace even though constitutive of historical human being.

In conclusion, Schillebeeckx seems to situate the gratuity of grace in the fact that it is *God's divinizing offer of Godself to us through Jesus Christ*, an offer that demands willing acceptance, an acceptance that in and of ourselves we cannot elicit unless inclined and moved by the saving God from within. As Rahner in his rejection of "D", so Schillebeeckx in his rejection of Seckler: the offer of grace cannot be made a constitutive element of nature as such, which at most is a possibility of being graced. The ongoing divine creative activity may be indivisible, but its effects in time are multiple and qualitatively different one from another. The gratuity of grace cannot be reduced to the gratuity of creation. Even if one agrees with Schillebeeckx's disagreement with Seckler,[73] one is nonetheless permitted to wonder whether, in his disagreement with Rahner, Schillebeeckx has not, by his recourse to what is fundamentally a traditional view of the matter, left the problematic where it was and still vulnerable to the charge of extrinsicism. Or we may wonder whether the difference between Rahner and Schillebeeckx that has emerged here is not more apparent than real. But to that issue we shall return.

---

[73]J. Alfaro, "Supernaturalitas fidei iuxta S. Thomam, II; Functio interioris instinctus," *Gregorianum* 44(1963) 731–787, incorporates the insights of Seckler's historical study of the *instinctus fidei* while espousing a view on nature and grace that is akin to Schillebeeckx's.

7

The Supernatural as Process: Reframing the Problem

Without exception the theologians studied up to this point have approached the nature-grace problematic from within the framework of Scholastic theology. Our study now turns to a thinker who, in his effort to reframe the problem, put aside the Scholastic structure along with its foundations in the Aristotelean worldview. Eulalio Baltazar's aim was to reconcile the immanence and transcendence of grace in the context of an evolving universe.[1] His study was exploratory. Hence by necessity it left many areas uninvestigated. What Baltazar hoped to achieve was a totally new approach to the supernatural through a philosophy that is suited to an evolutionary worldview.[2]

Baltazar's work moves through three phases. In the first he underlines the importance of the supernatural to ecclesial renewal and launches a brief survey of past and present handling of the problem.[3] This survey becomes a polemic which fires numerous broadsides at all previous labors, which are neatly bundled together as "Scholastic." Only Teilhard de Chardin emerges unscathed since the epithet does not fit him.[4] As for the two leading contemporary influences, de Lubac's work is inadequate and abortive, while Rahner's leaves the central problem, the reconciliation of immanence and transcendence, unresolved.

---

[1] E. Baltazar, *Teilhard and the Supernatural* (Baltimore: Helicon, 1966).

[2] Ibid., 8, 307, note 2.

[3] Baltazar maintained that the problem of the supernatural was the chief problem of the day and that Vatican II was convoked to come to terms with it. Ibid., 15-73.

[4] Nonetheless, even Teilhard and his commentators were not wholly pleasing to Baltazar. Ibid., 7-8; 29, note 30; 268-269.

The second unit presents a rudimentary philosophy of process sprinkled with Teilhardian insights.[5] Here is the philosophical overview that is to replace Scholasticism. Baltazar sees it as coherent with the biblical Weltanschauung and as an extremely apt underpinning for his theological elaboration of nature and grace. Armed with his process philosophy, Baltazar, in the third section of his work, undertakes a new understanding of the perennially tantalizing problem.[6] The immanence of grace to the human and sub-human levels of creation and of the incarnation to an evolving universe are explained by an analysis in terms of process that is held to be scripturally verified. We turn now to the specifics.

I. *The Case Against Scholasticism*

Baltazar's critique of the Scholastic formulation is addressed to its dualism, which conduces to a fatal extrinsicism. Aggravating this defect is its narrow focus on human redemption to the neglect of a more embracing cosmic redemption.[7] The supernatural must be seen as transcendent and immanent to humanity and its world, yet ever since the Baian controversy there has been a disproportionate stress on transcendence to the detriment of immanence. The reason is to be sought in the Scholastic view of human nature as a substance in which a variety of accidents may inhere. Only what is constitutive of the human essence is considered truly intrinsic to its being. In such a view the supernatural unavoidably appears as accidental and extrinsic, an accretion to human nature. Unavoidable too was a view of nature as autonomous and self-sufficient. Once the natural and the supernatural were seen as two orders extrinsic to each other, and the natural endowed with a radical priority making it the pattern of the supernatural, the door was open to the abuses of scientism and secular humanism which Christianity came so sorely to lament.[8]

---

[5]Ibid., 77–209.

[6]Ibid., pp. 213–329.

[7]Baltazar basically rehearses the deficiencies discussed above in our second chapter.

[8]Ibid., 46; 55–58. L. Dewart shared Baltazar's concern over Catholic theology's failure to do justice to divine immanence. "We confess the true God, both immanent and transcendent. But in real life we find it very difficult—often impossible—to live the contradiction, to hold on to both ends of the chain, confident that the two are joined, out of our sight, in God himself. Impaled on a dilemma. . .we instinctively opt for the safer extreme. . . . Our contemporary belief typically bears . . . only upon a transcendent God. We continue to believe in an immanent God . . . sincerely, but

Rahner attempts to remedy the situation by occupying a middle ground between the theologians of the schools and de Lubac.[9] He does not succeed. Rahner is simply more of the same; he offers not a solution but a reformulation of the problem. For he tries to render the supernatural immanent through an *existential* belonging to the category of accident. But the effort only issues in a more nuanced extrinsicism. As an accident the *existential* cannot be situated at the core of human being as Rahner claims it is. Only substantial matter and form as constituents of human nature occupy that privileged terrain. In no way does Rahner posit his existential as constitutive of humanity. Thus the most contemporary of modern Scholastic efforts to do justice to the immanence of grace as nature's highest perfection and deepest reality does not quite come off. Obviously theologians working out of the scholastic framework are caught on the horns of a dilemma begotten by their own system. To make the supernatural accidental is to make it purely extrinsic; to cast it in the category of the substantial, making it constitutive of humanity, is to sacrifice the dogma of gratuity. In defense of gratuity, Scholastics can never admit that grace is necessary to human beings. But if that be so, neither can they extol it as humanity's highest fulfillment. The accidental is always a perfection inferior to the essential. Moreover, the Scholastic view ought logically to charge God with contradiction, since God commands a nature to tend to an accidental perfection when the dynamism of created being is bound to tend toward its essential perfection.[10]

Actually it is the Scholastic who is snared in contradiction because of the contention that humanity can intelligibly exist apart from Christ and His grace. The argumentation is that what is necessary is owed and demanded. Therefore it is not necessary. This argument flies in the face of abundant scriptural evidence that without God the creature is meaningless. To affirm the contrary plays into the hands of the secularist.[11]

Nor is it only immanence that is jeopardized by the traditional view, but gratuity as well. Baltazar presents his own understanding of gratuity. First the giver must be totally free to present the

ineffectively. We confess it, but we do not mean what we confess." "God and the Supernatural," *Commonweal* 85(1967) 524. See also his *Future of Belief* (New York: Herder & Herder, 1966) 206–212.

[9]Baltazar classifies Rahner as a "moderate intrinsicalist."

[10]*Teilhard and the Supernatural*, 58–61.

[11]Ibid., 62–64.

gift, the beneficiary having no claim to it; secondly, the gift must be valuable to the receiver so that reception stirs up true gratitude. Further, the gift's capacity to inspire gratitude is proportioned to the desire of its receiver. Thus the greater the receiver's ordination to the gift, the greater the gratuity. Ordination is a necessary condition of gratuity. Scholastic theology admirably meets the first requirement of gratuity. But what of the second?

Christians believe that grace is an absolute necessity to human meaningfulness. In terms of its significance to humanity the supernatural is gratuitous. When belief is theologized, however, the Scholastic falls short of showing the significance of grace. Obviously the Scholastic views grace as a person's highest perfection. If so, then it should be admitted that humanity is intrinsically oriented to it as its deepest need. Otherwise, how can it provoke responding love and gratitude? On the other hand, if the grace-gift is merely accidental, God demands more than is granted when a total response to the gift is sought. Yet the Scholastic does insist that the supernatural is accidental, non-essential, non-constitutive. To protect the divine freedom the Scholastic devalues the meaningfulness of the gift for the creature by making it detachable from the creature's essential intelligibility. But how can true gratefulness, and therefore real gratuity, be verified where the gift answers to no real need, offers no radical fulfillment? Gratuity and immanence go hand in hand. The inability to fully recognize the latter is a slighting of the former.[12]

Finally, school theology's understanding of the immanence of grace is of no use today. True value, claim Scholastic thinkers, lies in the extra-temporal sphere. There lies the locus of the supernatural. This of course is patently unacceptable to Christians who share with their contemporaries an evolutionary world-picture and a healthy appreciation of terrestrial values. Nor does the watered immanence of Scholasticism appeal to nonbelievers. Whatever hope of acceptance the supernatural might find resides in its being a here-and-now reality, constitutive of humanity in the heart of its being. Such hope could never be engendered by even the best of Scholastic formulations, committed as they are to the perpetuation of extrinsicism. The Scholastics may loudly profess the immanence of grace. But they cannot gird it with credibility.

[12]Ibid., 65–68.

II. *A Philosophical Renewal to Ground Theological Renewal*

If Scholastic theology cannot adequately explicate the nature-grace relationship, the ineptitude ultimately stems from its employment of faulty philosophical tools. So it is that Baltazar tries to effect a transition from Scholastic philosophy to a philosophy of process. Here we can only distill some key ideas from the long second segment of his work.

To live in today's world one must be willing to see everything historically and evolutionarily. Even those realities traditionally considered as towering over the whirlpool of change evolve— dogma, the Church, philosophical and theological formulae.[13] At the physical level we have shifted from a Ptolemaic to an Einsteinian worldview and from static Aristotelean species to an evolving Darwinian framework at the biological level. The medieval ahistorical outlook has yielded to an evolutionary perspective. Baltazar's basic premise is that creation is now; species are evolving; reality is rough-hewn, plastic, and unfinished. In a word, all is in process. The intellect cannot arrive at the essential truth of reality today, but only at the end of all today's, the term of process. For absolute truth is synonymous only with the end of the process. Baltazar's fundamental perspective considers the medieval synthesis no longer viable. Perhaps the single most crucial task Baltazar set for himself was the replacement of the category of substance or essence with that of process.[14] He hoped to work out a philosophy of process that is Teilhardian, Copernican, Ein-

---

[13]Sounding the call to a process mode of thought with Baltazar were L. Dewart, *The Future of Belief* and E. Fontinell, "Reflections on Faith and Metaphysics," *Cross Currents* 16(1966) 15-40 and "Religious Truth in a Relational and Processive World," *Cross Currents* 17(1967) 283-315. Dewart and Fontinell shared with Baltazar the conviction that Hellenic metaphysics no longer present a viable philosophical worldview. Christian theism's future hangs upon its willingness to jettison classical categories and to forge new ones more congenial to contemporary life. Western Christianity, according to Dewart's thesis, has apostatized and no longer professes the belief that animated its culture and history. *The Future of Belief* was further elaborated in *The Foundations of Belief* (New York: Herder & Herder, 1969).

[14]*Teilhard and the Supernatural*, 77-90. Baltazar, Dewart, and Fontinell believed that as different as Husserl, Dewey, Heidegger, James, Bergson, and Whitehead may be among themselves, they share a world and it differs sharply from the substantialist world of Maritain, Gilson, de Lubac, Rahner, and Lonergan. According to Fontinell, metaphysical dualism that thinks in terms of underlying substantial essences that are only accidentally modified is no longer viable. For moderns reality is process and relationship, not structure and substance.

steinian, and Darwinian. The modest synthesis achieved made no greater claim than that it is probable.[15]

From the two basic approaches to reality derive two basic philosophical views; a philosophy of being and a philosophy of becoming. A philosophy of process, however, must consider becoming as more primordial. Nevertheless, process thinkers know that becoming terminates in being. Hence theirs is actually a synthesis of the traditional philosophies of being and becoming. Baltazar's process is not Heraclitean, since it does not view time as a directionless and interminable flux. Nor is it comparable to the process of Whitehead, Dewey, or James, though there are similarities, since it is not based purely on scientific ideas such as biological evolution, relativity physics, and quantum mechanics. It is Hegelian in that it terminates in Spirit, yet it is un-Hegelian and more Teilhardian in that its Omega attains its fullness in time.[16]

But what is process? Process for Baltazar is motion and change. More specifically, it is growth from within, immanent motion. And it is verified in all species. If the substances of things seem unchanging to us it is because of our myopia and the narrow time scale perceptible to us. We see objects, not processes. The category of substance was tailored to fit common sense observations of permanence. And to explain our experience of the perfecting activity proceeding from and happening to the subject we devised the categories of act and potency. Unfortunately, common sense experience was extrapolated. We came to think that regardless of time scales, reality conforms to our experience of it. But modern thought has detected the fallacy in this and has come to see everything in process, or better, to see that "all things are processes, not substances." The processes of individual species must be situated within the processes of larger time scales and all processes within the overarching process of the evolution of the universe whose ultimate meaning reposes in its Omega. In all this there is one perspective: all things are viewed linearly, all have

[15]Ibid., 97, 103, 193. Baltazar saw his work as exploratory and conceded it was too early "to present a perfect alternative to Thomism." He does not offer a complete philosophy of process; his selective treatment appeals only to categories useful for elucidating the nature/grace problem. Only via process categories can one move from the timeless to the historical. The Scholastic may accept evolution, but the logic of Scholasticism impedes its articulation.

[16]Ibid., 91–103. There is regularity in the world along with irregularity and novelty. But all is relative, not absolute. Change gives meaning to permanence. Permanence cannot be considered *the* reality so that change is merely apparent and accidental.

their alpha and omega, none are conceived as static points. And novelty is not the novelty of sheer flux so that each moment in a process is reduced to a new, discontinuous, and unrelated atomized element. It follows that the present is not the place of being, of the subject; it is rather the region of becoming. The future is the place of being, of the subject. In the present there is no subject apart from process. There is only process. Our world is in the making and humanity, continuous with it, shares the making and the being made.[17]

After postulating a shift from substance to process Baltazar calls next for a conversion from existence (the act of "to be") as self-containedness to existence as union, or sharedness. Existence is unitive; to be in process is to be united. A human being is, therefore, a being-in-the-world-and-towards-others. To be is always to-be-with. Being is never insular but always being-with-another. In the Aristotelean-scholastic frame of reference relation is the least respected category, the *debellissimum ens*.[18] This is so because Scholasticism considers relations a threat to substantiality; it implies dependence, and essential dependence implies loss of identity. But clearly, says Baltazar, there is no proper act of "to be" separate from its ground. All so-called autonomous substances are processes that enjoy existence only as a result of union. Further, no concrete reality is intelligible or exists apart from the evolutionary unity of the universe. Things are not simply born; they are born into a world. Nothing is its own ground; all creatures are locked in interdependence. The notion of substance as self-enclosed and self-subsistent is a pure abstraction. The biblical view supports the notion of being as relatedness when it stresses the fact that isolated from the covenant one is doomed to unauthentic being and death.[19]

So far we have seen that Baltazar considers existence a process. Process in turn is a "we"; not a succession of autonomous events, but a cooperation, a growth that is oriented and marked by an alpha, a middle, and a fullness, or omega. He adds now that process is also marked by qualitative changes or births to new

[17] Ibid., 104–120.

[18] Baltazar detects an inherent contradiction in a system that looks upon relation as the weakest of categories, yet employs it to theologize its highest reality, the Trinity. Ibid., 127.

[19] Ibid., 121–129. All this is especially true of the human person. The person is constituted by relationships to its various worlds. These relationships are internal, not merely extrinsic and spatial.

levels. Increase is not purely quantitative, simply a snowballing accretion. Nor is it only the actualization of what was already present potentially at the start, so that there is really nothing new.[20] Rather, increase in process is at the level of existence. It is creative and interior. Process is the search of being for its essence and true meaning. Present reality, consequently, finds its being and permanence in the future, not here and now; hence rationality and truth reside in the future, too, since being and truth are convertible. Only what is fully evolved is being; what is not fully evolved is non-being, though this does not mean non-existence. The reality of the present is hope, for the present is the region of reality that is unrealized. The present therefore is not fully real. The Greek view could, with its static outlook, situate being and truth in the present precisely because it saw things as already substantially finished and permanent.[21]

Creation is, then, a continuous process. Like a painting, it is completed not with the first stroke of the brush, but only with the final stroke. God and humans act as co-creators. The world is malleable, waiting to receive its finishing touches at our hands. One of the large implications of this perspective is that the knower and the known are both processes. Both, to the extent that the fullness of their being lies in a future dimension, are shrouded in mystery. Thus the real epistemological problem is the relationship of a knower and a known which are both evolving. Relating the two as static realities is a non-problem. There is no essence or noumenon lurking under present phenomena. Essential or noumenal reality is one with the omega of a given reality. To cling to the present and to look for substantiality there is an illusion. The Scholastic contention, therefore, that its epistemology affords absolute knowledge is tied to an outmoded cosmology. From our modern awareness we know that what we thought were eternal essences are simply moments or stages in an evolving process. The only unchanging basis of an unchanging knowledge of any given reality (process) is point omega. In relation to other stages it is absolute. At omega point no longer is there relativity. To be fully

[20]Here Baltazar is dependent on R. Johann, "The Logic of Evolution," *Thought* 36 (1961) 595–612.

[21]For Fontinell, too, essences are basically relational. Novelty is more than an expression of an immutable nature. Essences are novel and changing due to the continuous transactions within the relational continuum. Novelty does not threaten continuity, but it does foreclose the possibility of claiming to know reality's ultimate principles. "Reflections on Faith," 25.

evolved is to be unfolded, revealed. At omega the final presentation of being is achieved. It follows that an ontology built on the present rests on shifting sands. The only valid principle of intelligibility resides in the omega, which alone is fixed and unchanging.[22]

Finally Baltazar comes to his own understanding of the signification of truth. His concern is not with logical truth, the mind's conformity with reality, but with the authenticity or inauthenticity of process, with existential truth. In the Scholastic scheme of things all creatures are finished and in possession of their proper essence. Thus they are necessarily conformed to the mind of God. Hence they have ontological truth. But process philosophy sees realities in dynamic quest of their essence. We cannot, then, speak of them as in possession of ontological truth. Evidently, Baltazar wants to convert the notion of truth from content to direction. The truth of process is in the omega, for process tends to the other in order *to be*. In other words, omega is the ontological truth of process. The conformation of process to its other, its ground, renders it true to itself. There is another truth that corresponds to reality still in process; a reality tending in the right direction towards its omega is true. And this Baltazar terms methodological truth. In such a perspective truth is direction rather than content. And the aim of theologizing and of any worldview is to foresee, to give meaning and direction to human striving rather than to understand. Again, revelation bears this out. The Bible sees persons as pilgrims, sin as digression from the way, a missing of the mark. To lack truth is not to lack correct content, but to miss the true way. Revelation, consequently, is not ideas to be contemplated but a direction pointing the way. Hence we need a salvation history and a process theology, "not a thinking theology for contemplation."[23]

For Baltazar the stages of a process relate to their omega as symbol to reality. The moment attained does not point to itself but to a higher level. The higher is the reality of the lower and reveals the lower to itself; it holds the truth of the lower. The total direction finds its reality in the omega. Once we posit reality as

[22]*Teilhard and the Supernatural*, 140–171.

[23]Fontinell designates knowledge as "true insofar as it establishes or enables man to establish satisfactory relations." "Religious Truth," 310. Truth is predicated of personal experience insofar as the relations constituting this experience are conducive to humanizing life. Truth is existential and participational rather than abstract and representational. See also Dewart, *The Future of Belief*, 92–118 for a similar view.

symbol rather than form, the intellect's function must change. No longer is it the passive recorder, the spectator. "It is a gatherer of symbols." It is prophetic, predictive, believing, or imaginative, varying with the dimension of the future it is keyed on.[24] This too is confirmed by the biblical view of reality. For Israel the main event was aborning and the prophet's role was to read the signs of the times. The prophets, and the apex of their movement, Christ, are not purveyors of timeless dogmas, unchanging truths. They are the teachers of the true direction. They saw present facts and events as purely symbolic, harbingers of a higher reality.

Baltazar can sum up in paradox by saying that the present is not what it is. Reason in the present cannot grasp all the facts, which are not given to begin with. Hence it cannot judge what is true or false. Knower and known are partially evolved, thus partially present. Only the future sits in judgment upon the present. Today's statements about today are provisional, hypothetical, and subjunctive.[25] With this background we can now consider Baltazar's stance on the nature-grace dialectic.

III. *Grace in an Evolving Universe*

Baltazar's basic contention is that Scholastic theology exalted the transcendence of grace while condemning immanence to a theological limbo. In large part this was because Scholasticism began with a definition of the human being in terms of nature and then related grace to that nature. This methodology tailors grace to suit nature. It further presupposed one could, and had, zeroed in on the correct understanding of nature as essence. Methodologically, Baltazar proposes we commence with the requirements of grace and allow them to determine our approach to humanity.[26]

[24]Fontinell claims that faith, as belief bearing upon life in its comprehensive effort, does not give knowledge about God, others, or the world. It provides illumination, direction, meaning for human living. Theological propositions never inform us about God. They serve as limited, inadequate symbols. Objectivism must yield to symbolism. In knowledge there is no one-to-one correspondence between mind and reality, but rather a progressive transaction in which knowledge is a pathway to a more adequate relationship with reality. Cf. "Reflections on Faith," 35–40 and "Religious Truth," 301–314. Dewart, for whom Christianity has a mission but not a message, seems to be of the same mind. The difficulties engendered by these views are obvious. Cf. B. Lonergan, "The Dehellenization of Dogma," in G. Baum, ed., *The Future of Belief Debate* (New York: Herder & Herder, 1967) 69–91.

[25]*Teilhard and the Supernatural*, 172–209.

[26]Ibid., 215–216.

Thus Baltazar sets out to show negatively the inadequacy of a theology that first builds a definition of nature and subsequently brings grace to bear upon it. First, grace is a person's supreme perfection. This means that if it is so significant, it must find an ontological counterpart in one's inmost depths. But is human nature what is deepest in a human, as the Scholastics thought? Moderns find the deepest element is subjectivity. Is grace as the highest human perfection properly rooted in the deepest level if it is related to impersonal and objective nature? Secondly, if we ask what grace is, disregarding the traditional idea that it is an extrinsic, accidental determination elevating one to supernatural life, we must answer that it is love. To be graced is to be the recipient of God's love and of the capacity to love in return. Consequently, grace should be related to that dimension in human being which can respond to love. As intersubjective union, love is rooted in the uniqueness of two personal beings, not in what is objective and universal nature. Hence grace is addressed to a person, not to a nature. To approach humanity as a nature is to approach it purely as object, as thing, as "it". Thirdly, it does not suffice merely to situate grace at the deepest human level. One must also show it is central to this level. Here again Scholastic theology has not tasted success. The closest the Scholastic can make grace to nature is to term it an inmost accident. Nonetheless humanity remains intelligible in its absence. Such a formulation pays lip service to immanence.[27]

Baltazar next proceeds to show positively the greater adequacy of a processive and personalistic approach. Recall first that the perfection of being-as-process is in the other. Being is humble. It needs the other. Its fulfillment lies in the future and is attained by tending to it in love. Process requires an ongoing death and rebirth. Ontologically the "I" is feminine, mothering the new "I". Indeed the "I" becomes definable only in its relation to the Absolute Thou. Human depth resides in personality. Nature looks to the appropriation of what is necessary for physical survival or to the possession of impersonal goods that enhance natural perfection. But a human as person, participating in the presence of being to itself, "looks to the progressive fathoming by the finite self of the unique value, the unique Self," to communion with a Person who is the source of all personality. Evolution as an ascent toward consciousness should culminate in supreme conscious-

[27]Ibid., 214–223.

ness, i.e., in some type of hyper-personalization. Because personhood is, therefore, the deepest reality of the human, grace should be related to it, not to nature. If the Absolute Thou is the deepest level of all reality, the "I", which alone attains it, must be far deeper than objective human nature. One's depth is not what one holds in common with others, but what is uniquely one's own.[28]

Secondly, since grace is love, it ought to be related to a category that explains love. What responds to love is the person. Grace as love, therefore, must be related to subjectivity. In this way far greater immanence is achieved than could be had by keying grace to nature. But more is required. True immanence requires that the "I" be formally and ontologically structured for grace as its sole finality. Without this it is void of meaning. Grace must be situated at the core of personality. The "I" is a being-toward-the-Thou. Its very definition bespeaks ordination to the Thou, apart from which it is inconceivable. It was created for no other end prior to and apart from personal union through which a new "I" is begotten. The Scholastics stress nature as already endowed with essence and existence; Baltazar stresses only an "I" tending toward a Thou for its essence and existence. Moreover, if the orientation of the "I" toward a human Thou is deeper than that of nature to its end, then the "I" 's directedness toward the Absolute must run deepest, since God is the absolute Thou.[29]

Turning more specifically to humanity's orientation to grace as its omega, Baltazar sees grace as new life for the "I" in union with the Absolute Thou, in much the same way that the seed finds new life in union with its ground. The core of the seed carries the germ of life within; the core of a person carries ordination to divine life. Indeed this ordination is, so to speak, the very "substance" of the "I". In this way grace is truly immanent. Baltazar is aware that he has now, seemingly, put himself into a position that reduces the supernatural to the natural. Have we come full circle? Has immanence supplanted transcendence? What now of gratuity?

He feels however that he can extricate himself, first by analyzing the difficulties that have traditionally surrounded the notion

---

[28]Ibid., 224–231.

[29]Ibid., 235–236. Union that is personal requires a more profound and precise ordination than union that is natural. Binding two unique terms calls for a "closer fit" than is required at a generic or specific level.

of gratuity and transcendence. He begins by explicitly affirming that humanity has no exigency for the supernatural. But the Scholastics deduced from this that humanity could not be intrinsically ordered to grace. Such a conclusion is tantamount to negating immanence.[30] And yet are intrinsic ordination and gratuity necessarily contradictory? Baltazar thinks not. The I-Thou relationship (person-grace) thrives in a context of love, not justice. The "I" is not an Aristotelean nature. What is predicable of the latter is not necessarily predicable of the former. Baltazar's next move, therefore, is to analyze the I-Thou relationship to show that an intrinsic ordination to grace is not an exigency for grace.

In a love context the "I" cannot achieve its end alone. It is not a self-sufficient Aristotelean nature, but a being-to-the-other. Its end is union. Embedded in its ontological structure is need for an "other". In fact it would be contradictory for the Creator to produce a self-sufficient "I", since ours is a universe built on love. On the other hand, it may be objected that God creates in vain if the "I" is created without powers to attain its end. But not so, replies Baltazar, as long as God places sufficiency in the union of the "I" and the Thou. And this, in the context of love, is the case. In the Aristotelean universe self-sufficiency resides in the individual; in the Teilhardian universe, in the I-Thou bond. What it is to create in vain in the Aristotelean framework is to create properly in the Teilhardian framework. If God creates the "I" for love, God cannot make it self-sufficient. The divine exigency to create the "I" as insufficient exceeds the Aristotelean exigency to create a self-sufficing nature.

It follows that if the "I" is not self-sufficient, unable to attain alone the omega to which it is intrinsically ordered, then its end transcends its powers. In a word, grace, as humanity's sole end, is transcendent, supranatural, beyond natural capabilities. It follows also that in a love context the "I" has no exigency for the end it is intrinsically ordered to. The union is marked by bi-lateral freedom. If there is any exigency at all, it is that there be no exi-

---

[30]Baltazar finds Donnelly's work on the supernatural to be typical on this score (cf. chapter 2, note 2). The argument used by Donnelly and others, which, says Baltazar, derives from the Aristotelean notion of nature, is simply that any end without which a nature is inconceivable is owed to it. God must avoid the contradiction of creating a being without placing within its grasp the only finality for which it is made. The Aristotelean world, claims Baltazar, rests on justice and exigence or right, ontological or moral. The greatest work of love, the redemption, came consequently to be formulated in terms of justice. Ibid., 238–241.

gency. Gratuity is built into the I-Thou relationship. The "I" humbly waits and hopes for the advent of the Thou; the Thou is not coerced into union. All this would be lost by resorting to the context of nature where gratuity is obliterated when one speaks in terms of intrinsic ordination. Nature does not understand gratuity; it speaks the language of justice. Baltazar can only conclude that intrinsic ordination, far from obliterating gratuity, is a conditio sine qua non to render it real.[31]

Baltazar once more finds confirmation for his position in Scripture. What stands out there is the category of covenant as interpersonal union articulated as Father-child tie and conjugal bond. The foundation is love, not justice. He also notes that just as grace, love, person are primary in his analysis, so too in Scripture, covenant takes precedence over creation. The latter is in function of the former. Moreover, Scripture's description of the human-divine proximity in the conjugal image implicitly affirms the deep, intimate nature of humanity's ordination to God. Experience teaches that the more proximate the union the greater the ordination and vice versa. Scripture's delineation of the covenant relation is not metaphorical; in a very real symbolic sense, says Baltazar, it asserts that as woman is oriented to man (sic), so humanity is intrinsically ordered to God.[32] This ordination is constitutive, touching humanity's existence in the heart of its being. Scripture presents the "I" as lacking in self-sufficiency. Dissolve the covenant and the "substance" and existence of the "I" disintegrate.

This counters the Scholastic claim that humanity is not intrinsically ordered to the supernatural, that ours could be an uncovenanted world, and that humanity is thinkable apart from graced being. This pseudo-world is Scholasticism's basic building block; to it a very foreign supernatural is very awkwardly appended.[33] For the Scholastic, nature's ordination to its natural end is more intrinsic than the ordination of humanity to its graced finality. The former is constitutive, the latter an extrinsic append-

[31] Ibid., 232–246.

[32] Baltazar makes much of the "I" as feminine (e.g., ibid., 226, 245, 255 ff.) and draws upon biblical imagery to support his view.

[33] Intrinsic ordination notwithstanding, says Baltazar, the category of covenant excludes any exigence. Is God truly free if the creature's intrinsic ordination to grace must be fulfilled? Yes. Because in a love context the very meaning of the "I" is to call for the absolute Thou to give love freely. Otherwise it is not love. See ibid., 259–260, 263–264.

age. But if union with God is the closest possible, why term it accidental? What justification from within the law of human being sanctions the obligation to tend to a union that is extrinsic and accidental?[34]

Finally, Baltazar turns from the specific problems of person and grace to the more general problem of the relation of all creation to the supernatural, or more exactly, to the problem of the relation of the incarnation to an evolving world. Fortified by process thought he again does battle against dualistic ways of thinking. Baltazar sees the entire evolutionary line—matter, plants, animals, humans—as a Christ-line pointed to the incarnation. By the law of process, any historical process not issuing in a unique event is not process, but a purely quantitative growth. Every true process at a certain critical juncture evolves to a level new and qualitatively different from the preceding one. If humanity is in process, there is a point in history where there occurs an event that is supra-human and supra-historical. For a thing to remain itself it must become different. Further, since we judge any process by its omega, obviously evolution is a supernatural process. Only an Aristotelean who insists that nature attains its end solely by its own powers would, says Baltazar, claim that the Teilhardian view has reduced the supernatural to the natural. The objection has been sufficiently overpowered, he thinks, by the fact that every process needs its ground. God the Creator is Creator even now. Christ is not the natural fruit of the process, as though the evolutionary thrust attains the incarnation in and of itself. God's purpose is a world whose sufficiency is only in union. So the problem of exigency is handled here as it was in the case of person and grace. The evolutionary dynamism is a drive to union in the incarnation, where alone sufficiency and redemption lie.[35]

Again Baltazar appeals to a scriptural corroboration that shows creation as primarily soteriological rather than cosmological and only extrinsically ordered to the incarnation. In Scripture creation is the necessary condition for and consequence of Christ's coming, which is primary in the divine intention. Baltazar adopts the Hebraic notion that views creation and salvation as pertaining to the same order. Creation is structured for covenant in the

---

[34]Scholasticism, to avoid pantheism, cannot term the union substantial. For Baltazar, this underlines Scholasticism's bankruptcy. It cannot articulate the divine-human relationship since it lacks the conceptual tools.

[35]Ibid., 246–274.

fullest sense, i.e., creation is really a process of Christogenesis, the personal union of God and humanity in Christ and of all in Christ. Only thus can we exorcise the demon of dualism and make the incarnation immanent and meaningful to our world. There is not "in addition to the Christ-line of redemption another separate God-line of creation." The incarnation does not come from without; Christ is the within of our supernaturally evolving universe. That humans and other creatures are unintelligible apart from Christ is abundantly clear in Scripture. This, asserts Baltazar, is overlooked by the Scholastics in their one-sided understanding of gratuity.

Once more Baltazar insists that the point of departure is not an intelligible world to which the incarnation is a fortuitous additive; rather, grace and incarnation must be the points of departure. Starting with these givens, we derive the meaning of gratuity from them, not from a philosophical premise about the self-intelligibility of nature. The gratuity of creation derives from the primacy and gratuity of grace and incarnation, not vice versa. When grace and incarnation appear in a world intrinsically structured for them, grace is given to itself, not to some other reality demanding grace in such a way as to make it non-gratuitous. To make grace a detachable or bracketable accessory is to eliminate its immanence and its gratuity, for responding to no essential need, it does not evoke total gratitude.

Baltazar thinks his approach warrants the demolition of pure nature and of Rahner's remainder concept. If *Humani Generis* seems to assert otherwise it is only because its conceptual base is an outdated Aristotelean-Thomistic context. But the encyclical does not establish this as the only viable context. Hence Baltazar questions the encyclical's context more than its conclusion. In another context, one that starts with the incarnation rather than nature, God must create beings with whom the gifts of grace can be shared. Thus in a covenant context one may say that God could not have created humankind without structuring it for grace. In fact, to remove Christ and his grace is not simply to prune a part from the whole, it is to destroy the whole.[36]

What Baltazar's thesis boils down to is that there is but one order, the order of grace; and there is but one gratuity. In view of his personalism, his process approach, and his biblical corroborations, he feels that this one order should be termed the "natu-

---

[36]Ibid., 274–306.

ral" state of humanity. Sin is humanity's unnatural condition; grace, its natural completion.[37] The Western Church unfortunately could never adopt this terminology in its evangelization of the Greeks. To do so would have endangered gratuity. And so the polarization of natural and supernatural began. Unfortunately, says Baltazar, the necessities of evangelization fast became a theological norm and the nomenclature adopted determined our understanding. The result was that grace came to be seen as an accidental being, which, like color or weight, could be lost, human substance remaining unchanged. But on the I-Thou level loss of the grace-union is loss of the "I," a spiritual and eschatological death. Thus a semantic conversion, truer to the facts, would make it possible to bring the nonbeliever to see the rationality of the doctrines of grace and sin, as well as the Christian's concern for the world. The term "supernatural" safeguards the transcendence of grace, but victimizes immanence and portrays Christianity as a pie-in-the-sky flight from the arena of life.

Leslie Dewart found himself in basic agreement.[38] Once we conceive of nature as essentially and not merely existentially contingent, the concept of the supernatural, he alleges, is unnecessary to safeguard fundamental Christian belief in the contingency and gratuity of all divine-human relations.[39] The natural-supernatural distinction is merely a play on words. Grace continues to be what Christians always believed it to be, but nature ceases to be opposed to it. Indeed Dewart sees nature as endowed with an aptitude for grace. That is how nature was created. Essentially contingent, deriving its intelligibility from its factuality and historicity, nature is historically, not metaphysically related to grace. Grace as historical fact, God's presence to humanity, existentially qualifies in a definitive way the intelligibility of nature.

[37]For scholasticism, according to Baltazar, humanity's original condition was supernatural. The fall marked descent into a natural condition, similar to that of pure nature. Baltazar would call the fallen condition unnatural and the original condition natural. For him, redemption is restoration to a natural state. Does this make him vulnerable to the charge of Baianism? He thinks not. Baius considered the original condition a non-gratuitous elevation. But in the I-Thou context the term "natural" does not negate gratuity. Nor is nature the locus of the wound of original sin. Sin infects the "I", the person, for it is loss of the capacity to love. The wound is mortal, since without love, union and completion are unattainable. Ibid., 311–313.

[38]*The Future of Belief*, 206–212.

[39]Dewart detects a "necessitarianism" and an essentialistic immobilism binding together Hellenic ontologies so that they cannot conceive of the radical contingency of finite existents and hence they had no idea of a creation ex nihilo. Ibid., 152–170; 45, 208.

Dewart further notes that while one may wish to avoid terms like "naturalism" and "secularism" because of their pejorative connections, the fact is that post-Tridentine thought has tended to read Christian belief in terms of the temporal history of natural entities. "Natural" signifies "historically factual." Grace transforms spatio-temporal facts into ultimate truths by giving them a religious dimension. "The difference between a 'natural' and a 'supernatural' event or reality (or between the 'secular' and 'religious' explanation thereof) concerning any order whatever of reality from the amoeba to the ziggurat (or concerning any order whatever of explanation, from archeology to zoology) is not in the abstract spatio-temporal *content*, but in the existential historical *form* of the event or reality (or the ascertained explanation thereof)." In a word, a nonreligious order of daily events or scientific interpretations may disregard faith and revelation and claim to be absolute and self-sufficient. Truly Christian experience, however, whether scientific or commonsensical, is transmitted by faith. Faith enters not to judge what is true or false, but to interpret, to uncover the inner meaning, the deeper sense of the one and only "natural" truth. In this sense, Dewart thinks, it would not be altogether inexact to say that Christian reflection and experience are becoming naturalistic.

Dewart shows further convergence with Baltazar's position when he insists that nature is not something that determines a being to act in accordance with some immutable and constitutive principle of intelligibility. On the contrary. Nature is what emerges from the history that being makes or undergoes. In this light, the existence the gospel calls us to need not be seen as supernatural, as something alienating from humankind and its world. We are not called to a new existence that is superimposed on an independently evolving history; it is the same level of existence as that in which creation is now evolving. This historical evolution is under the aegis of God's free decision to be present to creation and to give Godself to humanity by becoming human. Grace is, then, a historical fact, God's breakthrough into history, a definitive actual event within a merely possible event.[40]

In the future we may not feel bound, concludes Dewart, to conceive of God as a super-natural being. As we slough off the Hellenic view of static and immutable essences, the Christian God will no longer have to perform super-natural feats to remain free,

---

[40]"God and the Supernatural," 527.

gracious, and gratuitously Self-giving. And so traditional belief can be asserted under new forms that make the notion of grace more meaningful than the notion of the supernatural has in the past. Grace will be better understood as the Self-bestowal of ultimate reality, as the true source of existence and creativity, "no longer God's cornucopia of immaterial plenty, but the alpha and omega of consciousness and praxis, existence and life."[41]

IV. *Reflections on the Supernatural as Process*

An evaluation of Baltazar's case for viewing the supernatural as process faces difficulties. It is no easy task to move from one system of ideas to another marked by a decidedly different focus and arrangement. Key ideas and words that were centuries in the coining become charged with ambiguity. The ambiguity is compounded as new worldviews, attempting to answer fundamental questions about reality, enter the philosophical stream. The problem is in the present instance further complicated by the fact that we are dealing with a daring and promising programmatic sketch that still needs fleshing out with argumentative detail, and even more, a firmer theoretical foundation.[42]

One thing is obvious about Baltazar's study. It is an effort to redefine the nature-grace co-ordinates. Because Scholasticism, it is felt, ends in a cul-de-sac where the nature-grace dyad is concerned, it deserves to be abandoned and replaced by a philosophy of process. So it is that Baltazar launched his ambitious effort to explicate the process philosophy he believed implicit in Teilhard.[43] There is much validity to Baltazar's critique. Yet too often it is marred by anti-Scholastic forays against straw men.[44] Too often the effort to impugn Scholasticism is a tilting at windmills.

[41] *The Future of Belief*, 212.

[42] The three thinkers referred to in this chapter admit that their work is tentative and exploratory. Cf. *Teilhard and the Supernatural*, 8, 97, 307, note 2; *The Future of Belief*, 7, 49f., 164, 171, 173; "Religious Truth," 301, 315. Certainly process theology has advanced a great deal in the years since their writing. This is so in Catholic as well as in Protestant thought.

[43] *Teilhard and the Supernatural*, 213.

[44] This seems true also of Dewart and Fontinell. On Dewart, cf. *The Future of Belief Debate*. Many positions attacked by Baltazar as Scholastic or Thomist cannot be acknowledged to be such. See e.g., 5, 26–28, 45, 55f., 70, 112, 125f., 130f., 134, 137, 161, 168f., 170f., 180–182, 190, 193, 216, 219, 221, 261, 275f., 278, 300, 311. The issue is aggravated when one uses "Thomism" and "scholasticism" as labels that cover diverse schools of thought and diverse eras. For a more careful and less simplified reading of this tradition, cf. W. Shepherd, *Man's Condition*, 31–93.

The target for Baltazar's lances are a naive realism or a formalistic conceptualism.[45] The surveyor of vast panoramas cannot do justice to important and intricate details. This, however, does not necessarily vitiate Baltazar's insights. For valid insights there are in the processive way of seeing things. In reality, Baltazar's is not a pure process system but a brew of process thought, existentialism, idealism, personalism, and even Scholasticism, all thoroughly seasoned with the poetic vision of Teilhard.[46] One may object that his situating of being and truth in the future renders the present world a shadow, every bit as illusory as Plato's sensible world, nothing but a fleeting symbol of the arch-type. Or one might see the purging of all permanence in favor of becoming as opening the door to nominalism or skepticism. And some might protest that to outlaw all Hellenic and Scholastic categories is to place severe restrictions on the theologian's choice of philosophical apparatus.

There is, however, a more fundamental issue at stake here. Baltazar's approach, it seems, is a manifestation of what may be called Heidegger's new-era syndrome, a radical simplifying and compacting of previous philosophical approaches developed to articulate the divine-human relationship. All are considered simple variations of the one very defective way of viewing knowledge, action, reality; defective because tied to the dichotomizing of subject and object, self and world.[47] A strong contrast is mapped out between preceding theories and one's own favored view of God and creatures. One's own conception is then announced as the radical principle of a new way of perceiving God and humanity. Critical alternatives are bruskly relegated to the junkyard for abandoned frameworks of the past. This strategy may awe some. But it will not sit well with critical thought. Plural traditions in philosophical and theological thought are done violence, as is the

[45]Transcendental Thomists, e.g., are hardly defenders of conceptualism nor representatives of the stark correspondence or spectator theories of knowledge attacked by Baltazar and Dewart. Nor in this was Thomas a "Thomist." But it should be noted that Dewart is unable to accept even the transcendental Thomist approach to knowledge. Cf. *The Foundations of Belief*, 499–522.

[46]Baltazar's view is colored by a naive optimism about the evolutionary line, history, human insecurity, and humanity's capacity to cope with it. Dewart and Fontinell share the same over-sanguine view of "man-come-of-age," which was common fare in the sixties. Too many sobering experiences count against this roseate vision. A more dialectical approach is needed.

[47]Baltazar read dichotomies into the tradition, e.g., matter as opposed to spirit. Cf. other examples in note 44 above.

painful analysis issuing in careful distinctions that feed the life-blood of thought. The new-era strategy distorts rather than enhances the fabric of philosophical and theological thought.

On the other hand, evolutionary theism proves attractive because it more adequately relates to contemporary experience and scientific endeavors. Process theism provides the believer with a felicitous elucidation of the gospel data and a medium for harmonizing religious and scientific explanations of our world. But evolutionary theism at the time of Baltazar's writing was in the midst of hard reflection upon methodology and theory formation so as to be able to lay bare the precise nature and limits of the coincidence of belief and evolutionary thinking along with the epistemological nature of general assertions of purpose in the evolutionary process. Philosophers, in other words, have been striving to uncover the logical theory and implications of biological and cultural evolution to which Baltazar's and Fontinell's theological views on the divine immanence in an evolving universe were definitely linked. The complexity of the philosophical labor to grasp the logic of evolution ought to communicate itself to the insistence that we correlate the meaning and immanence of the gracing of God with evolutionary theory. Some distance will have to be covered before such a correlation becomes fully functional theologically. And a theistic evolutionary reading of reality must undergo the discomfort of questioning before it becomes fully viable and achieves the significance we hope it will have for theology in an evolutionary and history-minded era.

The question, then, is whether the divine-human relation can be provided with a meaningful philosophical rendering other than that proposed by the process group. The question is not answered by an appeal to nominal biblical corroborations, nor by pointing to something accepted or suggested by evolutionary sciences. It can only be answered by further metaphysical analysis of process theism.[48] To become philosophically more viable, as we trust it will, process theism must, therefore, relate its propositions to pertinent alternative explorations. For example, is the assertion of an overarching purpose operative in the evolutionary line some-

---

[48]Theology can never free itself of metaphysics. Nor are all metaphysical schemes equally apt for articulating Christian faith. Any metaphysics must meet the criteria of appropriateness to the tradition and adequacy to experience. Moreover, a hazardous game is played in posing to the scriptures questions inconceivable to their authors and communities in an attempt to justify one's metaphysics.

thing more than a faith projection or extrapolation?[49] Does it function well in conceiving transitions from energy to life to culture, but only confuse when cast as *the* ontological key to the heart of reality? Is the meaning of evolutionary purposiveness purely hermeneutical or ontological as well? So much for Baltazar's general philosophical orientation. A detailed analysis of his processive view in all its postures and skirmishes with Scholasticism would take us too far afield.[50]

Turning now to Baltazar's attempt to restate the nature-grace coordinates, we ought first to note that it has much to recommend it. His aim is to reconcile immanence and transcendence in the context of an evolving universe and thereby render the supernatural relevant, immanent, central, and "natural" to our world; to place the supernatural at the heart of existence and thereby render it necessary to anyone who is to be truly human. The general realigning of nature-grace as person-grace was certainly necessary, though hardly a novelty among contemporary theologians. Baltazar might want to claim they are moving beyond their framework; nevertheless the personalistic bent is felt in Rahner, von Balthasar, Schillebeeckx, and especially Alfaro.[51] Baltazar's concentration on the concrete, existential, historical order with his stress on the primacy of the incarnation and grace as starting points is also laudable, but again, hardly revolutionary. At least since the writing of de Lubac some twenty years earlier, the main line of Catholic theology, as we have been seeing, asserted as much.[52] Contemporary Catholic theology did not see existing alongside the order of grace an order of creation that is distinct, independent, autonomous, self-intelligible, and capable of attaining its natural end by its own powers. To this extent, Baltazar's cry of protest against those who affirm the primacy of creation and make of the incarnation a divine afterthought was

[49]Cf. Baltazar's own brief remarks on this question in *Teilhard and the Supernatural*, 97-100.

[50]On the issue of dehellenization in the sixties, cf. J. Verbaar in *The Future of Belief Debate*. Verbaar shows that only someone innocent of history would trace Scholasticism back to Aristotle.

[51]Cf. chapters 4 and 6.

[52]Baltazar appears to misread Rahner. See e.g., *Teilhard and the Supernatural*, 293-297. Rahner's technical theology of nature and grace makes complete sense only when situated within his global theological vision. Cf. W. Shepherd, *Man's Condition*, 183-189.

largely in chorus.[53] The real value and the attractiveness of Baltazar's presentation lay in its dynamic, evolutionary perspective and in its effort to fit non-human reality into the creation-grace dialectic. In an age very conscious of the dynamism of history and evolution and questing for the unification of the religious and the secular, no theology of grace can afford to overlook a consideration of its cosmic implications, or cling to the static perspective rightly criticized by Baltazar. Again, the theme is not new but it had lain fallow.[54]

With regard to the specific problem of gratuity, Baltazar felt that having negotiated a transition from substance to process, he had liberated it from the antiquated worldview that only aggravated the problem by creating the phantom of exigence. However, Baltazar's application of process philosophy to the problem is marked by ambiguity. His notion of gratuity as the free bestowal of a truly significant gift is wholly acceptable. And his attempt to make meaningful the immanence of grace by affirming that persons are intrinsically ordered to it as essential and even constitutive of their being fully human is likewise acceptable. It is also the contention of Rahner and von Balthasar that historical humanity is unintelligible without grace; humanity needs it and is intrinsically ordered to it. Nonetheless, Baltazar's labor seems flawed from a Rahnerian perspective in its failure to distinguish humanity as such and historical humanity. His affirmations concerning ordination to and constitution by grace are true of historical humanity, but not, perhaps, of humanity as such. In this regard Dewart provides a precision not had in Baltazar's presentation; Dewart tells us that nature is historically, not metaphysically related to grace. If Scripture seems to confirm Baltazar's stance, it is because Scripture, obviously unconcerned with a theological formulation of gratuity, focuses only on historical humanity.

Nor does Baltazar's transposition from nature to person eliminate the problem. For Rahnerians, the absence of the distinction

[53]For a brief but accurate account of how the incarnation and creation were historically related in Catholic theology, cf., H. Küng, *Justification: The Doctrine of Karl Barth and a Catholic Reflection* (New York: T. Nelson, 1964), 123–147.

[54]The perspectives of Paul and Irenaeus are as relevant as ever. Cf. J. Sittler, "Nature and Grace: Reflections on an Old Rubric," *Dialog* 3(1964) 252–256 and K. Rahner's essays "History of the World and Salvation History," and "Christology Within an Evolutionary View of the World," both in *Theological Investigations*, V, 97–114 and 157–192.

mentioned above, coupled with the repeated affirmation that grace is constitutive of personhood, despite Baltazar's stress that the person is by nature open and incomplete of itself, turns de Lubac's "monstre de l'exigence" loose to haunt us once again. The possibility of a world order other than we have is, no doubt, a marginal theorem relative to the existing order; but the theorem is necessary, according to Rahnerians, to do *full* justice to the transcendence of grace and the double gratuity at stake.[55] The human being as person is structured for personal union. This, however, does not necessarily imply that the union must be with the tri-Personal God as such. It does not mean that God, in addition to giving the creature to itself, must give Godself to the creature, that God *must* make the "offer of a new, additional level of existence."[56] That, however, seems to be the thrust of Baltazar's thinking, given his understanding that all being is being-to-another. In this connection Baltazar informs us that the premise of *Humani Generis* "is that God starts with creation first as an act in and for itself, intelligible apart from the incarnation and grace" and that "given this set-up . . . God must be able to create intelligent creatures without ordering them to the beatific vision." It seems, more precisely, that the premise is simply that a wholly other kind of world plan is possible.

Baltazar's strenuous effort to skirt the metaphysical dualism inherited from the past, then, will not seem sufficiently nuanced to some.[57] Yet a charge of pantheistic reduction would be unwarranted.[58] Union, as Baltazar tells us, citing Teilhard, does differen-

---

[55]Dewart presents this double gratuity well. Cf. his "God and the Supernatural." Baltazar is preoccupied with the unity of the present order and is blind to the double gratuity.

[56]Ibid., 527.

[57]Baltazar's statements that grace is constitutive of human being are never sufficiently honed as they are in Rahner. Cf., e.g. *Hominisation: The Evolutionary Origin of Man as a Theological Problem* (New York: Herder & Herder, 1965) 77–78. For Rahner God is an integral element of all secondary causation without, however, "forming an intrinsic component of the finite being as such." Were God an intrinsic component of human being, there could be no true transcendence, for humanity would already be in itself all there is to be. Cf. also W. Shepherd, *Man's Condition*, 166–176.

[58]However, ill-considered statements such as "We believe it is not necessary to have a remainder concept of nature in order to safeguard gratuity if we start with the incarnation as the principle reality" (*Teilhard and the Supernatural*, 293, 300), are at best ambiguous and at worst destructive of any distinction between nature and grace. If all is grace, then nothing is. Dualism is to be rejected but not the duality of the saving God and the graced human. Moreover, Baltazar seems to confuse a remainder concept of nature with a pure nature that is self-sufficient to achieve its natural end (ibid.,

tiate.[59] (This, as de Lubac pointed out, is in the best Scholastic tradition.) But Baltazar's desire to redress our sins against immanence seems to blind him to the distance intervening between the Creator-Savior and the saved creature. Then too, in Baltazar's world of process where grace is related to person, it seems we must somehow attribute greater permanency to the subject than he seems willing to allow. Otherwise there is no abiding other related to God and the process itself seems ultimately evacuated of meaning. Existence may be a process of sharedness and to-anotherness. But "the principle of union is unity."[60] It is not easy to see, therefore, what prevents Baltazar's position from deterioration at times into a superficial historicism.

The ambiguity does not stop here. Baltazar is certainly correct in emphasizing that there is but one order; that presently there is no supernatural order juxtaposed to a self-sufficient order of natural reality. But we have also seen Rahner, von Balthasar, and Schillebeeckx maintain that grace is so pervasive it is well-nigh impossible to clearly delineate what in the human phenomenon pertains to the sphere of grace and what to the sphere of nature. Dewart does too. Now Baltazar also emphasizes that where there is one order there is but one process with one term, one omega. In the present order of grace the end-all and be-all of creation is union with God. There is no quarrel here. But all this leads Baltazar, unlike the others, to a kind of undifferentiated consciousness that demolishes any distinction between science, philosophy, and religion, between the sacred and the profane.[61] Quite legitimately he wants to elaborate Teilhard's vision of the phenomenon of humanity as including all lesser phenomena. We might ask however, whether Teilhard would have any appetite for an omelet which indiscriminately blends science, faith, philosophy, and theology. Teilhard did not dissociate or dichotomize, but he did distinguish. Distinction is not divorce nor return to a double-tiered world.[62] Failure to distinguish is reversion to a

293). The latter construct he labels "Thomist" even though historical study hardly attributes it to Thomas.

[59]Ibid., 127.

[60]This was an accepted axiom of the schools. Cf. Thomas Aquinas, *ST*, II–II, 26,4c. If nature was portrayed as autonomous and self-sufficient, it was not to affirm that it has no need of the other, but that the person had the wherewithal for development through personal union. Cf. J. Alfaro, "Persona y gracia," 8, note 7.

[61]*Teilhard and the Supernatural*, 326–329.

[62]H. de Lubac, *The Religion of Teilhard de Chardin* (New York: Desclée, 1967), Chapter 11.

primitive consciousness that in failing to do justice to the autonomy of the orders of reality has too often worked havoc in the
history of Christianity. Many of Baltazar's questions in this area
are legitimate. They have been posed before. But his own presentation does not elucidate them.

We might sum up in this way. The Scholasticism berated by
Baltazar is a primitive and decadent brand. The Baltazarian
process philosophy constructed to replace it is quite different and
insightful to be sure. But in the end, Baltazar's approach, purged
of its confusion, does not seem, at least where the nature-grace
problem is concerned, so radically different from what many of
his peers working within and without the old framework were
proposing. Baltazar is close to Rahner in his view that grace and
creation are related as the contingently-is and the hypothetically-
necessary; that humanity is ontologically oriented to grace; that
this orientation is constitutive of humanity and a condition sine
qua non for true gratuity.[63] Baltazar's theology to this extent seems
separable from his philosophy. No one may rule a healthy pluralism out of today's theology. There is room for a number of theologies, each with its own philosophical underpinning. The
contrast between Baltazar and the other theologians reviewed by
us is a case in point. But our verdict must be that Baltazar's bold
pioneering, and welcome application of process thought to the
supernatural, leaves us with many questions.[64]

Baltazar provides a fine propaedeutic to a new formulation of
the problem. We are told that humanity is intrinsically ordered
to the covenant and that grace is constitutive for it; that God is
not bound to bestow covenant love, nor can humanity demand
or attain it by its own power. This core reasserts the immanence
and transcendence of grace. Baltazar's process thought has not
provided us with more light than his predecessors, neither has it
given us less. Indeed, some will judge that he has added to the

[63]We might add that W. Shepherd, who took Rahner's entire theology to be a theology
of nature and grace, asserts that Rahner "better than anyone else, has carefully worked
out the metaphysical and theological complexities of the relationship of God to man
on the basis of an evolutionary and unified view of the world process." *Man's Condition*, 24. See also 51, 97, 121, 194–199, 232–233. Process thinkers, with some justification, today find this an exaggeration, to say the least. See the critique of Rahner
in Chapter 8.

[64]Since Baltazar's writing, process theology has come more and more into its own.
The literature is voluminous. In the forefront of this mainly American development
have been Charles Hartshorne, John Cobb, Schubert Ogden, and David Griffin.

confusion. Yet we must admit that his introduction of process thought as a framework for dealing with this problem was a bold move that augured well for those to follow. Process thought was to be espoused by a growing number of Catholic thinkers.

8

The Graced Horizon:
The Gratuity and Universality of Grace

In the preceding chapters we have mapped out a typology of approaches to the systematic problem of nature and grace. Our immediate purpose was to expose in their similarity and dissimilarity the array of alternatives that appeared on the Catholic theological scene in the two decades following *Surnaturel*. The theologians treated were truly representative. They typify the most significant approaches to this thorny issue in the last four decades. Moreover, the lack of total agreement among them affords a contrast that is illuminating. As a group they are something of a period piece, for their work is a reflection of the theological revival Catholicism came to know beginning in the pre-World War II period and culminating in Vatican II and its immediate aftermath.

Our further purpose in laying out a variety of theories was to test our modest hypothesis that, while various theologians spoke of gratuity in their own way, nonetheless, the general approach to the gratuity of grace underwent a change. Our exposition of and reflection upon the views of those theologians who were the focus of our investigation does seem to bear out the hypothesis. Let us state more explicitly why this is so, and in so doing sum up our investigation to this point.

I. *A Changed Perspective on Gratuity*

A noticeable shift in emphases came to characterize the post counter-Reformation Catholic theology of nature and grace. Aware of the past ravages of extrinsicism, theologians took an approach to the relationship of nature and grace that is much more historical, and personalistic. Since humanity exists for grace, the incarnation and the call of all to union with God in Christ are now the points of departure rather than an abstract notion of human nature. God's gracing encompasses all else. Creation stands in function of grace, for the grace of Christ conditions human possibility.

Two things follow in the wake of awarding primacy to grace. There is a tendency to stress humanity's total historical situation rather than dispositive additions to or modifications of human being as a result of its vocation to union with the Trinitarian God. In other words, interest turns from humanity as it is in itself to what it can freely become. This broadened historical perspective, focusing on the totality of the human situation, gives fuller play to the social dimensions of grace and militates against the narrow individualistic concerns of the past. In view of this changed perspective a more personalistic tonality is injected into the problematic. The nature-grace pairing yields to a grace-person pairing. Naturalizing tendencies are eschewed. For this reason these theologians, more successfully than their predecessors, eluded the nemesis of "natural desire" and "exigency."

Given the focus on the concrete, historical order with grace as the starting point, concern with what-could-have-been is relegated to a secondary position. The possibility of pure nature, which had been inflated almost to actuality, becomes a marginal theorem. Notions of pure nature or of humanity-as-such have their heuristic value, but they no longer serve as basic building blocks in the theology of graced humanity. The gratuity of grace thus comes to be interpreted not in terms of a pure, ungraced being, but in terms of existing graced creatures. The possibility of other world orders may heighten the intelligibility of gratuity. The argumentation, however, no longer moves from that possibility to graced actuality. Rather, the possible is known only through the real. The real occupies center stage with other possibilities cast in secondary and supporting roles. As Lonergan noted in the heat of the controversy over *Surnaturel*, the crucial issue had become a test of strength between the static formalism of a closed conceptualistic and essentialistic approach and the more dynamic openness of the intellectualist and existential tendency. That issue was resolved in favor of the latter.

So it is that recent theology has been better able to articulate the immanence of grace without collapsing the distinction between nature and grace. But nature and grace are not at all dualistically understood as two autonomous, self-sufficient, and self-intelligible orders thrown by an intruding God into a co-existence that only highlights their discontinuity and opposition. A concerted effort has been made to purge Christian understanding of the dualism that marked the past.[1] Humanity came to be viewed as unintelligible apart from Christ and his grace. Creation finds meaning only in Christ. From the outset God wills Self-communication in Christ. There is no question of sin forfeiting grace and thereby moving God to *then* send the Christ to restore humanity to its original condition. Humanity has been the hypothetically necessary element enclosed in God's incarnational plan from the start. There is then a true sense in which grace is constitutive of humanity. There is more to humanity than nature. Elevation to the supernatural and an absolute and unconditional ordination to the full life of grace are components of creation. This in no way stands against the gratuity of grace. They are components because creation is as it is. And gratuity covers God's structuring of reality as we find it. That God decided to create in order to be other than Godself and thereby share the divine inner life, and structured humanity accordingly, renders grace and the creature's ordination to it no less gratuitous. Grace continues to be, more so than creation, unmerited, unowed.

Moreover, so far reaching is the permeation of grace on all levels of existence that the "natural" never comes to be siphoned off and the two experienced in their own pure reality. The "natural" is patient of no easy circumscription and is best considered a conceptual and theological residual. Grace, on the other hand, is experienced in all the love and labor, all the joy and misery that characterize the human condition. Nature and grace may be thematically distinct, but in lived experience lines of demarcation are not easily drawn.

In this context, then, grace is seen as gratuitous relative to historical humanity, not to some possible being. Gratuity does not reside in the fact that grace is the conferral of a new and higher nature upon a human nature already complete and autonomous in itself. The sad irony in such an understanding, as we have seen, is that it jeopardizes the gratuity it claims to protect. For it fails

---

[1]To avoid the dualism and formalism of the post-Tridentine era, theology today eschews the centuries old terminology of "natural" and "supernatural." Biblical and patristic categories such as "new creation," "covenant," and "life," "love," "filiation," etc. have come to be preferred.

to do complete justice to the unique quality of grace. Rather, grace is itself the completion of humanity's incomplete being, far exceeding whatever relative fulfillment it could fashion for itself. Only if graced does humanity become and remain truly human. Theologians explain in different but complementary ways the transcendence of grace. For some it is the immediacy of the knowledge-love relationship that God calls humans to. God's Self-donation signifies that God sees more in human beings than creatures or servants, and has turned to them in a love surpassing that of creation, in which the creature is given to itself. As de Lubac insisted, the Self-gift of the divine Persons can never be in response to an exigency in humans. Some, like Alfaro, place the transcendence of grace in its personalizing impact. Grace introduces the human person into a set of personal ties proper only to the three divine Thou's that leads to a personal self-actualization totally transcending that achieved on a merely creaturely level. Still others, like Schillebeeckx, emphasize that grace is God's divinizing offer of Godself in Christ, coupled with the offer of the very possibility of the free, personal acceptance that must greet this offer.

In every case gratuity is related not to some hypothetical being, but to historical humanity. Although in any hypothesis the gracing activity of God remains free and unexacted, concern is with the actual order of things, with the fact that even in this present economy God owes it neither to Godself nor to humanity that God's Trinitarian life be shared. Even though humanity's being graced is simultaneous with its coming into being, the gratuity of grace is retained. Created personhood in no way exacts grace from God. On the other hand, God cannot be said to be meeting God's own demands upon Godself in ordering humanity to grace, even though God does so in granting grace and glory once it is decreed that humanity be so ordered. Ultimately grace is never in any way owed by God nor won by humans. To say that God owes grace reduces to the fact that God has freely decided to be present and engaged with humans and their world. One cannot overestimate the debt owed to Henri de Lubac in this regard. He it was who stressed the wholly hypothetical character of pure nature and its inability to do full justice to gratuity and immanence because it totally prescinds from the concrete, historically situated being of humanity. We must consider how this changed perspective on gratuity has had an impact on the theological formulation of the supernaturality of grace.

II. *Negative and Positive Formulations of Gratuity*

In the past the notion of the supernatural typically evolved through two phases or moments. The first furnished a definition of the supernatural as that which transcends the capacities and exigencies of all created natures and even of natures that could be created. The supernatural is neither a constitutive nor a derivative of any nature; nor can it be exacted by nature. Summarily, it is that which is unowed to nature, a superadded gratuitous gift; *donum naturae indebitum et superadditum*. Having drawn this definition, attention was given to the reality of the gift itself. In this second phase the definition of the supernatural was more positive and concrete, whereas in the first it was negative and abstract. Ordinarily, the supernatural gift bestowed was defined as a here and now sharing in the divine life meant to reach maturation in the intuitive vision of God. For some the focal point was the beatific vision, which, together with the means necessary for its attainment, the light of glory, sanctifying grace, the virtues and gifts, actual graces, and revelation, formed the heart of the supernatural. Others refused to consider grace, which makes one the child of God, merely as a means to vision. For them grace was already the beginning of eternal life. In this view, divine adoption, making one heir to the divine Parent, was the central element in the notion of the supernatural. Only subsequently are grace and the virtues considered as conditions necessary for salutary action.[2]

There is validity to both these formulations, the negative and the positive. But do they not labor under the grave deficiency of failure to say all that needs saying? To begin with, the positive formulation usually assumed a secondary position. Before introducing the notion of participation in the divine life, a wholly formal and abstract gratuity preceded. And it focused on the essential structure of human nature as totally divorced from any historical context or world process. This was dictated by a concern to eliminate from the outset any vestiges of Baianism, which claimed that the endowment of original justice was due to the first parents in their condition of innocence. But there is a drawback in placing the negative formula first. Surely, in the framing of

---

[2]Examples of this approach to the supernatural are found in the manuals in use prior to Vatican II. See e.g., D. Palmieri, *Tractatus de Deo Creante et Elevante* (Roma: S. Cong. de Prop. Fide, 1878), 272–405; C. Pesch, *Praelectiones Dogmaticae*, II (Frieburg: Herder, 1895), 76–79; G. Van Noort, *Tractatus de Deo Creatore* (Amsterdam: C. Van Langenhuysen, 1912), 48–60; I. Sagues, *Sacrae Theologiae Summa*, II (Madrid: Bib. Auct. Cristianos, 1952), 736–742.

definitions it is legitimate sometimes to begin with a purely formal and abstract idea, one emptied of all concreteness. To communicate its true meaning and relevance, however, the formal idea must at least carry within it the seeds of that meaning. In the present instance such does not seem to be the case. For one can speak abstractly of a perfection that transcends the exigencies of a nature without stating precisely *how* that transcendence is a perfection and how it is truly significant for this particular being. Thus the negative formulation speaks abstractly of a gift considered valuable by reason of its gratuity, but in no way tells us *how* and *why* precisely this gratuitous gift should be of significance to the entity in question. Gratuity, as Baltazar noted, is meaningful only when it is the quality of a gift that corresponds to a need or a directedness in the beneficiary. But the definitions of gratuity and supernaturality deriving from the negative propositions were so abstract and so far removed from being deduced from the inherent logic of any concrete reality that one may wonder whether the formulae hold anything more than a purely nominal and grammatical sense. The real gratuity of grace is not expressed in such a negative formulation, especially when it is isolated from a positive formula which touches upon the unique quality and meaning of grace. It was these shortcomings that lay behind von Balthasar's difficulties with the negative formulation.

Nor can we overlook a further drawback in granting priority to the negative formulation. The impression is given that nature enjoys a temporal priority over grace. Most theologians intended only to assert a logical priority or a priority of hypothetical necessity. But the weakness of syntax and the strength of their emphasis on the abstract resulted in a failure to translate their intentions. Nature was portrayed as endowed with a conditional openness or obediential potency, humbly awaiting the call to grace. There is humanity, and *then* there is graced humanity due to a new, free decision by God, Who, for one reason or other, decreed an additional perfection for creatures. The meaningfulness and utility of such a portrayal is nil when all readily contend that never was there a time when humanity existed outside the order of grace.

On the other hand, the fullest understanding of gratuity, it is claimed by some, must recognize that a myriad of world orders is enveloped in the divine creative virtuosity. This was the basic assertion of the *Humani Generis*. Refusal to allow the possibility of other options diverse from the actual order, at least from our perspective, is considered a gratuitous theological assertion. This in no way implies, as the extrinsicism of the past could have led one to believe, that God could refuse to grace the present order. Nor does it imply that the present creation is neutral toward being graced, so that its graced condition demands a second divine decree of elevation in addition to creation.[3] A double gratuity so ambiguously put could only create the mistaken notion of two temporally separated divine actions and a dualistic extrinsicism with all its disastrous practical consequences.

The possibility of diverse world orders, then, is relevant, but only indirectly, to the structure and gratuity of the actual order. God could, according to some, have created an ungraced order to which God would not communicate Godself. That its creation would derive from but one creative act does not mean the present order derives from a double divine action. As noted earlier, the complex prodigality of created effects is not the measure of divine action. A more complex order requires no more divine actions than a less complicated one.[4] The divine largesse is not poured out piecemeal in successive increments, but through the evolutive unfolding of the one indivisible decision in which God commits Godself to humanity.

It would seem, then, that to arrive at the proper significance of gratuity, one must develop it by a consideration of concrete nature and its intrinsic orientation and intentionality. Historical humanity should be the starting point. In fact, concrete humanity has been the concern of recent Catholic theology. Its attention is given, not to pure nature, but to historical humanity as spirit endowed with freedom and self-transcendence. Yet this alone, on closer analysis, would not yield a notion of the special gratuity in question. Even with historical humanity as the beginning point one does not arrive at a notion of gratuity proper to the Trinitarian Self-gift, but at most at the gratuity of the creative action.

---

[3]The impression was often given that the postlapsarian human condition had reverted to a state of pure nature. In this perspective the incarnation became a divine afterthought which allowed for the re-elevation of humans.

[4]In general, it seems safe to say that in the period we have studied most Catholic theologians who took up the question did not want to go so far as de Lubac seemed to go in claiming that humanity in another order would be essentially other than it is now, that it would not be humanity at all. This opposition does not imply that in a graceless world humanity would be exactly as it is. God's commitment to Self-communication constitutes the special character of this order. Without it, any other created order that might exist would be, it seems, different. Today there is probably a growing number who would plead a reverent agnosticism about all such speculation or who would consider a graceless world impossible. See section IV below.

The Christian notion of the supernatural and its special gratuity is not explicitly grasped unless the total historical situation is recognized for what it is. Gratuity, therefore, is best understood in light of the historicity of the incarnation and the divine summons to share the divine life.

This explains recent theology's effort not only to modify the formulations of the past, but to change their usual order as well. The formulation of Rahner and Vorgrimler in their *Theological Dictionary* reflects this shift in perspective and formulation and better respects the thought sequence that provides a more meaningful understanding of gratuity. Accordingly, "the supernatural in the strictest sense is that which, insofar as it is a participation in the Spirit and life of God (2 Pet 1:4), transcends the powers and exigencies of any created spiritual nature (to the extent that these powers and exigencies are necessarily given with such a nature): grace and the beatific vision."[5] Even within the context of an anti-Baian or anti-reductionist polemic, this formulation seems more adequate.

Note that the matter does not rest with an inversion of the customary propositions defining gratuity. The formulations themselves needed sharpening. Hence the statement of Rahner and Vorgrimler is not content simply to say that participation in the divine life surpasses the claims and capacities of creaturely nature, but that it exceeds those of any created spiritual being (*Geistnatur*). And even greater precision is added when the formulation continues: "it is a free gift of God in Jesus Christ, even prescinding from the need of pardon for our sins." Brief as it may be, it embodies those refinements resulting from the reconsideration of the nature-grace problematic that were among theology's chief concerns between 1946 and 1966. As such it more adequately frames the understanding of gratuity and retrieves the pre-counter-Reformation insights of Aquinas.[6]

As a result of the renaissance in Scripture, patristic, and medieval studies, there was also a greater awareness that too often in the past the Christological character of grace, both in its inherent character and in its mediation, had been ignored and at

---

[5]K. Rahner and H. Vorgrimler, "Supernatural," *Dictionary of Theology*, 2nd ed. (New York: Crossroad, 1985), 490–491.

[6]On Aquinas and the supernatural, cf. H. Rondet, *The Grace of Christ: A Brief History of the Theology of Grace* (Westminster: Newman, 1967), ch. 12 and R. Haight, *The Experience and Language of Grace* (New York: Paulist, 1979), ch. 3.

best poorly and at worst not at all integrated into the notion of gratuity. If theological propositions were to faithfully embody the content of the Christian message, they had to restore to their due place the historical elements of its primitive tradition so often lost in the formalism and abstraction of post-Tridentine theology. That humanity is saved by faith in Christ and called to share in the life of God through union with Christ, this is the Christian tradition. If the supernatural was, as the heart of Christianity, to resume its rightful place for the believer, these concrete elements had to be factored into the propositions attempting to frame its reality.

In connection with the appeal to the concrete, historical situation of humanity, the lag between what humanity is and what it can and must become, between its being and its perfection, and the need for personal decision in this context, permit us to distinguish and unite the natural and the supernatural.[7] A human being, the *imago Dei*, called to the *similitudo Dei*, is constituted by a relation to its source. Not only participation in the divine life, but one's very existence is the gift of God. Herein lies the double gratuity. Divinization by grace is marked off from creation because it is a transformation that, unlike creation, calls for total conversion in response to the saving God. And yet without that conversion one remains God's creature, the *imago* called forever to become the *similitudo*. The abiding, real possibility of entering the Trinitarian existence as *similitudo Dei* through a free conversion is what moves some to distinguish in humans a compound gratuity. If the real possibility of transfiguration into the *similitudo Dei* is an endowment over and above being the *imago Dei*, it is because its actualization is contingent upon free conversion which implies a before and after, and which itself knows the Self-manifestation of God as the condition of its possibility. What affords ground for distinction likewise provides ground for unification. As *imago Dei* one must freely become the *similitudo Dei* to which one has been interiorly destined in order to realize oneself fully. Failure to become the *similitudo Dei* is the negation of personal being, the abortion of humanization. This again points up the need to refine our formulations by recognizing that the subject of graced existence is the person as a free spirit, capable

---

[7]What follows should not be taken to imply that nature enjoys a temporal priority over grace. The Christian indicative precedes the Christian imperative. More will be said on this below in the epilogue.

of conversion. Simply to say that the supernatural is not due to created nature does not suffice to indicate what distinguishes the gift of grace from the gift of nature and colors the former with its own special gratuity. Strictly speaking, one does not freely receive or accept existence. But one does, and must, freely receive and accept grace. The supernatural must be theologized over against the spirit created in freedom and transcendence.[8]

Further concretization, therefore, was achieved in redefining the gratuity of the supernatural by an appeal to the crucial, historical mediation of Christ. It is in and through Christ that God communicates life and it is only through the option of faith in Christ that this life becomes a vital reality for any individual.[9] Justification, a new creation, filial adoption, the gift of Spirit, resurrection, all are claimed to be mediated through the life, death, and resurrection of Jesus. The destiny of the Christian is to reproduce in his or her existence the image of Christ. It is in Christ that all things find their source and goal, cosmologically and soteriologically. This Christological emphasis gives the "supernatural order" a much less abstract quality. Precisely this type of emphasis was wanting in the more abstract treatments of the post-Tridentine centuries.[10]

The supernatural, according to the renewed theology, is the communication of Godself to humanity in and through the Word become man. It is humanity sharing in the divine life through the mediation of Christ. And the supernatural order is that directedness and meaning given to human life and history through the coming of Christ as the presence of God in the world. This perspective more clearly delineates what the classical negative formulation of gratuity (*donum naturae indebitum et superadditum*)

---

[8]Cf. Aquinas, *ST*, I-II, 5, 5, ad. 1.

[9]This has been a basic Christian confessional claim. Of late it has come under increasing qualification and in some cases denial. There is a growing body of literature on the question of the uniqueness and normativeness of Jesus Christ. For a good survey of opinions that puts forth a thesis of its own, cf. P. Knitter, *No Other Name: A Critical Survey of Christian Attitudes toward the World Religions* (Maryknoll: Orbis, 1985).

[10]This silence is partially explained by the fact that questions "De ordine supernaturali" were treated before the incarnation and redemption. A *Loci* approach to theology did not promote a synthetic theological overview in which a more Christological approach to grace could be developed. Grace was conceived metaphysically as the divinization of nature but little was said (apart from the mystics) of grace as assimilation to Christ. Cf. K. Rahner, "Current Problems in Christology," in *Theological Investigations*, I, 149-200 and "The Eternal Significance of the Humanity of Jesus for Our Relationship with God," in *Theological Investigations*, III, 35-46.

struggled to assert with little success. The formulae are concretized now by the introduction of Christ's mediation and the human option of faith (explicit or implicit) in Christ. The gratuity of God's Self-donation now becomes linked to the historicity of two contingencies: the appearance of Christ and the faith commitment of individuals. The terms "supernatural" and "super-added," disagreeable as they are to modern ears, would achieve, it was hoped, a certain meaningfulness in that they designate the contingent newness that is the historical fact of Jesus Christ and the humanity recreated in him through faith. It is only in this historical perspective that the notions of supernaturality and gratuity could avoid becoming mere abstractions and achieve concreteness and universality. Perhaps, too, it is in this way that new light is shed upon the age-old problem of the natural desire for the supernatural. Such a desire is probably recognized for what it is only in the process of a conversion entailing death to self and the option of belief. Then it is recognized that this orientation may be ignored, but never erased. It serves to affirm the correspondence between the inner logic of human existence and of Christian history. Extracted from the historical and personalistic context envisioned here, natural desire for the supernatural, as noted before, through its appeal to the "naturalness" of the desire, tended to underestimate the weight and importance of a free faith-decision.

Having viewed the nature-grace unity in terms of the Irenaean notion of the human person as *imago* and *similitudo* Dei, which stresses the Christian imperative, the need for a subjective acceptance of grace, we must now consider the Christian indicative, or the objective fact of the presence of grace prior to any free act on the part of the person.

III. *Karl Rahner's Graced Horizon*

We turn again to Rahner's theory of the supernatural existential. In the theory of the existential we have the single most significant Catholic contribution to an understanding of the nature-grace dialectic in the twentieth century. The existential, however, has not always been clearly understood. This accounts for some of the disagreement it has occasioned. A profound theological theory that forms the heart of a coherent theological synthesis is often reduced to a slogan. A clear understanding of Rahner's existential moves us closer to a better integration of nature and grace and a more meaningful approach to gratuity. Perhaps, too, a deepened understanding of the Rahnerian position will lead us to conclude that those objecting to it may not be as divergent from Rahner as first appears.[11]

Rahner's supernatural existential did not derive simply from his desire to resolve the dilemma created by the controversy surrounding *Surnaturel*. It is more correct to see it as growing out of his early work on the metaphysics of knowledge and forming a central element in his global theological vision which had been in the making since the writing of *Geist in Welt*.[12] Only within this framework can it be adequately understood and related to the perennial and technical nature-grace problematic.

Rahner's metaphysics of knowledge aimed at showing how one actually knows and what the ontological conditions for knowing are.[13] He wanted to elucidate the process involved in knowing, not the fact that there are extra-mental realities. Rahner sees being itself as a participating constitutive element in all human cognitive and affective activity. To know a particular object is to know the total context in which it is situated. Since the knower's appetite for intelligibility, for understanding, is unlimited, the context within which one knows particulars must itself be infinite and unrestricted. However, being, which is co-known when finite ob-

---

[11]W. Shepherd, *Man's Condition*, 97–100, maintains, with some justification, that Rahner's theology is disjointed. On the one hand, Rahner treats the technical doctrine of nature and grace within a traditional post-Tridentine framework and on the other hand, constructs a synthesis that can only be termed a theology of nature and grace "within the context of a modern, non-static, unified, historical evolving view of the universe." Hence there is a clash of thought-styles within his theology. In Rahner's synthesis the relationship of nature to grace is not considered one isolated locus. Rather, the conceptual apparatus supporting the union of the two is the fundamental pattern undergirding his entire theological vision. Yet Rahner's technical treatment of the problem is in the fashion of the older loci theology. And his handling of it is in terms "drawn from the traditional, hierarchical, static, layered view of the world." There is much to be said for this thesis. As we shall see in the following section, there are some who think that the criticism does not go far enough and that Rahner's entire enterprise is flawed by an incapacity or unwillingness to break out of the classical mindset.

[12]The strength of Rahner's position is its foundation in a metaphysics. At the same time, it is its weakness for those of another, not to mention no acknowledged metaphysical persuasion.

[13]For good elaborations of Rahner's metaphysics of knowing, cf. J. Bacik, *Apologetics and the Eclipse of Mystery: Mystagogy According to Karl Rahner* (Notre Dame: University of Notre Dame, 1980), chs. 3 and 4; A. Tallon, *Personal Becoming* (Milwaukee: Marquette University, 1982), chs. 1 and 2; M. L. Taylor, *God is Love: A Study in the Theology of Karl Rahner* (Atlanta: Scholars Press, 1986), chs. 3–5. Above all, see T. Sheehan, *Karl Rahner: the Philosophical Foundations* (Athens: Ohio University, 1987).

jects are known, and which grounds both the objects of knowledge in the world and the subject's capacity to know them, cannot itself be objectified. Being-itself can only be characterized as an infinite, *a priori*, non-objectifiable horizon against which limited, finite, particular objects appear. The very possibility of cognitive life is founded in the subject's reaching out toward the unlimited horizon (*das Woraufhin*) or scope of being. This anticipatory thrusting (*der Vorgriff ad esse*) is included in every act of knowing. Being, the unlimited scope of all possible objects of knowledge, is itself grasped only in a preliminary, anticipatory, and non-objectified way in any particular cognitive act. In Rahner's theory the thrust toward being, the *Vorgriff*, one's reaching out beyond oneself and all particular objects, constitutes the subject's *a priori* cognitional structure. In it is rooted the knower's dynamic orientation to or longing for (*Begierde*) the world of possible objects. The orientation is actualized in each single instance of knowing. Being thus acts as the formal object toward which the intentionality of the knower is directed.[14]

Now the metaphysician may wish to designate this infinity of being, the formal object requisite in knowing and willing, as "God."[15] This would mean that being itself, God, is present in all successful instances of knowing as an unconceptualizable background, a participating factor. Thus God is the transcendental referent (*das Woraufhin*) of knowledge without becoming patient of objectification. But if one is to know more about being itself than simply that it is the condition for the possibility of human intellection and affectivity, there is need for a Self-revelation on the part of God. One cannot make a direct projection out of one's limited experience to an understanding of infinite being. The human spirit is, in Rahner's view, open to this fuller manifestation of being that it is asking about and striving for, and of which it already has an anticipatory awareness.

Rahner's metaphysical investigation thus defines the conditions of a possible revelation and shows that the human being is an obe-

---

[14]The influence of Maréchalian Thomism and the Heideggerian turn to the subject-in-the-world as the starting point of metaphysics is in evidence here. Employing the methodology of transcendental deduction, Rahner is concerned with how things stand empirically and the conditions grounding the possibility of things being the way they phenomenologically appear. More specifically, he is concerned with the dynamism responsible for humanity's insatiable quest for knowledge and the structure of human spirit-life.

[15]For a vindication of this identification, see J. Bacik, *Apologetics*, ch. 8. and M.L. Taylor, *God is Love*, 70–80.

diential potency for historical revelation, a spirit who must listen in history for the possible Self-manifestation of God in a human word.[16] In doing so Rahner has laid the foundations and structured a framework for his theological synthesis which is basically a theology of grace. In that synthesis he will repeatedly assert the constitutive presence of the Christian God to all simply in virtue of their cognitive and affective life. The already existing formal conditions of human knowing and loving will not be ignored in event of a Self-revelation by God. But this bond is not by itself a proof of God's existence nor an argument that revelation is required of God because of the nature of humankind. Should God have remained in silence, God would have been only the infinite horizon encompassing all knowing and questioning, the ultimate mystery that envelops all. It remains to be seen what the precise character of this directedness to the infinite *Woraufhin* of transcendence de facto is. Whether God be more than the *a priori* ground of spirit-life can find an answer only in revelation.[17]

At this point Rahner's notion of transcendental revelation links the notion of God acting as the horizon of knowing to that of God communicating Godself to humans in categorical or special revelation. The notion of transcendental revelation is a key to a fuller understanding of the supernatural existential. Categorical revelation makes the unlimited scope of being something more for the believer, permitting it now to be interpreted as the presence of God and the ground of Christian hope and love. The special or categorical (*Kategorical*) revelation that is Christ assures us that God is more than the metaphysical condition of the possibility of human knowing and loving. The "more" is a transformation of the unrestricted horizon of being. Even though transcendental revelation is understood and articulated fully only in the light of Christ, God's categorical or historical revelation, it must nonetheless be grasped as a real Self-communication of the Trinitarian God. What this amounts to is that God, whether one realizes it or not, as the transcendental *a priori* condition of human cognitive, affective, and conative activity, is actually the triune God revealed in the incarnate Word. The horizon of being never was nor will be, objectively speaking, nothing more than

---

[16]For the full exposition of this, see Rahner's *Hearers of the Word.*

[17]Unless the face of God is believed to be turned to humans in gracious Self-revelation, there can be no answer to the questions whether God exists and whether the horizon of infinite Being can be identified as God.

the metaphysical condition of human life as transcendent spirit. Hence transcendental revelation serves as the horizon of the human spirit and is itself grace.[18] In a circular movement categorical revelation makes transcendental revelation known for what it is and is the condition of its possibility while transcendental revelation is hypothetically necessary for the reception of categorical revelation.

Rahner will not reduce revelation to categorical revelation, embodied in the Jewish and Christian testaments. God's salvific will is universal, co-extensive with the totality of human life. Consequently, the order of grace knows a similar catholicity. All are offered grace. This Rahner explicates through his metaphysics of knowledge. Through the subject's *Vorgriff*, the drive toward self-transcendence through knowledge and love, the all-embracing horizon of being conditions all knowing and loving and is even constitutive in their realization. God as transcendental horizon is the quasi-formal cause and ultimate term (*Woraufhin*) of personal existence, known and chosen or rejected in every human act. Categorical revelation, however, brings awareness that the horizon encompassing all human life is the saving God. The universal and perduring offer of grace demanded by God's universal salvific will leads us now through categorical revelation to interpret the horizon of human activity not merely as being-itself but as God in the act of communicating Godself. Grace is now the quasi-formal cause of the human spirit. Thus the supernatural existential that marks historical humanity's situation is seen to be God's ever-present offer of God's own Self. So it is that grace, transcendental revelation, and supernatural existential express one and the same reality.[19] The supernatural existential refers to the abiding divine immanence in which God offers to humanity Godself and the possibility of the free response of faith.[20]

[18] "Because actual, concrete action is also a 'natural' knowledge of God, it is an ethical act; in the factual order of salvation it is 'elevated' by supernatural grace and is concretely also faith. Supernatural grace constitutes a transcendental horizon for freedom and knowledge which is, along with its willing acceptance, already a factor implying an unthematic, general (*transzendentalen*) revelation." K. Rahner, "Observations on the Doctrine of God in Catholic Dogmatics," in *Theological Investigations*, IX (New York: Herder & Herder, 1972), 140, note 14. See also K. Rahner and J. Ratzinger, *Revelation and Tradition* (New York: Herder & Herder, 1966), 13–15.

[19] Rahner is explicit on this identification. Cf. "History of the World and Salvation History," in *Theological Investigations*, V, 103–104.

[20] "Christianity and the non-Christian Religions," 124.

Since the mode of God's saving presence is as *Woraufhin* of transcendence but more than simply as the transcendental metaphysical condition for human activity, then concretely the horizon of historical humanity is divinizing grace as causal and participative in all cognition, volition, and action. The gracing of humanity is never purely forensic in Rahner's view. The graced human condition means that the triune God dwells in all and assumes an active role in the human situation. There is a convergence between the simultaneous agency of God and humans. The Trinitarian God as horizon, as quasi-formal cause, is not such simply for so-called "supernatural" acts, so that grace would have no effect upon a whole stream of so-called "natural" activities, which constitutes the bulk of human living. The Self-offering God Who incarnated divine love in Christ, must be the horizon, the quasi-formal cause of *all* human loving and knowing without exception. The calling of humanity to a supernatural goal means the *a priori* formal object, the horizon whereby the objects of experience are grasped, is the triune God. And because the horizon is transcendental, it is affirmed even when explicitly rejected. God, therefore, without becoming an intrinsic constituent of the finite being as such, is a necessary element in humanity's secondary causation. The human person's constant reference is to an all-pervading horizon that remains distinct from the finite order of things. As the all-embracing horizon and term, as goal and cause of the finite spirit's intentional dynamism, the Self-revealing God is immanent to all human activity, grasped in anticipatory and unthematic fashion, yet transcendent and apart from the finite.[21] God gives Godself and becomes present in one's unreflexive consciousness as the horizon within which all objects fall and which itself is the reality necessarily co-known, though not as object, in all acts of knowledge and love. God revealing becomes the condition for the possibility of every human act and is immanent to it. But it remains a human act.[22]

[21]"A direct presence of God belongs to the nature of a spiritual person, in the sense of an unsystematic attunement and an unreflected horizon which determines everything else and within which the whole spiritual life of this spirit is lived. This direct presence to God belongs to the nature of a spiritual person as the ground which, though not allowing us to grasp it completely in a reflex manner, is nevertheless the permanent basis for all other spiritual activities and which, on this account, is always more 'there' than everything else." "Dogmatic Reflections on the Knowledge and Self-consciousness of Christ," in *Theological Investigations*, V, 209.

[22]*Hominisation*, 69–86. Rahner avoids a theology of interventionism and the problems it entails. See M.L. Taylor, *God is Love*, ch. 6. It is axiomatic for Rahner that

Since the contention here is that the God Who graces is present to the human spirit as quasi-formal actuating cause, and since this is also Rahner's denomination of the presence of the indwelling Trinity in uncreated grace, we now see that for Rahner uncreated grace, general revelation, and supernatural existential are equivalents.[23] Transcendental revelation is uncreated grace as present to all in their cognitive, affective, and conative existence. Far from there being any question of mere forensic imputation, God through uncreated grace is present to all as participating in their activity. It should be clear by now that Rahner did not initially devise the existential as a tertium quid between nature and grace, as a nebulous linking reality void of content and meaning. The existential is now understood to refer primarily to God's activity, rather than to some component added to human nature. This does not mean it is without implications for human being.[24] The divine gracing activity effects in each person a horizon, which, while it may not be materially different from what it would be in an-

"the radical dependence and genuine reality of the being that has its origin in God increase in direct and not in inverse proportion." *Foundations of Christian Faith: An Introduction to the Idea of Christianity* (New York: Seabury, 1978), 79.

[23] See "Some Implications of the Scholastic Concept of Uncreated Grace," in *Theological Investigations*, I, 319–346. This does not mean that the offer of grace has met with willing acceptance in every-individual. All are offered divine friendship. But human freedom remains. The supernatural existential means the presence of the spirit to all so that they are objectively justified. But subjectively one can still reject the gift offered. See "The Concept of Mystery in Catholic Theology," in *Theological Investigations*, IV, 36–73.

[24] Shepherd seems so concerned with the divine activity and humanity's objective situation that he tends to undervalue the effect of the situation on humanity's inner constitution. Shepherd's statement that "the supernatural existential refers to the activity of God, not at all to man's make-up" is difficult to understand. For Rahner, the two are inseparable. Nevertheless, it is true that Rahner's early writing stresses the existential as a reality or a predisposition in us while his later writing focuses on the divine saving presence to all forming the condition for openness to God. The earlier writings focus on human *being*; the later on the human *situation*. More will be said about this below. See M.L. Taylor, *God is Love*, 127, note 50: "Within the context of Rahner's original discussion of the concept, his proposal of a supernatural existential does not solve the problem it was intended to solve (how grace can be intrinsic . . . and yet unmerited), but merely poses the same problem on a different level. Rahner could be asked, in relation to his original formulation of the concept, how the supernatural act whereby God imparts a disposition towards grace (the supernatural existential) is both intrinsic . . . and yet unmerited. The result . . . would be assertion of an infinite number of such predispositions toward the supernatural activity of God. But when the supernatural existential is understood as the offer of grace itself, then this problem of infinite regress is removed." See also B. van der Heijden, *Karl Rahner: Darstellung und Kritik seiner Grundpositionen* (Einsiedeln: Johannes Verlag, 1973), 21–41. More will be said about this in the next section.

other order of things, is certainly quite different in its formality. Here there may be a convergence with Seckler.

Uncreated grace as supernatural existential is the metaphysical condition of an orientation of humanity to God that finds fulfillment in the glory of vision. As such the existential is constitutive of humanity's present situation and cannot but have ramifications for human being. For this situation creates in one a new horizon. New not in the sense of an additive connoting temporal sequence. But new in that such a horizon, constitutive of historical humanity, is in no way constitutive of humanity as such. Due to God's graciousness the finite spirit finds itself a different being in a situation different from what would have obtained were God not so present to it as supernatural horizon.[25] In a word, as uncreated grace, the supernatural existential means that one is endowed with an *a priori* horizon that is a component in all one's activity, since all activity is permeated by cognition and affectivity, which in turn are grounded in self-transcendence through the *Vorgriff*, the preapprehension of the horizon that is the God continually offering Godself.

God imparts this Self-communication in a twofold way: through transcendental and categorical revelation, the latter being the full articulation, consummation, and condition of the former. It is transcendental revelation, through the uncreated Self-gift, that establishes the supernatural existential of humanity's actual situation.

To this point we have asserted that Rahner's horizon analysis moves from being to mystery to the God Who graces with Self-bestowal. It remains now to point up the incarnation as specifying the supernatural horizon. The human person as self-transcendent being reaches for the infinite which it can recognize as necessarily involved in all its activity as spirit. It is not unthinkable that being, as the scope of all possible objects, could be more than that. But only faith can resolve whether in fact it is to be considered more. The possibility conceived here is really the conceivability of a God-incarnate. For it seems credible that the mystery that is being, the human horizon, should be able to communicate itself in a way intelligible to those bound by space, time, and history. It is not absurd in the quest for self-transcendence to search out the possibility of God's perpetual and

---

[25]"Christianity and the non-Christian Religions," 131–132.

yet historically localized communication of Godself.[26] Such a localization would definitively manifest God as God's own Self is and make known the nature of the human horizon. God's gracious presence to all as horizon is ultimately guaranteed only through the Christ event. In Christ is an immediate divine presence, according to Rahner, that completely reveals and renders irrevocable the perpetual presence of the God of transcendental revelation, for the incarnation signifies God's definitive commitment to the world process.[27]

We have already stated that God's decision to communicate Godself effects an ontological difference. It need not be, but is a fact that the unlimited horizon that all tend to and which is involved in every act is the divine gracing presence. The drive to self-transcendence is assured fulfillment in the immediate vision of God. The human world is constituted in this very precise way. Now it is the revealing Word's incarnation that manifests fully the significance of humanity's present horizon. It is Christ's role to reveal that the horizon which is immanent yet transcendent is the saving God. And since creation stands in function of the incarnation, and anthropology of Christology, this gratuitous horizon would not be were there no historical and human embodiment of the Son. Christ by his historical presence renders God's presence to humans in uncreated grace efficacious and definitive. Only in Christ is God's transcendental revelation recognized and interpreted for what it is. Transcendental revelation, objective justification, the universal indwelling of the Spirit, uncreated grace—all of these are the abiding supernatural existential that shapes the human condition and affects its structure and being. And all of them are the one reality contingent upon God's will to the communication of God's own Self by becoming other than Godself in the humanity of Jesus.[28]

[26]Cf. "Thoughts on the Possibility of Belief Today," pp. 12–14 and "Christology Within an Evolutionary View of the World," in *Theological Investigations*, V, 174–175.

[27]"Christ is the point in the world process at which the self-expression of God becomes the self-transcendence of the world as man embodies it. Creation and incarnation are the two phases of God's one single decision to give himself over into that which is not himself. Both Christ and uncreated grace merge the developmental history of self-transcendence and the self-communication of God; but the former is the ontological condition for the latter, because God's decision had to become actually embodied in order for the cosmos as a whole to become part of his own life." W. Shepherd, *Man's Condition*, 197.

[28]"The connection between incarnation and uncreated grace in which God bestows himself supernaturally on man, is not merely de facto, but essential. . . . All will con-

Christ, as eternal expression of God's design of Self-donation, as God's special revelation is the fulfillment of transcendental revelation. Neither can be considered apart from the other, the former being the condition for the latter and logically prior. It is Christ, who by his death, and resurrection, and return to God, sends God's Spirit, thus manifesting and founding the universal presence of the saving God. In this Christological framework the "supernatural existential means that God as the horizon of general revelation and as uncreated grace is present to man in the mode of the Holy Spirit . . . the indwelling of the Holy Spirit *is* uncreated grace, *is* supernatural existential . . . Objective justification, the fifth equivalent term, simply means that man is ontologically justified by the presence of God prior to any acceptance of it on his part, though his freedom means he can fail to actualize it in love. . . . The supernatural existential is identical with God's supernatural justifying grace insofar as it is enduringly offered."[29] It is important to note that for Rahner the grace making possible free acceptance of God's Self-offer is identical with the grace that justifies. One need make no appeal to the addition of a new formal object for the faith option. Why? Because the God of general revelation and of uncreated grace, which is objective justification, is already the formal object of all human activity. Rahner does not view actual grace as an intermittent reified reality bombarding persons from time to time. It is identified with objective justification. God's Self-communication effects its own acceptance.[30] This view is quite

cede . . . that the human nature of Christ must also be intrinsically divinized by what we call justifying grace . . . we can then understand why the divinization of the human nature of the Logos by grace necessarily implies the call of all men to supernatural fellowship with God. And hence it is not too daring to suspect that there is also a necessary connection from the other side: if there is to be a grace as a supernatural participation of man in the inner life of God through God's real Self-communication to man, there must be also an incarnation. . . .'' "Dogmatic Questions on Easter," in *Theological Investigations*, IV, 131–132.

[29]W. Shepherd, *Man's Condition*, 206–209. "Without doubt man is through God's salvific act in Christ, already objectively and in himself (not only in the sight of God) different from what he would be if he is (or were) simply a sinner and nothing else (supernatural existential). Ordinary theology has no name for this 'subjective' condition which is given only through 'objective' redemption *prior* to subjective decision and sacrament, and which nominalism would have to deny, while ordinary theology does have a name for the opposite condition: original sin." K. Rahner, "Rechtfertigung," *Lexikon für Theologie und Kirche*, VIII, 1043. Rahner sees two existentials in tension: objective justification (supernatural existential) and original sin. See "Existential, Übernaturliches," *Lexikon für Theologie und Kirche*, III, 1301.

[30]K. Rahner, "Gnade," ibid., IV, 994–995.

different from an older one that saw the offer of grace as transient and present only when the gospel is preached or when revelation as historical tradition is present in some way. Humans are affected by the offer of grace not only now and then; the permanent offer of grace is an ever-present, inescapable factor of the human condition.

We see, then, how Rahner has considered God's Self-gift in the light of his metaphysics of knowledge. Uncreated grace is the human horizon and gives meaning to the supernatural existential. Every human life is acted out within the pale of this existential. God is present always and to all, in all activity, as participating horizon of possibility. Explicit Christianity reflexively acknowledges this situation and welds together a believing community that attempts in its own fumbling fashion to shape an existence in accord with it. An anonymous Christianity is the contrast, and it is into this category that, for Rahner, the vast majority of humankind may fall. Without acknowledging the name of Christ, and perhaps even while rejecting it, one may, by accepting oneself as a person, by a fundamental decision to pursue the moral good, and above all by the effort to live a life of love, simultaneously be responding positively to the presence of God within. In this way those not explicitly Christian subjectively accept objective justification in accepting the situation God has placed them in. The affirmation of oneself in one's situation with all its duties is implicitly an affirmation of absolute value and meaning. For Rahner, if a value is affirmed, absolute value is implicitly and simultaneously affirmed, because God, source of all value, is the pervading horizon involved in all knowing, willing, and doing. Ultimately it is love that constitutes the anonymous Christian, love that comes to one through the actuating presence of a grace-communicating God. Through love of one's neighbor, one becomes open to the totality of reality, because ethical acts have the triune God as transcendental condition and because God, through his quasi-formal actuating causality, participates in all moral activity so that it is ultimately meaningful and salvific. Love therefore is the translation of life's given direction.[31]

In the light of all that has preceded, the distance separating Schillebeeckx and Alfaro from Rahner does not seem so great as

---

[31]On Rahner's anonymous Christianity, see above, chapter 4, note 40. See also "Atheismus," ibid., I, 988; "Reflections on the Unity of the Love of Neighbor and the Love of God," in *Theological Investigations*, VI, 231–249.

it had first appeared. Schillebeeckx insisted that the real term of God's summons to personal union is a person's situation, which seems to mean concretely the "state of grace" or a condition of sinfulness. Yet this is so only because human persons, especially adults, can never be found in a neutral stance before God. Such "states" are consequent upon and conditioned by (and Schillebeeckx seems to admit as much) acceptance or rejection of the *instinctus fidei*, the ubiquitous presence of grace, or more precisely of God offering Godself to humanity. God, Schillebeeckx told us, is always there wherever we turn, always ahead of us. Is this position basically so different from Rahner's? It seems not. For Rahner, Schillebeeckx notwithstanding, the supernatural existential is not a "disposition" for the offer of uncreated grace. It is the offer itself, present continually since God is one's enduring *Woraufhin* of transcendence. It is difficult to see what grounds Schillebeeckx has for viewing the existential as an extrinsic ontological imposition bereft of personalistic and psychological import. Quite the contrary, harmonious as it is with Rahner's metaphysics of knowledge. Alfaro, too, while not dissenting from Rahner, has emphasized the personal and psychological aspects of grace. Alfaro sees humankind constituted in a supernatural economy because of the possibility for it of the highest type of personalization through divinization by grace, which is enduringly offered by God Who does not cease to address humans. In this sense, he admitted, one can speak of a supernatural existential. Again, is this not basically the meaning of Rahner's existential?

If the existential is seen simply as a disposition prior to habitual and actual grace (taken in what has become their customary sense) it is only because it is misunderstood to be an accidental ontological modification to dispose people for the offer of grace, or worse yet, as simply the "natural desire" for God. Surely the existential, as uncreated grace, is prior (at least ontologically) to sanctifying grace (as it is traditionally understood), which it conditions and effects. And, as we have seen, there seems no reason, in Rahner's view, to distinguish the existential, insofar as it is God's abiding offer of Godself, from actual grace. We can only conclude that the differences between these theologians may be more apparent than real.

To conclude, Rahner's is a tightly reasoned position. His notion of humanity as the grammar of God's Self-expression is fully articulated in his Christology. But Rahner's Christology is intelligible only when understood as the categorical articulation of

God's transcendental revelation through uncreated grace. And finally, his notion of the *Woraufhin* as uncreated grace and objective justification receives its proper formulation only in terms of his own metaphysics of knowledge. In this carefully and coherently woven theological tapestry is found the true meaning of his supernatural existential.

IV. *Critiques of Rahner's Technical and Synthetic Theologies of Nature and Grace*

We turn now to a consideration of some of the more important critiques leveled at Rahner's technical doctrine of nature and grace and, indeed, at this entire theological enterprise. To begin with, William Shepherd feels there is some equivocation about the supernatural existential. At times it appears reduced to a part of human being so that its cosmological reference is lost and "its significance as a concept describing God's active and gracious relationship to man (is) compromised."[32] Rahner, like his Catholic predecessors and contemporaries, assumes in dealing with the nature/grace problematic the double gratuity affirmed from the thirteenth century on: creation and elevation. Further, his existential is not an ad hoc solution to a particular problem, an imaginative invention to bridge humanity and the gracing God. Even less is it a polemic offered in defense of gratuity. Rather it is a necessary element in his comprehensive theological overview. The existential refers to God's activity as structuring a situation which cannot but leave its mark upon human being by way of a horizon that need not be as it is. God's decree does not remain extrinsic. God's activity and its effect in the person are both to be maintained. Justice is done to both in Rahner's synthesis. If the latter appears to receive the emphasis in Rahner's technical doctrine of nature and grace (though this is not at all evident), it certainly does not neglect the former. There does not seem to be in Rahner any "equivocation," as Shepherd thinks, between his *doctrine* and his *theology* of nature and grace, nor two divergent concepts of the existential. There are only different emphases.

To say that for Rahner concrete human quiddity is constituted of nature and the supernatural existential so that the existential appears to be a "part" of human being is simply another way of saying that historical humanity is different because its situa-

[32]*Man's Condition*, 239.

tion is different. The horizon of human cognition, volition, and action cannot simply be identical with that of humanity-as-such. This in turn is only to say that God's actual turning to humanity is God's own free and gratuitous decision to be active for and upon people in a way that cannot be demanded. God's activity and the difference it makes in human being go hand in hand. Rahner's technical doctrine no more "divorces man's being from his entire condition or situation" than does his theology. We cannot agree with Shepherd that Rahner's direct treatment of nature and grace "makes supernatural elevation refer solely to man's being" and that "precious little is said about God's activity."[33] God created with a view to Self-communication through the incarnation. In creating, God structured a being that would be open to this Self-impartation by endowing it with the Spirit as the unlimited horizon and transcendental condition of all its activity. God's continuing creativity sustains that horizon, that supernatural existential which is the offer of Godself. But it is immanent and effective in us of a modification that would not be in another world order. This is Rahner's position both in his technical doctrine and in his theology of nature and grace.[34]

A second defect that Shepherd detects in Rahner's technical presentation is a double-gratuity-talk that gives the impression of a time-lag between creation and elevation, as though the existential were granted at a historical point that postdates creation. No doubt one must affirm a double gratuity and in so doing avoid as best one can language suggesting a chronological caesura between the two. Rahner never holds for a time sequence of any kind between creation and gracing. They are simultaneous. The notion of nature existing historically in an ungraced condition is wholly foreign. Never does God see historical nature as neutral, so that God must opt for or against elevation. If nature has any priority over grace, it is only the priority that any hypothetically necessary moment has in a process. What Shepherd objects to is Rahner's use of "temporal recipient language" (implying the notion of a recipient in the non-historical sense) to resolve the dilemma of gratuity. Such "recipient language," Shepherd thinks, posits, as *logically* required, a nature that has no unconditional and unfrustrable ordination to grace, when actually Rahner knows

[33]Ibid., 241.

[34]Shepherd himself leaves the impression that the existential is a modification of human being. See ibid., Chapter 10, passim.

and asserts that *historically*, elevation of a pure nature never occurs. Shepherd sees this as "vacillation between a hypothetical pure nature and historical, concrete nature." To his mind it is "incompatible with the way Rahner himself sets out his theological doctrine."[35] For Shepherd, this hypothetical and logical leap from pure nature to graced nature beclouds the issue and does not explain God's actual creative activity. To that extent it is irrelevant to *this* world. Generally, Rahner is, Shepherd feels, concerned with historical nature, where creation and gracing are simultaneous. But there are times when reversion to nature as a logical priority implies a temporal double gratuity in a logical sense. In these instances a misleading temporal language is in evidence. And it connotes temporal succession of ontologically different epochs. For Rahner conceives of a pure nature existing in some nonhistorical, logical sense which is consequently made the recipient of elevation to the supernatural order, "which is to say, elevation to the actual historical order of things."[36]

Now Rahner certainly stands for a double gratuity. But there are no grounds for reading temporality into that twofold gratuity. Rahner never sees creation, even in a logical sense, as lying in wait for God's decision as to what is to happen to it. Creation always lies within the pale of grace. It is always the otherness to which God is ever communicating God's own Self. To the extent that one finds temporality lurking behind Rahner's formulations it seems explainable by the inherent inability of human syntax to express the divine creativity. Creation and gracing flow simultaneously from the one gratuitous decree of God that terminates in a human condition endowed with a dual gift: its own otherness from God and its infinite horizon participative in all its spirit life, the presence of the gracing God. In the first moment of human existence human being came to know a supernatural dimension in terms of which it is absolutely and unconditionally ordered to personal union with the Trinity. There is, as noted before, no need to appeal to two distinct divine actions to explain the human condition.

When Rahner does introduce a notion of nature in a hypothetical or seemingly ahistorical sense, it is only to more fully explicate the gratuity of grace.[37] Into this sphere of abstract distinction,

[35]Ibid., 243.
[36]Ibid, 246.
[37]Shepherd acknowledges this. Cf. ibid., 250.

projected only to provide a richer understanding of the concrete, there is no call for injecting the issue of temporality. Moreover, the hypothetical notion of nature is for Rahner, as for his contemporaries, a secondary matter, heuristically employed only to highlight the depth of God's free love in gracing humanity. There is no avowal of a real leap from hypothetical nature to actual graced nature; there is simply the contention that an ungraced world is possible, that the actual economy is not the sole possibility, that there is a difference between humanity-as-such and historical humanity.

The crux of Shepherd's difficulty seems to lie in his assumption that there are times when Rahner moves from the possible to the real, though usually his attention is riveted upon the real. Actually Rahner passes to the possible only through the real, which for him is paramount. Hence his endowment of nature, not so much with a logical priority as with the priority of hypothetical necessity, should not be construed as connoting a time-lag between creation and gracing.[38] What Rahner is dealing with is a theological concept of nature, which he feels is necessary not only to safeguard gratuity, but the distinction between nature and grace. Double gratuity implies no time lapse, but simply that humanity-as-such is not necessarily to be inserted into the order of grace. In truth, logical priority is given by Rahner to graced nature. Ungraced nature, as a possibility, is logically posterior. Shepherd's own perception of human being as a complex reality of nature and grace says as much.[39]

This leads us to what are perhaps more serious critiques of Rahner's thought. Some have criticized the anthropocentrism of Rahner's approach to nature and grace and the risk of reductionism that it runs, so that Christianity becomes a humanism.[40] It is true that Rahner's entire theology is marked by an anthropocentric methodology. This can already be seen in his *Spirit in the World* where he develops a metaphysics of knowledge that attempts to wed Thomistic principles to the Kantian Copernican revolution.[41] Human existence, more specifically, the human

---

[38]A typical expression of this is found in Rahner's essay "Questions of Controversial Theology on Justification," in *Theological Investigations*, IV, 217–218.

[39]*Man's Condition*, e.g., 244, 249, 252f., 255.

[40]A. Kelly, "God: How Near a Relation?" *Thomist* 34 (1970) 208; J. Moiser, "Why Did the Son of God Become Man?" *Thomist* 37(1973) 301–302.

[41]*Spirit in the World*, 406.

knower as dynamic questioner is, for Rahner, the chief focus of philosophical reflection. "For human beings the ontologically first and fundamental case or paradigm of a being and of its fundamental properties is found in the being himself who knows and acts."[42] What is meant by the basic metaphysical realities such as being, truth, goodness, and mystery is known by reflection on our own human operations. The knowing process is not one of mere conceptualization restricted to an ideal order cut off from the real world of physical entities. We are most in touch with reality in appropriating our interior acts of knowing and willing. Thus metaphysics has to be an analysis of human being because the question of being, with its universal and necessary properties, is essentially one with the question of the nature of human existence.[43] Turning to the philosophy of religion in *Hearers of the Word*, Rahner, making use of the basic insights of his philosophy of knowing, does not begin by searching out an objective, external revelation. Rather, his approach is anthropocentric. Persons are viewed as finite spirits listening in history for a fulfilling word from the mystery that envelops them. All this is carried over into his theological method, for "dogmatic theology today must be theological anthropology."[44] We know about God only by knowing about ourselves and our humanity. Only by plumbing human experience in all its depth do we come to grasp the significance of particular Christian doctrines.

Rahner sees himself developing the anthropocentrism already at work in Aquinas, maintaining dialogue with Descartes and Kant, and continuing the pioneering work of Blondel, Rousselot, and Maréchal in challenging the narrowness of modern subjectivism. Rahner, therefore, makes the modern turn to the subject, but all the while insisting that the human being in all aspects of its existence is referred to the absolute mystery, God. Reductionism, "mere humanism," results not from starting with the human, but from a failure to probe it deeply enough. The human creature is essentially open to the absolute and inevitably related to it. One does not find a place for the absolute only after analyzing humanity in a purely natural way. Concrete humans are from the beginning immersed in the absolute mystery. Rahner's basic

[42]*Hominisation*, 81.

[43]*Hearers of the Word*, 36. See also M. Heidegger, *Being and Time* (New York: Harper & Row, 1962), 26–35.

[44]K. Rahner, "Theology and Anthropology," in *Theological Investigations*, IX, 28.

understanding of persons as always already oriented to the gracious mystery is the powerful lens that he employs to examine all theological issues. It affords him ground for dialogue with nonbelievers, a consistent and organic theological synthesis, and an idiom for communication of the Christian vision. The charge of reductionism is hollow and stems from a failure to grasp Rahner's project. Far from reducing Christianity to a humanistic scheme, Rahner's approach may rescue us from imprisonment in our finitude by revealing the dimension of mystery hidden in everyday experiences accessible to all.[45]

We must also note that Rahner's theological approach has been criticized as too individualistic and insufficiently interpersonal.[46] Salvation seems too private and too worldless. The criticism contends that political, social, and eschatological elements are insufficiently attended to in Rahner's thought since it centers on the individual subject thrusting toward the absolute mystery. Some further argue that Rahner's metaphysics concentrates excessively on abstract knowledge, misses the dialogical nature of human existence, and therefore lacks grounding in the interpersonal dimension of life. The gist of these criticisms is that Rahner's starting point is misplaced, because he is not attentive to the communal and political dimensions of experience.[47] All this is alleged of his technical doctrine of nature and grace and of his synthetic theology of nature and grace. Moreover, since the interpersonal is so highly valued today, any theology that does not give it sufficient weight quickly loses interest for us and must be considered inadequate.

Aware of the objection, Rahner himself has offered a double response. First, he should not be judged solely on the basis of his early works *Spirit in the World* and *Hearers of the Word*. Secondly, he has provided a framework which is open to development and interpretation in terms of historicity and the interpersonal.[48] What follows his foundational works has, cer-

---

[45]For two excellent efforts at a mystagogy to deal with modern insensitivity to mystery, cf. J. Bacik, *Apologetics and the Eclipse of Mystery* and J. Haught, *What is God? How to think about the Divine* (New York: Paulist, 1986).

[46]See J. Metz's Foreword to *Spirit in the World*, xvii–xviii.

[47]E. Simons, *Philosophie der Offenbarung: Auseinandersetzung mit K. Rahner* (Stuttgart: Kohlhammer, 1966), 1972; A. Gerken, *Offenbarung und Transzendenzerfahrung* (Dusseldorf: Patmos, 1969); S. Ogden, "The Challenge to Protestant Thought," *Continuum* 6(1968) 243.

[48]See Rahner's introduction to *Herausforderung des Christen: Meditationen—Reflexionen* (Freiburg: Herder, 1975).

tainly, provided a counterpoint to their formality, abstractness, and orientation toward the human knowledge of material objects. Rahner seems correct in his contention that his theology is open to social and communal dimensions. For Rahner, the person's transcendental relationship to being can be mediated only by experience. All things, events, persons are possibly revelatory. All finite reality can and must serve as catalyst for the movement from transcendental to categorical awareness of the absolute mystery. Hence the interpersonal, the historical, the political, and the institutional are at least seminally present in Rahner's analysis from the start. Among the myriad of mediating elements some are more able than others to bring us to confront ourselves and the mysterious *Woraufhin* that engulfs us. In Rahner's mind, personal relations know this power in a preeminent way. We cite but one example of Rahner's contention that relations to other persons are essential to self-realization.

> Yet since knowledge (being itself already in act) attains its proper and full nature only in the act of freedom and therefore must lose and yet keep itself in freedom in order to be completely itself, it has a fully human significance only once it is integrated into freedom, i.e., into loving communication with the Thou. *The act of personal love for another human being is, therefore, the all-embracing basic act of man which gives meaning, direction, and measure to everything else.* If this is correct, then the essential *a priori* openness to the other human being, which must be undertaken freely, belongs as such to the *a priori* and most basic constitution of man and is an essential inner moment of his (knowing and willing) transcendentality. This *a priori* basic constitution (which must be accepted in freedom, but to which man can also close himself) is experienced in the concrete encounter with man in the concrete. The moral (or immoral) basic act in which man comes to himself and decides basically about himself is also the (loving or hating) communication with the concrete Thou in which man experiences, accepts or denies, his basic *a priori* reference to the Thou as such.[49]

Personal relationships are not just one of numerous mediating factors; they are demanded by the very essence of human being. Knowledge and freedom basically came to realization in and through encounter with other persons. Rahner rooted the interpersonal clearly in the essential, *a priori* structures of human be-

---

[49]"Love of Neighbor and the Love of God," 241.

ing, especially in his middle and later works. It is difficult, therefore, to accept the suggestion that his theology is held prisoner by a private, individualistic anthropology with no opening to the social and political dimensions of life. Rahner does provide a transcendental grounding of the dialogical principle of intersubjectivity.[50] Certainly, Rahner never wrote an elaborate philosophical account of human intersubjectivity. His discussions of the interpersonal are always evoked in connection with or in preparation for discussions of Christology, grace, God, or some other topic. This does not mean his appropriation of the principle that the personal Thou is mediation of the being-with-self (*das Beisichsein*) of the subject is inadequate.[51] It cannot be over-stressed that for Rahner relatedness to others is essential to human being. The other does not exist alongside, but is a necessary moment in self-realization. The transcendentality implicitly affirmed in all human activity does not consist of two moments, a return of the subject to itself and an openness to being as such and therefore God, but three. The necessary relatedness to other persons is also a transcendental dimension of human being. Rahner states that

> . . . these three relations of the subject, to itself, to God, to other persons do not simply stand side by side and separate from one another like the relationships the individual subject has to different contingent states of affairs or to objects of a posteriori experience, but are necessarily given together as mutually conditioning in every act of the spiritual and free subject (whatever this act may be), even if unthematically and unreflectively.[52]

Relatedness to the other may assume different forms (love or hate) but in every case the Thou is there with the I necessarily. In Rahner's view, love for the other is the authentic realization of human freedom. The act of personal love for the Thou is the "basic act" (*der Grundakt*) that provides meaning, direction, and standard for every other act.

[50]See K. Fischer, *Der Mensch als Geheimnis: Die Anthropologie Karl Rahners* (Freiburg: Herder, 1974), 199 and A. Grun, *Erlösung durch das Kreuz: Karl Rahners Beitrag zu einem heutigen Erlösungverständnis* (Münsterschwarzach: Vier-Türme, 1975), 15.

[51]"Love of Neighbor and the Love of God," 241.

[52]"Experience of Self and Experience of God," in *Theological Investigations,* XIII, (New York: Seabury, 1975), 128.

226 The Graced Horizon

To all this must be added other factors. Rahner has written widely on social and institutional themes and has called for a "practical theology" that would bring to bear a theological reflection on society. He has been a contributor to the Christian-Marxist dialogue and has attempted to integrate socio-political themes into his transcendental method. One can only conclude that Rahner's programmatiç theology is open to the interpersonal and institutional aspects of human existence. If he did not develop these aspects as fully as theologians of liberation, it is only because Rahner is a man of his own world and era. No one can (or has to) do everything. Moreover, it is safe to say that political and liberation theologies borrowed much of their intellectual capital from Rahner.

Perhaps the most telling and important criticism of Rahner has been made by Mark L. Taylor.[53] Taylor argues that Rahner's account of the assertion that "God is love" is inadequate at three points. First, his view of the relativity and non-relativity of God is incoherent. Secondly, his view of the freedom or gratuity of the divine love entails God's not being essentially love of others, which is incoherent with the tradition and with human experience. Finally, his view of divine love is unbalanced insofar as divine love, unlike human love, does not involve for Rahner a passive moment in which God is open to and determined by creatures. All this, says Taylor, indicates a more basic inconsistency in Rahner's thought. Rahner does not carry through the modern turn to the subject, which is his methodological starting point. Rahner's notion of God involves categories not drawn from what he considers the fundamental *existentiell* human experience. His idea of God is imposed upon his understanding of fundamental human experience; it is not derived from it. Some essential elements of the relativity, freedom, and love revealed in basic human experience are negated when the three are analogically predicated of God. The negation, argues Taylor, contradicts Rahner's own criterion for the proper predication of analogical attributes to God. In elaborating his critique, Taylor's own espousal of process thought must be kept in mind.

To begin with, Taylor contends that an essential dimension of love, as it is understood in our experience, is denied when Rahner analogically attributes love to God. In human love both lover

[53]M. L. Taylor, *God is Love*, 193–332. The critique follows an excellent exposition of Rahner's theology of God and humanity and is followed by a suggested alternative theology of God.

and beloved reach authentic self-realization through interrelationship. Human love is, according to Rahner, the opening of oneself and the ecstatic giving of oneself to the other. However, Rahner's concept of divine love differs substantively from human love. Divine love, as human love, is certainly a free, ecstatic self-giving that enables the self-realization of both God and the creature. But Rahner does not assert a passive moment in the divine lover, a moment that in the human lover is the flip side of the active moment. An essential aspect of human love, being affected by the love bond, is denied in Rahner's account of divine love. It is doubtful, therefore, that the categories used in Rahner's view of divine love are derived from the basic human experience of love.

There is also inconsistency within Rahner's view of human and divine freedom, according to Taylor. Rahner's view of divine freedom differs significantly from the understanding of freedom he derives from transcendental analysis of basic human experience. For Rahner, freedom is a free subject's capacity to realize itself, to choose itself, and to take possession of itself.[54] As noted above, freedom, taking possession of oneself, is realized only through the mediation of other free persons. Freedom is the ability to constitute oneself in and through relations to others.[55] This is a positive approach to freedom. Rahner, however, understands divine freedom in a negative as well as a positive sense, for he maintains that God "cannot need finite reality, called the world, for otherwise he would not be radically different from the world, but would be part of a larger whole."[56] God can freely constitute Godself independently of any relationships to others. For Rahner, this is so in regard to both the divine creative and Self-communicative activity. Both are gratuitous acts. Again Rahner adduces a negative understanding of divine freedom. God could have withheld from creatures the divine Self-communication, could have remained the remote, hidden, silent, asymptotic *Woraufhin* of human self-transcendence. God would still be God in a posture of Self-refusal and in a world without grace. A human subject is free only in the positive sense of being able to constitute itself as this or that kind of person in relation to others. God is free in the negative sense as well to constitute Godself outside of reference to any others. We can only conclude, according to Taylor, that

[54]*Hearers of the Word*, 123.

[55]K. Rahner, *Foundations of Christian Faith*, 65.

[56]Ibid, 85.

given Rahner's own analysis of human experience, it is not clear how the negative view of freedom arises from the basic experience of freedom implicitly shared by all human persons.

These views of divine love and divine freedom are evidence that, for Rahner, relatedness to others is not essential to God, though it is for humans, who are constituted by their relations to others. Human *Beisichsein* or subjectivity is always being-with-another. Not so for God, who has chosen to create and grace the world with divine Self-communication when it could have been otherwise. The relativity of human being is essential. The relativity of God to the world, whether as creator or as savior, is gratuitous and accidental. Again, this appears to negate an essential datum of fundamental human experience from which Rahner claims to derive his concept of God.[57] In our experience we always find ourselves in relationships to others. Rahner himself notes there is no region of the self into which we can retreat and escape relatedness to others.[58] Yet Rahner does not view God as constituted by relatedness. Hence divine personal being differs radically from human personal being as we experience it. But Taylor goes farther. To suggest that Rahner's views of divine love, freedom, and relativity significantly differ from his understanding of human love, freedom, and relativity does not amount to showing an inconsistency in Rahner's thought. Taylor, therefore, attempts to show that Rahner's formulation of the concept of God violates his own principles of appropriate reflection on God and is at odds with his own view of analogy. Therein resides his inconsistency.

For Rahner, "Analogy means that a concept, without losing the unity of its content, undergoes a real variation of meaning as it is applied to different individual beings or to different realms of being."[59] There must be real variation in the meaning of the concept drawn from human experience when the concept is employed in reference to the divine. Divine love is enduring and faithful, unlike human love. God is free in relation to all others in a way that humans are not. God's relativity to the world in consequence of the incarnation does not cancel divine transcendence and immutability. To affirm that God is free, loving, and related is not to univocally predicate freedom, love, and relativity of God.

[57]Cf. M.L. Taylor, *God is Love*, chs. 1 and 2.

[58]"One Mediator and Many Mediations," in *Theological Investigations*, IX, 176.

[59]"Analogy," *Dictionary of Theology*, 8.

But the question is whether the essential meaning, the "unity of content" of love, freedom, and relativity applied to God analogically is retained when, in Rahner's hands, these concepts undergo "a real variation of meaning." If the essential meaning of a concept drawn from our experience is not retained when the concept is predicated of God, there is equivocation, not analogical predication as Rahner defines it. It does seem, according to Taylor, that an essential aspect of love, freedom, and relativity is removed when these predicates are attributed to God by Rahner. They are, therefore, applied equivocally, not analogically. In each instance something essential to love, freedom, and relativity, viz., real or internal relatedness to others, is not predicated of God. This appears arbitrary. To view divine love as wholly active and exclusive of any passive moment, or divine freedom as the negative freedom of God to find self-realization independently of any relatedness to others, or God as a subject able to exist devoid of all relationships to any others is not merely to vary the meaning of love, freedom, and relativity, but to use them in a very different, even equivocal sense.

In denying the essential relatedness of God to others, Rahner is not merely "protecting" God from some human imperfection or defect. Certainly, one cannot analogically predicate of God the limitations that characterize human intellection. But real relatedness to others, as even Rahner contends, is not a human imperfection, but a constitutive of human being's essential, positive nature. Relatedness is a necessary condition of human self-realization, not an obstacle to or limitation of it. Thus Taylor finds it difficult to fathom, given Rahner's definition of analogy, why relatedness as an essential dimension of humanity should not be predicated of God in some appropriate fashion if God is loving and free. Rahner's concept of God seems to conflict with his principle that there is a commonality between infinite and finite that makes reflection on and talk about God possible.

> The ground of a reality that exists must beforehand possess in itself in absolute fullness and purity this reality that it grounds. For, otherwise this ground could not be the ground of that which is grounded at all; for, otherwise, it would finally be the empty nothingness that—if one takes the term seriously—would express nothing and could ground nothing.[60]

[60]*Foundations of Christian Faith*, 73-74.

For God to be the ground of the finite, and especially of human being, God must possess, it seems, in absolute fullness and purity that real relatedness which is essential to finite reality, and especially to human being. Yet, for Rahner, God to be God must stand essentially free from all relations to other realities. At this point inconsistency enters. He denies God is essentially related to others while enunciating a principle that indicates that God as ground of the finite must appropriately yet essentially be related to others.

The implications of all this for our problem of nature and grace can be more explicitly stated. For Taylor, God cannot be God without creating a graced world. This must be so if God is love, for to love is to-be-to-another. God must create *some* world, though there is no necessity that God create a *particular* world. Between God and the world there must be a mutuality whereby all finite realities are affected by God, and God in turn is affected by them. Moreover, pure nature is not just a possibility never realized. It is a contradiction. To be a creature is to be loved by God. God would not be God unless God loved some conceivable world, necessarily made actual, in a supremely intimate way. The God who is love must create some world and must communicate Godself to the intelligent beings in that world. Gratuity resides not in creation and redemption as such but in *my* redemption and creation. For while there must be some order that is created and redeemed, it does not have to be one including me or just this species of intelligent being. In a word, for Taylor, God, as love and as essentially related and constituting Godself in and through relatedness, must create some world, and having created it must grace it. How different this is from Rahner's view. For Rahner, God, while essentially unrelated to others, has freely chosen to relate to a world. God could have chosen not to love this world in a fully personal way. God's love for others is not, for Rahner, God's primordial possibility, but merely one of God's many possibilities, though one in fact actualized. God could have remained merely externally related to the world as the creator-God. It is in the divine Self-communication that God contingently comes to be really related to the world, while yet remaining, inexplicably, unrelated.[61] Rahner views the relativity of God as a free self-limitation of God's primordial mode of being as nonrelative. Incarnation, he realized, involves more than a nominal relationship to creatures. In contrast to the doctrine of creation, or a

---

[61]On this entire issue of divine relativity, see M. L. Taylor, *God is Love*, chs. 6 and 7.

metaphysical doctrine of God, the incarnation adds, contingently, relatedness to others of a God who, in the essential divine nature is unrelated. For Rahner, it is talk of the divine Self-communication that affirms that God has freely chosen to become related. His formulation of the incarnation as Self-expression, Self-alienation, Self-externalization of God conveys a God essentially Self-possessed (*bei sich selbst*) but freely opting to relate Godself to creatures. It is through the Self-expression of the triune God in Jesus that God freely, contingently assumes real relatedness.

But Taylor argues that God as related cannot be derived from God as unrelated. "Either the relatedness of God affirmed in the doctrine of the trinity or the incarnation is a relatedness of God in Godself or else these doctrines express merely verbal affirmations of God's relatedness."[62] If essentially God is love, then appeal to the incarnation to ground relatedness is specious. God in Godself in every divine state is already constituted in relatedness to creatures. There is no need to add relatedness to an essentially unrelated God. Talk of incarnation or Trinity or grace is an expression of God's essential relatedness, not a demonstration of it. The real relatedness implied in talk of God as love is not a special theme of Christian theology; it is its only theme, indeed its basic ground.

The fundamental reason for Rahner's difficulties, according to Taylor, is his failure to fully take the turn to the subject. He fails to conceive God solely on the basis of categories drawn from the basic experience human persons have of themselves as persons. Rather, he uses categories that cannot be derived from that experience, thereby repudiating his own call for a turn to the subject. Rahner holds that the turn to the subject, wherein fundamental human experience furnishes the starting point and paradigm for all philosophical and theological analysis, must also inform any adequate understanding of God. Rahner felt that a conception of God based on categories taken from the experience that the human being has of itself as a free subject had not yet been arrived at. Rahner's theology was an effort to forge just such a revisionary concept of God. But it seems to Taylor that Rahner did not follow through on the turn to the subject. He clearly maps out the starting point, the *existentiell* experience the person has of itself as a free subject, but at a crucial point his notions of divine love, freedom, and relativity seem to import categories not

[62]Ibid., 397.

found in the basic human experience of the self. His concept of God outrightly denies the experience of the human self as essentially related. But there is no experiential data to warrant a love that does not know a passive moment, or a free agent that can constitute itself independently of other persons, or an individual that can exist without real, internal relatedness to others. This is why Taylor considers the categories called upon by Rahner to conceive the divine reality to be imported from without and imposed rather than derived from our radical experience of ourselves as persons. Rahner is drawing upon the traditional and classical notion of God as radically *a se* and non-relative. He does not fully heed his own call to construct a concept of God on the foundations of our experience of ourselves. Perhaps unaware of this, he provides no justification for it.

William Shepherd, as noted above, argued that Rahner's theology is "disjointed." His basic theological synthesis (an enterprise of nature and grace) is conceived and executed within the framework of a modern, evolutionary, historical view of the universe. But his technical doctrine of nature and grace is worked out "using terms drawn from the traditional, hierarchical, static, layered view of the world."[63] Taylor argues that something similar may be said of Rahner's conception of God. Rahner proposes, on the one hand, that God be conceived in categories drawn from the experience humans have of themselves as persons instead of in categories drawn from the world of things. This leads Rahner to a revisionist stance; he reconceives doctrines by abandoning altogether or reshaping Scholastic categories. The God-world relationship, for instance, is rethought in terms of personal dialogue, grace in terms of quasi-formal causality, or in terms of interpersonal communication. On the other hand, he retreats back into the traditional view of God as unrelated and understands divine love, freedom, and relativity in ways incoherent with our immediate experience of our personal being. There is, therefore, an unrelieved tension between Rahner's revisionism and his actual formulation of the doctrine of God. The classical view of the unrelated God is behind his contention that there need not be a creation and even given a creation, it need not be graced. Rahner is caught between the subject-oriented approach of transcendental philosophy and the substance-oriented approach of the Thomism in his Catholic background. It is perhaps impossible to reconcile

[63]W. Shepherd, *Man's Condition*, 25.

233 The Graced Horizon

transcendental Thomism and the subjectivist principle (what we have called the turn to the subject).[64]

Certainly, Taylor's is the most serious critique of Rahner to date. It probes to the heart of the underlying issues where it challenges Rahner's philosophical foundations and his ability to carry through his anthropocentric methodology. Taylor is correct in detecting an obvious tension between Rahner's Scholasticism and his transcendental philosophy. The two are bound together in an uneasy marriage. It would be surprising if at various points along the way disharmony did not show its face. Rahner's theological instincts and insights do sometimes (e.g., concerning the possibility of change in God due to the incarnation) seem too much to bear for the mode of thought and categories he has inherited. At these points there appears to be a reneging, even a loss of theological nerve and ironically, a reversion to a position of the *Schultheologie* Rahner's entire theological project generally opposed. In this connection, it must always be kept in mind that Rahner is a transitional thinker in a transitional period for Catholicism. Given his background and time it is to be expected that we should find in his theology a Scholastic sediment that surfaces from time to time. Nonetheless, Rahner proved himself an invaluable mediator for twentieth century Catholicism which has been holding tightly to the classical mindset while being drawn willy-nilly into the world of modernity.

Therein lies the much larger and deeper problem that Taylor's critique unearths. The core of the problem is that these two positions, Rahner's and Taylor's, rest finally either on the classical preference for the absolute and the unchanging or on the modern preference for relativity, change, and the utter sociality revealed in our concrete experience. If one accepts process philosophy as furnishing the metaphysics and the categories deemed most adequate for doing theology today, then Taylor's critique of Rahner will be perfectly welcome. On the other hand, if one finds process thought too problematic, then one may be content with Rahner, whose categories sometimes prove brittle and whose insights are sometimes pushed to the breaking point.

[64]S. Ogden makes the same criticism of B. Lonergan's theology in "Lonergan and the Subjectivist Principle," *Journal of Religion* 51(1971) 155–173. Ogden thinks that despite Lonergan's endorsement of the turn to the subject, the crucial categories he employs to conceptualize God do not derive from an analysis of human experience. L. Dewart brings a similar charge against Rahner and Lonergan. See "On Transcendental Thomism," *Continuum* 6(1968) 389–401.

234 The Graced Horizon

Of course, one may search for a third way. But the immediate question is which of these two metaphysics, Thomistic or Process, provides the more appropriate and more adequate conceptuality for interpreting Christian faith. Which is more in keeping with the tradition and which is best able to articulate our basic experience of ourselves as persons? One must also ask in dealing with Rahner whether a modernized Thomism, Transcendental Thomism, is truly possible.[65] These are questions very much debated today by theologians attempting to reconstruct a doctrine of the Christian God. In an interpretative and historical study such as this we cannot engage in a dialectical study of these important and difficult metaphysical issues that are critical to the choice of a worldview.

[65]See M. L. Taylor, *God is Love*, 332, note 10.

Epilogue

I. *Sacred and Secular Intertwined*

A renewed Catholic theology of revelation sees it as God's Self-disclosure in history through word and event for humankind's salvation. God communicates Godself, not ideas about Godself. But does this Self-manifestation and donation come as an alien element injected into history? Or is it somehow the answer to the perennial questions and aspirations that burn deep in the human heart? On the one hand, it is difficult to see the value in a revelation that is a *deus ex machina* having no real relationship to human existence. On the other hand, simply to claim revelation is the answer to the human search for meaning runs the risk of reducing the divine revelatory action to identity with human thought and history. The horns of the dilemma can be eluded if we bear in mind what has been stressed throughout our study: the gratuity of grace and human openness to a horizon of absolute mystery that transcends humanity and its world. The mystery that permeates human life in the world and constantly holds it in its grasp is the answer to all questing, yet it is not concocted by humanity. It is always the unowed and the unexpected.

Dynamic intentionality, as we have seen, the source of human self-transcendence, is concretized in acts of knowing, willing, and doing by which humans make for themselves a world and a history. Yet despite the shape of their history or their world humans remain open-ended, directed to a horizon of Mystery, never sealed off within the limits of empirical experience. The human condition verifies this. Human reach always exceeds its grasp. The new continually beckons. Hunger and longing range beyond the edge of this world, beyond even the most intimate and satisfying of personal bonds. A plumbing of human needs reveals a need, a depth, that knows no end. In this context the grace that is revelation is God's coming to fill the human spirit's openness by incorporating it into Christ so that it now enters the Trinitarian family and becomes by grace conformed to Christ. Human response is also initiated by the same divine Self-gift. The response elicited by the Self-disclosing God carries the human subject beyond the limits of its capacity to understand and to love the Mystery living in the horizon of human existence.

But in a secularized world how should a believing community understand, communicate, and live its awareness of God's universal gracing presence?[1] Any theology of nature and grace must achieve such an understanding of their relationship that one can give oneself fully to the secular task and find and experience God precisely there and not merely in peripheral areas of crisis or church-going. The need is imperative since the secularizing process has swallowed up much of the ground once occupied by the "religious." This is why the old chestnut of the sacred and the secular is in final analysis the problem of nature and grace. For the future, therefore, theologies of nature and grace will very probably continue to stress and refine inclusive viewpoints such as Rahner's and the insights introduced by the neo-liberal theology of the early sixties. Awareness and appreciation of transcendental revelation will assume increased importance in an age where institutional and explicit Christianity no longer occupy the place they held before the demise of Christendom and the advent of secularization.

The possibility of conceiving an anonymous Christianity, a notion offensive and unacceptable to some, grew out of a new understanding of the nature-grace dialectic. Despite the objections raised against it, its basic premise seems valid. Humanity and its world do not form a self-enclosed reality to which grace is appended as a foreign element. Creation knows an inner pointing to grace, in which alone lies its fulfillment. Human beings are so structured that should they freely accept and open themselves to their dynamic intentionality and its transcendent horizon, they already render themselves affirmatively related to the God Who reveals

---

[1]Secularization is the process whereby human life and institutions in the industrialized world have come to be largely free of ecclesiastical control, both jurisdictionally, doctrinally, and in terms of social control. Though economic and political factors are important causes of secularization, the crucial element may be humanity's critical appropriation of its own intelligence. The result is a secular society marked by a pluralism of ideologies in which Christianity is no longer predominant.

Godself, even though the reality of revelation and grace is not called by those names, or is, perhaps, even rejected.

Because of the universal presence of grace, then, Christians cannot see the secular world as a hostile arena. Sin notwithstanding, there is no purely secular reality over against grace. The catholicity of grace will not allow for the categorization of the world simply as pagan or non-Christian, even if it is, by reason of its sinfulness, marked with an ambiguity and a darkness that deter the embracing of all it is and does. The distinction of nature and grace is no thoroughgoing dualism between good and evil. Christians and their Churches, though marked by the same ambiguity, struggle to recognize and cooperate with the working of the Spirit continually breaking through in all phases of human existence and assuring ultimate victory over sin. The confidence of the Christian does not stem from naiveté in the face of evil, but from the consciousness of having been grasped by a reality that transforms everything.

This in no way makes the role of explicit Christianity superfluous. Nor does it baptize a crass stress on an immanence that rules out of court all transcendence. Radical immanentism, not attaching sufficient significance to human openness, sets an arbitrary and restrictive cap on the experience of "secular man." If God's Self-donation and revelation are accessible to all who open themselves to the horizon that transcends them, then the God of grace and revelation can be met in all the secular dimensions of life. Existence, in all its moments, is itself the locus of grace. As Barth put it: "What is Christian is latently but fundamentally identical with what is universally human."[2] This provides broadness of vision and confidence in collaborating with a world of people who may not wish and do not need to bear the name of Christian and yet who, in their life and work, at least implicitly, acknowledge the Mystery absolutely transcendent to the cosmos and absolutely near to it in the grace of Christ. As for themselves, believers must realize their reflexive Christianity in its pneumatic and institutional elements can truly sustain a vertical relationship to God only if it is complemented by, translatable into, and expressive of their horizontal relations with others in building the human city, thereby bringing all of nature under the full sway of grace.

In fact it is the catholicity of grace, the comprehensive union of grace and nature, and the unity of love of God and love of

[2]K. Barth, *Christ and Adam* (New York: Harper & Row, 1957), 8.

neighbor that grounds the catholicity of the Church's concern to involve itself in the totality of life. The shape assumed by the Church's catholicity and involvement will vary from era to era, from culture to culture. The very fact that grace does universally penetrate the total sphere of nature precludes any attempt to incarnate Christianity without regard for given historical and cultural factors. In a secularized culture, however, the Church can no longer concretize the relationship of grace to the secular realm as it did in a past which was informed, at least externally, by a Christian ethos. Our cultural forms have been transformed and this necessarily affects Christianity's search for and reinforcement of the presence of grace already operative in the secular. As early Christianity was to express itself in Hellenic culture, so must Christianity today, because of the catholicity of grace, come to grips with the bewildering idioms of a secularized world.

In other words, the future life and theology of the Church will have to articulate in new ways the existing unity of nature and grace. This will entail a double task. First, careful attention will have to be paid to the lineaments of contemporary human experience and of the culture the Church finds itself in, for they disclose where the presence of grace is already operative in nature and what the Church may effectively do to foster it. Secondly, the Church must engage in theological reflection upon itself (its scriptures and traditions) to attain a sharpened consciousness of its own identity and what it entails and how it may preserve grace from oblivion and repression as it permeates the world.

We now see that the Christian indicative—the existential unity of nature and grace, the universal presence of a supernatural existential, the ongoing immanence of the Spirit to all—is weighted with practical implications. This indicative is the factual unity of grace and nature, a contextual reality that Christian life and theology work out of even before it is a goal they work toward.[3] This was the basis of Bonhoeffer's "holy worldliness" and of Tillich's "belief-ful realism." More is involved here than a self-serving ecclesiastical strategy for survival. Rather there is an awareness of the universality of the grace-nature union which points to Christ and of the need for the Church to respond creatively to that indicative and to affirm the reality of revelation both inside and outside the Church.

Christianity may find itself increasingly in diaspora in a pluralistic world society. Especially now Christians must trust in the efficacy of God's general revelation to each and every person. They will give themselves to the quest for a better planet, all the while remaining skeptical about the significance and success of utopian schemes in a world where sin as an existential conflicts with grace. They will not be disconcerted by the seeming chasm between the universal presence of the supernatural existential and the diminishing significance of the Church from an institutional standpoint. They can accept secularity, indeed embrace it, aware that it is permeated and transformed by the grace it mediates.

II. *The Cosmic Dimension of Grace*

We have seen where the problem of nature and grace has come from and where it presently is. What might be the shape assumed by future theological discourse upon the relationship between nature and grace? And what posture will the Churches assume in the light of present and future theological reflection? In an era where humanity has to a degree unknown before critically appropriated its own intellectual capacity to manipulate nature, and where human consciousness is marked by an unprecedented historical awareness, it would seem that the theology of nature and grace must in the future become even more dynamic and cosmos-ranging in its perspective. A static, ahistorical, individualistic, other-worldly approach must yield more and more to a dynamic, historical, social, and this-worldly view of grace. This means that it must be more closely linked to Trinitarian, Christological, and eschatological doctrines. Rahner, probably more successfully than anyone, initiated such an integration with no small success. He attempted to throw the integration of spirit and matter into a Christological and eschatological context. Christ becomes the archē and the telos of all movement in the cosmos, the immanent force that impels the evolution of humanity and its world to their consummation.[4]

What must be better understood is the fact that existence in a graced order not only renders the being of humanity different

---

[3]Christian existence is also marked by an imperative, for humanity is always *simul iustus et peccator*. But the priority goes to the indicative. If the imperative is divorced from the indicative, Christian life falls prey to the discontinuity and extrinsicism that has plagued the nature/grace relationship. The imperative alone gives the impression that humanity is simply called to become what it is not, and perhaps has no reason to become. Only with the indicative can it be called to recognize and be fully what it already is. The affirmations of tensions like nature/grace, sin/redemption should not slight the fundamental priority to be awarded the prevenience of grace.

[4]K. Rahner, "Christology Within an Evolutionary View of the World," 157–192.

but that it also makes a difference in the cosmic process itself. In other words, the orders of world and grace must be seen as compenetrating one another, not as simply juxtaposed, or at best, blended in the enclave of the individual's faith.[5] Authentic human existence is a fulfillment, a maturing of existing humanity, not an extraneous addition made by an invading entity standing over against it. Graced persons do not find salvation in a vertical, Platonic escape from the world that is their home and an element in their self-definition. Rather they find it only by involvement in and development of their environment in preparation for the ultimate divinization of all creation and by horizontal relationships in the world with their neighbors.[6]

To a large extent this type of future development may be contingent upon the continuing advancement of a more sophisticated process theism than we have hitherto had. Talk of an evolutionary perspective is easy. Detailing its ramifications for theology and vice versa is another matter. For one thing our universe, far from manifesting a clear unity of purpose, seems to be a plurality of purposes, some of which are at loggerheads. If there is progress, there is also regress. If there is harmony, there is also conflict. To the extent that there is an overarching divine telos embracing all other purposes, and that is a basic contention in our theologies of nature and grace, it can hardly be viewed as implying that the human race is a cast of characters, and the world a set of stage props, forming together a pre-planned scenario in which all lives and actions are nothing more than the predetermined unfolding of what was in the playwright's mind from the start. Our world is a scene of too many random contingencies to fit that pattern. Human freedom must be taken more seriously. Moreover, if God is immanent to and participating in the finite cosmic process as humanity's graced horizon, then future theology must work to a better understanding of the meaning of God's co-creative work with and in human beings. We must also note, however, that humanity's own relationship to its world has changed.

---

[5] In the present context "nature" is used broadly to denote not just human nature, but the whole created order in distinction from its creator. Thus it refers to society, culture, nonhuman creation, organic and inorganic. It is the public environment of communicating persons. "Nature" is the world of created realities whose expectation is as yet unfulfilled. Cf. J. Hefner, "Politics and the Ontology of Nature and Grace," *Journal of Religion* 54(1974) 119–137; J. Carpenter, *Nature and Grace: Toward an Integral Perspective* (New York: Crossroad, 1988).

[6] Cf. K. Rahner, "Love of Neighbor and the Love of God," 231–249.

Today humans can do with nature, at least in principle, things heretofore unimaginable. This is something new. More than ever, the biblical injunction to "have dominion" over the earth has been realized. With science and technology humanity has made an assault on the basic structure and process of its world. This changed relationship of humans to the social and physical environment that is the extension of themselves has large implications. When humans and their world were companion creatures the notion of creaturehood was quite easy to formulate and to live with.

But nature as experienced today, especially in the West, is less an occasion for submission to Providence than it was. Nor is it an experience of the manifestation of an alien Power. Nature is less provocative of gratitude and obedience than it had been. Now it is seen as an invitation to the application of intelligence and the construction of tools whereby it may be mastered and conformed to the human will. Humanity's conscious relationship to nature is one of initial but not so much of continuing, direct dependence. Modern people live in direct dependence on human science, institutions, and instruments. It is difficult therefore to count as one's blessings the kindness of nature or its God. Nature is only a supplier of material for human artifacts. Humans see themselves more as masters than as beneficiaries of nature. The will of God as read in creation is not, as it often was, the governor of human action. Humans build up and tear down not according to divinely dictated purposes, but according to their own. No longer a spectator of a nature that controls human destiny without rhyme or reason, a more accepting rationality has yielded to an intelligence that systematically attempts to remodel the world.

In this situation one finds no easy path from nature to God and grace. To the extent that for humans today there is no outside mind or will dictating its commands through nature and calling for submissive obedience, they themselves by their own intelligence must mark out goals. This, it seems, must have some bearing upon the theology of nature and grace. The older question of the will's power as argued under that rubric must be broadened and deepened by inquiry into the relationship between grace and the social process of the intelligent quest for humane and civilized values. Grace now finds humanity more easily in its dependence on the human community in quest of life and good. God is found in nature not by reason of consciousness of immediate dependence upon its process, but by awareness of dependence on one's neighbors in the mastery of it. This is an insight that had much to do with the development of the liberation theologies pursuant to the mid-century nature-grace development that we have been examining.

Once the total environment becomes more malleable to human designs the notions of creature and creation become more difficult and complex. It is one situation when humanity finds nature calling the tune, its fate controlled by the celestial bodies, and it is something else again when humanity is probing into outer space and when a string of atoms can be made to dance their proper steps to human orchestration. There is good and ill in the new. But the important thing to note is that the very concept of nature has been broadened and radically changed. Any theology of nature and grace failing to factor this change into its considerations will hardly be of much use. So closely linked are humans and their environment that their changed relationship cannot but influence human self-definition. This in turn cannot but affect the relationship of graced creatures to the Creator-Savior. The human situation has outrun the world-view within which the theology of nature and grace was constructed in the past.

Moreover, it is paradoxical that with the increased technologizing of nature humanity has come to know a certain alienation from its world. We are well aware of the pervasive influence that co-existence with one's neighbors exercises upon one's selfhood and upon one's relationship to God. We accept the fact that any theology of grace neglecting that fact is faulty. This explains to some extent our concern with sin as alienation from the community. But the notion should be extended. Humans are alienated from their physical world and from themselves as well as from their social world. One alienation influences the other. Together they create a kind of lostness that can make God-talk, moral feelings, and awareness of grace, end, purpose, and meaning evaporate.[7] Humanity's being situated in nature is an essential aspect of its social history. The two are mutually dependent. Distance from neighbor shrinks and perverts the self and its relation to God; but the same is true when the earth is estranged. It is true that the gracious God addressing humans is properly responded to only when one realizes and acts upon the importance of the love-relationship to the neighbor. We are much aware of that. But we fail to sufficiently weigh the importance that caring

[7]Cf. J. Bacik, *Apologetics and the Eclipse of Mystery.*

for the world of physical nature has for humanity's grace-bond with God and neighbor. It is to Teilhard's credit that he strove to endow the categories of personalization through grace with a cosmic dimension.

Human beings are never isolated atoms. The full richness of graced human selfhood is understood only in a symbiotic relation with the human community and the physical world as well. The human and subhuman levels of creation share a common destiny. The distant galaxies may not (at least not yet) be part of human history; but they may share a common source and end with humans. Human relationships to the world, therefore, can never be neutral, or at best merely utilitarian or aesthetic. They are also ethical. More is at stake than a romantic concern for nature. Precisely because of humanity's vastly increasing power to control its environment, the future is becoming more problematic. And this is the point of entry for our understanding of a supernatural existential. Its translation into the ethical realm is required for a humane handling of our world. Not only do humans use the earth; they care for it and prepare it for the fulfillment intended in God's good time. Humans simply cannot grace and save themselves while losing or debasing the world. Here then is an area that future theological considerations of nature and grace must continue to address. Our concern with the problem of gratuity—really a concern with the immanence and transcendence of God's presence to humanity—should not remove from view numerous other fertile but underdeveloped areas also touched by the universal gracing presence of God.[8] The catholicity of grace, its penetration into every dimension of existence in which the community of persons works out its destiny, will probably receive continued attention in the future, both theologically and pastorally. Reflection upon catholicity, essential in any theology of nature and grace attempting to grasp the cultural and cosmic aspects of

---

[8]The union of nature and grace can receive no adequate treatment apart from Christology and eschatology. Irenaeus in the West and Gregory of Nyssa in the East elaborated a Christology which embraced a comprehensive view of humanity and its world in their relation to God. Theology's recession from the world of nature and of politics has many causes. Science, in its success at explaining the data of the everyday world, is one of those causes and it forced theology to retreat to a higher ground where it concerned itself with a very individualistic treatment of the relationship of the Christian to God and a very narrow and restricted morality. On the whole problem of relating grace to the physical and social worlds, cf. B. Meland, "New perspectives in Nature and Grace," and J. Haroutunian, "Toward a Piety of Faith," both in P. Hefner, ed., *The Scope of Grace* (Philadelphia: Fortress, 1964), 143–161 and 165–182 respectively, and J. Carpenter, *Nature and Grace.*

the nature-grace unity, seems especially pressing now. The challenge is comparable in urgency to that faced by post-apostolic Christianity, viz., the challenge of allowing for the expression of Christian life and meaning in the cultural idiom of the world, which in our case is a secularized world.

Our epilogue indicates the new vistas already opened by a renewed theology of nature and grace and the tasks that lie ahead. The unity of nature and grace is the very heart of Christianity and of all human life. For that reason the theologizing of it will never be at an end. The effort to grasp and live the meaning of this unity between God and the world of creatures will always assume a variety of forms, pastoral, theological and religious, that will ever manifest the Church's living awareness that God has communicated Godself in history through Word and Spirit, who draw together the varied strands of life and bring them to the heart of God where all searching and expectation find satisfaction and completeness.

Index

Extrinsicism, 16, 55–58, 63, 75,
76, 86–87, 92, 94, 102–103,
113, 123, 129, 163, 168, 170,
171–172, 196, 202, 239n.3

Finality, double, 29–30, 34–37,
45–48
Fontinell, E., 173n.13 and 14,
176.n21, 177n.23, 178n.24,
188n.46, 189

Grace, experience of, 53, 86,
92–93, 101–102, 107, 138,
153–154, 160–161, 165–166,
198, 211; immanence and
transcendence of, 135–144,
160, 168, 169–170, 171,
178–181, 184–185, 191–192,
194, 197, 199, 237, 243; as
quasi-formal cause, 138n.7,
210–212, 216, 232; sanctifying
and actual, 158–159, 164,
215–216, 217. *See also* Gratuity of grace
Gratuity of grace, 23–24, 42–43,
47, 56, 63, 74–75, 78, 82, 90,
102, 114, 118–121, 124, 130,
133, 140–141, 144, 159, 168,
171–172, 180–185, 191, 194,
196–206, 207, 219–221, 230,
243; "from above," 115–121,
130; negative and positive formulations of, 126, 200–206
Gutwenger, E., 50n.2, 121n.12,
134n.33

Heidegger, M., 106, 109–111,
188, 208n.14, 222n.43
Human nature, 16–17, 52, 76,
91–93, 107–108, 114, 116–117,
121–123, 143–144, 179; definitions, 93, 96, 103, 108; historical and as such, 20n.14,
78–81, 90, 94–95, 134,
152–153, 165, 168, 191, 221;
historicity of, 105–106,

110–111, 113, 202–203; quiddity, as distinct from, 88, 90,
94–95, 97, 98, 99, 108, 113,
122–123, 127, 129, 143, 201,
218–219, 239–244; remainder
concept, 94, 107–108, 113,
122, 129, 131, 133, 166, 184,
193n.58. *See also* Nature, pure
Humani Generis, encyclical,
59–60, 62, 63, 70, 103, 126,
133, 184, 192, 201

Immanence, method and doctrine of, 61–62
Incarnation, 53, 96–98, 141–142,
170, 183–184, 190–191, 197,
198, 203, 205–206, 213–215,
230–231, 233
Instinctus Fidei, 145–163

Jansenius (Jansen, C.), 13,
18n.11, 56n.9, 74n.19, 86

Kant, I., 51, 221, 222
Kuhn, U., 62n.22
Küng, H., 100n.40, 191n.53

Lindbeck, G., 88n.8
Lonergan, B., 50n.2, 54n.7,
82–83, 84, 112, 113n.64, 131,
178n.24, 197, 233n.64

Malevez, L., 20n.15, 24n.17,
28n.25, 50n.2, 57n.13, 76n.26,
79n.30, 80n.33, 108n.50,
109n.54–55, 123, 126n.21,
131, 132n.30
Maréchal, J., 7, 50n.2, 51–52,
208n.14, 222

Natural, the, 24, 36n.29, 42–45,
56, 92, 107, 165, 185, 198n.1
Nature, pure, 29, 42–44, 47, 52,
56n.9, 58, 64, 67, 72, 73,
74–76, 78, 80, 87, 113,
116–117, 119–120, 122,